Tes

I have known Diane for many, many years and I've watched her grow from someone with HUGE limiting beliefs about herself and success to a woman on a mission! She is a passionate messenger with a powerful message. Her enthusiasm for life is contagious. And anybody who has the privilege to work with her will forever be blessed by her gifts.

**-Sean Smith, Certified Master Results Coach
Founder of EliteCoachingUniversity.com**

I thoroughly enjoyed my mentoring process with Diane Burton. She was such a great encourager and always knew just what to say. The most important part was rediscovering my "WHY!" It caused me to look at my business and the women I came in contact with in a different way. I am still making that mind shift, but Diane really made me search and dig deeper and question my reasons for doing what I do. In fact, she brought up questions that I would never think to ask myself that revealed to me some of my core strengths which have been profitable as I have progressed.

The very first call I had with Diane, I felt the presence of God and knew for sure I had made the right decision to have her as my mentor. She would start each session by telling me to take deep breaths and then she would begin our session in prayer. This really touched my heart that she started our time like this. I realized this was probably the only time in the week that I began my day taking deep breaths.

Not only did I feel she was my mentor, I felt I could tell her anything and she always had a perfect solution. I really felt like she was my best friend and ending our session has been difficult. Thank you, Diane. Words can't express the thanks for the things I feel in my heart and am applying to my life.

-Love and appreciate you, Mary S

I want to tell the world how very much your tele-class has helped me. I have changed not only the way I eat, but the way I think about myself, and every day gets better. I can say that without a doubt, if I had not taken the tele-class "The Master's Masterpiece," I would still be stuck at the bottom of my well with no self-esteem or self-confidence or knowledge that I am a wonderful, worthy creation of God. I am beautiful to Him and that I can take better care of His Masterpiece by taking responsibility for my food and drink and life choices. Diane Burton is an angel sent by God to help us understand that we CAN do ALL things through Christ who strengthens us. I would recommend this to EVERY woman I know, because I know there is something there that we all need to hear and apply to our lives. Thank you, Diane, for being my angel."

PS–I have lost five pounds since starting the class.

- Debbie

The moment I met Diane, I couldn't help but fall in love with her. She has a depth of character that is beautiful and a joyful spirit that is both refreshing and contagious. With the creation of the Master's

Masterpiece she is bringing God's grace and presence to the table–literally. I am excited for her work to be available to groups all across North America and encourage anyone who has struggled with their weight or an issue that's weighing them down, to seek out Diane for her wisdom and guidance.

-Patricia

Diane's class has truly been an enjoyable, thought provoking, feel good class! Through God's word, she has inspired me to look at myself as a masterpiece. As God's masterpiece, I am not without humanly seen flaws. But as humans we are unique and beautiful in a way only God could create. Just as we are to feed our mind with God's word and to grow ourselves spiritually, I believe we are to feed our physical bodies, not just healthy food, but by healthy living. Healthy living includes exercise, having healthy relationships with a spouse and friends, and to laugh! It means to strive to improve everyday physically and mentally. Healthy living also includes being grateful in all situations as Paul was in the book of Philippians. This class has helped me challenge myself more in new ways! Thank you Diane for a great class!

- Jinger

Your coaching has been immeasurable for me. I will admit that it was a leap of faith to know if it would be "worth it" or not, and many things I have invested in turned out to be not as beneficial as I had hoped throughout my Direct Sales career. However, your coaching has been extremely helpful just in the fact that you have helped me think different thoughts, and look at things differently than I have in the past. There are so many times that I knew in my heart of hearts that something just didn't "feel" right in my thought processes, but I couldn't put my finger on it. You have helped me dig in and pick it apart to figure out where the "hang up" was. Many times I think we just take what others say and believe it without thinking through if this is applicable for us or not. I have not bought into as much as some, but am still prone to do so at times. You have helped me not feel "guilty" about not "buying in" to every idea or thought process that is out there. Some are great, but some are just not for everyone. I appreciate all the times that you have taken extra minutes to go over a sticky thought and haven't watched your clock to say we are done in the moment we needed to talk it through. I will definitely recommend you to anyone who is committed to improving their life!

-Sincerely, LaVonne

Working with my coach Diane Burton has helped me to clarify my personal "stumbling" blocks that had begun to sour my spirit and hold me back from my desired accomplishments. Through her stimulating and thought provoking questions, I have been able to uncover belief patterns that were not supportive or even true. It is amazing how incorrect thinking and wrong feelings can so easily begin and take captive our potential! Thank you, Diane. I look forward to continuing our work together in the future as well!

-May your days be blessed, Maggie H

Diane is a genuine and very caring person who I highly recommend as a coach. She is very positive and optimistic, and has excellent listening skills. Diane has coached me over several months and has taught me about how to treat the masterpiece God gave me. I always feel better after our sessions.

-Linda

I have had the pleasure of working with Diane for several months. She is a very caring, loving, genuine, and enthusiastic coach. She takes the time to find out what your needs are as a client. Diane uses different tools from her toolbox to help her clients cope through their pain. I have become a better person and have been able to grow as a person since working with her. Thank you Diane, for your dedication.

-Emily

Diane has shown me through her story what I'm doing to myself by carrying the mean/fat girl on my shoulder. She reminded me how my body is God's temple, not to hurt it by my negative thoughts/comments or starvation/depravation and over indulgences. She has taught me to be thankful for what I do have and to take care of myself internally and externally.

-Maggie

The class was very encouraging and uplifting. I wish I had been offered all this information when I was a teenager so I could have painted my masterpiece more carefully all these years! We all need to realize how special we are to God, our Creator, and this material did just that. Because of this series of lessons, I will strive harder to better understand His love for me as an individual. I think that if some felt uncomfortable about the weight and lifestyle part, it is because they don't want to hear of their responsibility to God for their health and body. We do have a stewardship with our health that I believe the American culture has squelched. Your classes always make me feel perked up and more energetic for my day to day service to the Master. Thank you for all you do.

-Sandra

<hr/>

I want to tell you how much I enjoyed the class. It's so bizarre the subject came up "The Master's Masterpiece." I came across an article several months ago similar to this subject. It got me to thinking about my priorities. Then I thought, "Yeah, all of this is on loan until God returns. So what am I doing about all this? Nothing, Not a Thing! I'm letting my body go, and in the meantime, feeling sorry for poor me." My mind has to change and I said, "Wake up and smell the roses!" So slowly I am working on my list. I enjoyed the class and how it helped to wake me up again.

-Donna

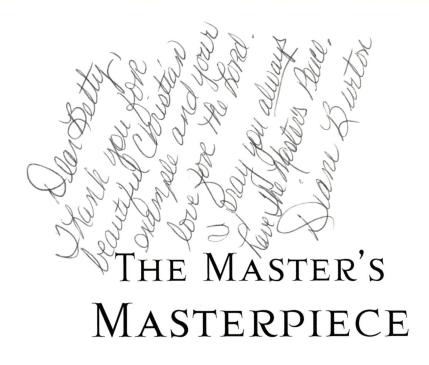

The Master's Masterpiece

A Preacher's Wife's journey from a broken and fat masterpiece to the Master's Peace

Diane Burton
2013 Grief Coach Academy Coach of the Year

Copyright © 2014 by Diane Burton 2013 Grief Coach Academy Coach of the Year

The Master's Masterpiece
A Preacher's Wife's journey from a broken and fat masterpiece to the Master's Peace
by Diane Burton 2013 Grief Coach Academy Coach of the Year

Printed in the United States of America

ISBN 9781629524368

All rights reserved solely by the author. The author guarantees all contents are original and do not infringe upon the legal rights of any other person or work. No part of this book may be reproduced in any form without the permission of the author. The views expressed in this book are not necessarily those of the publisher.

Unless otherwise indicated, Bible quotations are taken from The Holy Bible, English Standard Version, copyright © 2001 by Crossway, a publishing ministry of Good News Publishers. Used by permission. All rights reserved.

Scriptures marked NKJV are from the New King James Version. Copyright 1979, 1980, 1982 by Thomas Nelson, Inc. Used by permission. All rights reserved.

Scriptures marked NIV are taken from the HOLY BIBLE, NEW INTERNATIONAL VERSION. Copyright © 1973, 1978, 1984 by International Bible Society. Used by permission of Zondervan Publishing House. All rights reserved.

Scriptures marked KJV are taken from The Holy Bible, King James Version. Copyright © 1972 by Thomas Nelson Inc., Camden, New Jersey 08103.

Scriptures marked NAS are taken from the NEW AMERICAN STANDARD BIBLE®, Copyright © 1960, 1962, 1963, 1971, 1972, 1973, 1975, 1977, 1995 by The Lockman Foundation, LaHabra, CA Used by permission. All rights reserved.

Scriptures marked TLB are taken from The Living Bible. Copyright © 1971 by Tyndale House Publishers, Wheaton, Illinois 60187. All rights reserved.

The Amplified Bible, containing the amplified Old Testament and the amplified New Testament. 1987. The Lockman Foundation: La Habra, CA

Published by permission. Originally published by NavPress in English as THE MESSAGE: The Bible in Contemporary Language copyright 2002 by Eugene Peterson. All rights reserved. (The Message Bible Online)

Scriptures marked NCV are taken from the New Century Version (NCV) The Holy Bible, New Century Version®. Copyright © 2005 by Thomas Nelson, Inc.

Scriptures marked NRSV are taken from the New Revised Standard Version Bible, copyright © 1989 the Division of Christian Education of the National Council of the Churches of Christ in the United States of America. Used by permission. All rights reserved.

Scriptures marked NLT are from the New Living Translation copyright© 1996, 2004, 2007 by Tyndale House Foundation. Used by permission of Tyndale House Publishers Inc., Carol Stream, Illinois 60188. All rights reserved.

Scriptures marked WYC are from the **Wycliffe Bible**, copyright© 2001 by Terence P. Noble.

This book contains the opinions and ideas of its author. It is solely for informational and educational purposes and should not be regarded as a substitute for professional medical treatment. The nature of your body's health condition is complex and unique. Therefore, you should consult a health professional before you begin any new exercise, nutrition, or supplemental program or if you have questions about your health. Neither the author or the publisher shall be liable or responsible for any loss or damage allegedly arising from any information or suggestion in this book. Any similarity between the names and stories of individuals described in this book to individuals known by the readers is purely coincidental. The statements in this book about consumable products or food have not been evaluated by the Food and Drug Administration. The author or publisher is not responsible for your specific health or allergy needs that may require medical supervision. Any recipes in this book are to be followed exactly as written. The author or publisher is not responsible for any adverse reaction to the consumption of food or products that have been suggested in this book. While the author has made every effort to provide accurate telephone numbers and Internet addresses at the time of publication, neither the publisher or author assume any responsibility for the errors or the changes that may occur after publication.

www.xulonpress.com

Dedication

When I was thinking about whom to dedicate my book to, the first person who came to mind was my mother, Claudia Petty. When I told my mom about training to become a Grief Coach, she was so thrilled. I actually debated about telling her for a while, because she already thought I had too many irons in the fire; however, she seemed so proud.

My mom has always encouraged me, although as a child and young teenager, I didn't always see it as encouragement. However, as I matured as an adult, I realized she was doing what she felt was best for me. When I wanted to begin a direct sales business she and my dad loaned me the money to get started. She then was a great customer and at the age of 62 she joined my team. At the age of 65, she became a widow. Instead of feeling like her life was over, she moved to the town where my sister lived and became very involved with her new church just as she always had been: jail ministry, helping with the babies in the nursery, having the college girls over for meals, taking food to those in need, sending cards and notes to the sick and those needing encouragement, speaking at ladies events, helping teach Bible classes, taking sick people to the doctor and being a mom and grandmother. I called her the Energizer Bunny® because she was so active. At the age of 87, she was still driving and would go to another town about fifty miles away to visit and help with her older sister. She also would pick up other elderly ladies who couldn't drive anymore and take them to church.

In June 2011, my mom wasn't feeling well. When she shared this with me, a red flag went up. My mom never complained about being sick, so when she told me what was going on, it sounded serious. Because of her being so independent, I kept begging her to let me come make sure she was okay. (I lived 2 1/2 hours away.) She kept telling me she was okay and was supposed to go back to the doctor the next week. Three days later, on a Sunday night, she called and asked me to come so I could go with her to the doctor. I grabbed some clothes, packed quickly, and started on what was going to be a journey like I had never had before.

I arrived at her home about 11:30 p.m. and knew when I saw her something was seriously wrong. We were finally able to get her to her doctor on Monday afternoon. She was put in the hospital that evening, tests were run and the next day we were told she had cancer and the doctor helped us understand how serious it was. She and I both started to cry. Then she suddenly wiped the tears and said, "I don't know why I'm crying, I have a mansion in heaven waiting for me." It turned out to be colon cancer and she died 5 1/2 weeks later. She was in the hospital three weeks and at home with hospice care for 2 1/2 weeks.

My mother taught us how to die. During those 5 1/2 weeks, she never complained, even though she couldn't have any food or water in the beginning because she couldn't keep anything down; and only an occasional sip the last two weeks of her life. She also had surgery so the doctors could find the cancer and see if there was anything they could do. She was so brave through it all. She asked me the second day she was in the hospital to have her visitors sign her journal; she wanted to remember who came to visit her. I thought it was an odd request; however, I am so glad we did. We counted the signatures and she'd had over 600 visits. Many came several times to visit; some even came every day.

The words "she taught us how to die" were used describing her. One young man whom my mother had mentored even asked how she could be so peaceful knowing she was going to die. The nurses would come to her room to feel her peacefulness. When friends from church would come get a hug from her, she would ask different ones to take on one of her "jobs" –sending cards, picking people up, taking care of the babies, the jail ministry, etc. She was also known for helping with missionaries when they came to town, being sure they had a car to drive. She sent them e-mails and handwritten cards. While in the hospital, she received a card signed by the women she taught in her jail ministry. Her whole focus during this time was being sure others were taken care of.

After we got her home for hospice care, I asked her if it made her sad to know she was leaving us. She said at first it did; however, she was now ready to go. I can't say it was easy to let her go; however, I know she is with God. I miss picking up the phone and talking to her while I'm getting ready for the day or while I'm traveling. She always wanted to know what her children and grandchildren were doing and their travels. She would write this information on her desk calendar and we knew she was praying for our safety and for us to make wise decisions.

My mom wanted to leave one last gift/legacy for her children and grandchildren. We ordered Bibles and she wrote a note and signed one for each of her three children and seven grandchildren. You can see the pen in her hand and a Bible on her lap. It was a hard task because she was so weak and it took her several days to get them signed. The grandchildren's were signed first and I was so afraid she would die before she got to mine. She lived long enough to sign them all and I treasure that Bible. We gave the Bibles to the grandchildren at her visitation. I also have a picture of my grandson (her great grandson) asleep that night with my Bible wrapped in his arms, so sweet.

xv

The Master's Masterpiece

Thank you, God, for allowing Claudia to be my mother and thank you mom, for being such an amazing Christian example and for leaving a legacy. I love you!

The Watcher
She always leaned to watch for us,
Anxious if we were late,
In winter by the window,
In summer by the gate;

And though we mocked her tenderly,
Who had such foolish care,
The long way home would seem more safe
Because she waited there.

Her thoughts were all so full of us-
She never could forget!
And so I think that where she is
She must be watching yet,

Waiting till we come home to her,
Anxious if we are late-
Watching from heaven's window,
Leaning from heaven's gate.

Margaret Widdemer

Acknowledgements

When I first wrote the lessons and taught "The Master's Masterpiece" to my ladies Bible class, I knew I wanted to make it into a book so the message could be shared with others. I knew there were other women in this world who had issues surrounding their weight like I had. I also knew these issues caused a lot of pain and grief. I have been so blessed by people who have encouraged and poured belief into me through this process.

I first want to give God all the glory. This book would not have happened without Him. He has entrusted so much to me and I pray I am using the talents He gave me to the max.

Thank you, Ken, my wonderful caring and generous husband, for encouraging me every step of the way and for the lessons you teach and preach every Sunday. You have blessed me since we married in 1975.

Thank you, Jennifer and Justin, my amazing children, for blessing my life from the day you were born and encouraging me in this endeavor. It has been a joy to watch you grow and mature into amazing adults.

Thank you, Sue, for being my friend and my mentor and for pouring belief into me since the minute I met you in 1988. Thank you for being there when I called in December 2010 about becoming a grief coach.

Thank you, Sean, for being my first business coach and for helping me when I was first struggling with my direct sales business. Thank you for teaching me the "Mirror" and the "I Did & I Didn't" exercises and for being such a great coach and trainer.

Thank you, Aurora, for your encouragement and gentle push to write a book, this would not have happened if you hadn't expected it from me. Thank you for being my grief coach trainer and for helping me to release

xvii

the "fat girl." I have grown so much since being a part of your academy and learning about "The Master's Masterpiece."

Thank you, Joe, for being a business coach, sharing what a masterpiece really is, and for telling me the story about the broken urn.

Thank you, Lynell and Charlene, my two very special girlfriends at church for keeping my "secret" about becoming a grief coach until I was ready to share it with the world. Thank you for the encouragement you have been. I am so blessed to call you friends.

Thank you, Kathy and Teresa, for your friendship and believing in the possibilities and for reading the first chapter and giving me your opinion as to whether what I have is worthwhile.

Thank you, Tish, for being my sister and encouraging me through our mother's illness and death. Even though we didn't always see eye to eye growing up, I can say I have the best sister in the world. Thanks for reading and giving me your input as I've worked to put this book together.

Thank you, Carl, for being my big brother and for being an encouragement to me through mother's death and on this journey as a coach. I am very blessed to have such a great brother.

Thank you Linda, Lynell, Teresa, Kathleen, Sandra, Tish, Charlene, Pat, Sue and Donna for proofreading chapters of this book.

Thank you, Dr. Larry Keefauver and Pam McLaughlin, for being my book writing coaches. I have been writing this material and trying to figure out how to get it into book form for two years. Thank you for taking my material and pulling it together. You have been so kind and gracious with your encouragement and belief towards me. You have made me think I have the best material ever written.

Thank you, Michael at Xulon Press, for patiently taking the time to talk to me about publishing my book. I was so pleased to find a Christian publishing book company who would work with me and help me get it into the right hands.

Thank you Karen and all my Direct Sales Sisters . You have added so much value to my life. Your friendship is priceless and my life has been blessed more than you will ever know.

TABLE OF CONTENTS

Introduction–From a Broken Master-P.I.E.C.E. to the Master's P.E.A.C.E. . . . . **xxiii**

Chapter 1–Am I Really God's Masterpiece? **27**
Answer 1: Understand You Are Unique
Answer 2: Realize In God's Eyes You Are A Masterpiece
Answer 3: Love the Body God Gave You
Answer 4: Admit You Are Made in the Image of God

Chapter 2 – Does God Really Care What I Eat? **33**
Answer 1: Understand You Were Bought With a Price
Answer 2: Realize You Are No Longer Your Own
Answer 3: Remember Whose You Are
Answer 4: Admit Your Disobedience Is Sin

Chapter 3 – Why Did God Make Me This Way? **45**
Answer 1: Acknowledge You Are Fearfully and Wonderfully Made
Answer 2: Acknowledge God Knows All About You
Answer 3: Acknowledge You Cannot Hide from God
Answer 4: Acknowledge God Has a Plan for Your Life

The Master's Masterpiece

Chapter 4 – How Can I Keep From Failing at Every Diet I Try? 57

Answer 1: Understand He Has Given You What You Need
Answer 2: Know It's Not Beyond What You Can Bear
Answer 3: Realize Gluttony Does Not Honor God
Answer 4: Enhance Your Health with Moderation

Chapter 5 – Why Do I Turn to Food for Comfort? 71

Answer 1: Discover the Mindset Behind Your Choices
Answer 2: Face Your Circumstances
Answer 3: Find the Stuff Beneath the Stuff
Answer 4: Learn to Break Food's Control

Chapter 6 – Why Me? 86

Answer 1: Learn to Focus on Your Inner Self
Answer 2: Discover Your Weight Grief
Answer 3: Let God Heal Your Broken Heart
Answer 4: Be Anxious for Nothing

Chapter 7–Am I Disrespecting God When I Eat Unhealthy? . . . 102

Answer 1: Cherish Your Masterpiece
Answer 2: Respect God, Your Creator
Answer 3: Develop a Healthy Respect
Answer 4: Develop a Healthy Respect for Food

Chapter 8 – How Can I Stay in Control? 122

Answer 1: Display the Fruit of the Spirit
Answer 2: Commit Your Daily Life to God
Answer 3: Get Self Out of the Way
Answer 4: Realize It's All About Him

Chapter 9–How Can I Keep My Commitment? 142

Answer 1: Be Willing to Make a Decision
Answer 2: Be Willing to Live with Integrity
Answer 3: Understand There Is No Plan B
Answer 4: Realize Daily Decisions Do Make a Difference

Chapter 10 – How Can I Love Myself?. 158
Answer 1: See Your Ideal Weight from the Inside Out
Answer 2: Admit God Loves You Even if You're Overweight
Answer 3: Monitor Your Self-Talk
Answer 4: Replace Negative with Positive Affirmation

Conclusion 173
Answer 1: Master the Guilt
Answer 2: Change Your Brain Pattern
Answer 3: Put Off the Old and Put On Your New Self
Answer 4: Respond to God's Promises

10-Week Devotional Journal. 175
Personal or Small Group Guide

Strategic Daily Plan 271

My Daily "I DID" and "I DIDN'T" Sample Journal. 275

Weight Control Tips 279

Recommended Reading. 283

About the Author 285

xxi

Introduction

FROM A BROKEN MASTER-P.I.E.C.E. TO THE MASTER'S P.E.A.C.E.

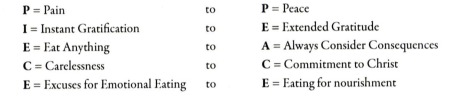

P = Pain	to	**P** = Peace
I = Instant Gratification	to	**E** = Extended Gratitude
E = Eat Anything	to	**A** = Always Consider Consequences
C = Carelessness	to	**C** = Commitment to Christ
E = Excuses for Emotional Eating	to	**E** = Eating for nourishment

My story starts when I was a little girl. I was always petite until the age of six – seems like a young age to suddenly begin to gain weight, but it happened. I never knew if it was because I ate a lot or inherited "the fat gene." However, for the next several years, the battle of being overweight happened. I was a happy kid; however, the older I got, the more weight I put on. And, yes, I was eating a lot of food. I found I really liked how food tasted – one bite was never enough. I really enjoyed the church potlucks, too. I would be sure I was first or close to being first in line, I would pile my plate high, and then go through the line at least two more times. By January of my senior year in High School, I weighed over 200 pounds.

My parents tried so many things to help me lose weight. However, the more they pushed me, the more I resisted. I didn't want to be fat; I was miserable. What's interesting is people thought I was so jolly. Have

xxiii

you heard fat people are jolly? I was jolly on the outside, but on the inside I was hurting.

My senior year in High School I worked in the afternoon at a local bank. One day, some of the ladies at the bank were talking about wanting to lose weight and were going to join a group to help them. I was invited, I accepted, and it was there I made the decision to lose weight. I began an eating plan and by the time I graduated from High School, I had lost several pounds. I continued to lose the weight, started college, kept the weight off during college, and now forty-two years have passed and I have kept the weight off.

However, it's been a battle and this is where the thoughts for this book have come into play. After many years of keeping the weight off, I still thought of myself as the fat girl. I struggled with self-esteem issues. I remembered the degrading names people called me. I remembered how I embarrassed my family. I remembered how people thought I was stupid because I was fat. I have a wonderful husband of thirty-eight years who is a minister, two beautiful children, their spouses, two grandchildren, and a very blessed life. Yet, I was constantly aware of the fat girl still living in my brain!

Through a business coach, Sean Smith, I had the privilege of meeting Aurora Winter, the founder of From Heartbreak to Happiness® Grief Coach Academy. After talking with her, I became very interested in helping women through the grief associated with weight issues. I enrolled in her academy and began the process of learning how to be a grief coach. Using her PEACE® Method, I had a huge breakthrough surrounding thoughts around my weight. In about twenty minutes, Aurora helped me shift my thinking and I have been a different person ever since. I even had a friend share how she saw a difference in me after the event! Because of this breakthrough, I began writing thoughts to help others through the grief associated with weight.

As a Christian, I believe God is my partner and will guide me as I go through life. However, I had not allowed Him to really help me with this issue. As I have studied and written the lessons for this book, there are scriptures that have come to mean so much to me. The scripture for the theme of this book is Ephesians 2:10, "For we are God's masterpiece. He has created us anew in Christ Jesus, so we can do the things He planned for us long ago" (NLT). **We are God's Masterpiece!**

Ephesians 2:10 in the English Standard Version says, "For we are His workmanship, created in Christ Jesus for good works, which God prepared beforehand, that we should walk in them." **We are His Workmanship!**

I discovered I was created by God and He created me with a plan to do good works. As I thought about my body as God's masterpiece, I realized I wasn't taking care of it the way God wanted me to. I realized He has big plans for me and when I don't take care of the body He gave me, I can't be my best for Him.

My prayer is this book and the ten-week devotional journal section at the end will be an encouragement and will guide you to realize just how special you are to God and to take better care of the masterpiece He made—you.

Note: The ten-week devotional journal section can be used as an individual or small group study guide. In using the journal, read through the entire chapter before you begin Day One of each week. Then, each day will review for you portions of that material and give you ways to think about, process, and act upon that material.

**If you don't have an issue with weight, but you have some other form of addictive behavior, this book and journal could be helpful to guide you through your challenge and help you overcome.

Chapter 1

AM I REALLY GOD'S MASTERPIECE?

For we are God's masterpiece. He has created us anew in Christ Jesus, so we can do the things He planned for us long ago. (Ephesians 2:10 NLT)

The dictionary says a masterpiece is a "work of outstanding artistry, skill or workmanship." It is a person's greatest piece of work! It is done with mastery skill! In Ephesians 2:10, I am called God's masterpiece!

How in the world can I be God's masterpiece when I am overweight and out of shape? How can I be God's masterpiece when I don't even like who I am? Why do I have this flaw of being fat? Isn't a masterpiece a work of art–priceless, worth more than I would ever be able to afford?

When I read the definition of masterpiece from the dictionary, it says to me I am the work of an outstanding artist! God is that most amazing artist. Every time a person is born, it is another piece of God's greatest work, and you are one of those great pieces of work!

The first time I read I was God's masterpiece it made me feel He had made something very special when He made me. However, I also thought a masterpiece was something perfect – no flaws, nothing wrong with it. So then I began to question how could I be God's masterpiece? I have imperfections, I have flaws, I sin, I have trials and tribulations. I found out many others were asking those very same questions so I began to look for the answers.

Answer 1: Understand You Are Unique

One day I was sharing with a business coach, Joe, about being God's masterpiece. He asked me if I knew what a masterpiece was. I shared I thought it was a one of a kind work of art. He shared that was a true statement. However, he went on to explain that an artist would put a flaw in his work of art no one else knew about. By doing this it would increase the value of the piece of art by making it one of a kind, unique; a masterpiece.

How many times have you looked in the mirror (sometimes even using a magnifying mirror) to find your flaws believing they made you a lesser person? I remember a client asking me if I could see a particular flaw on her face. Even looking very closely, it was almost undetectable. She admitted she'd found it while looking in a magnifying mirror! I shared with her that people don't look at us with a magnifying mirror. We don't see the flaws on others that we see on ourselves when we are looking in a mirror!

Yes, we do want to look our best. We want pretty skin and to look presentable. However, I believe many times we get so caught up with how we look on the outside and the flaws we see we forget about looking for the good God gave us. We forget to look inward at who we really are. God looks at our hearts (see 1 Samuel 16:7).

Ask Yourself:

What do I see when I look in the mirror?

Do I see a Masterpiece?

Do I see flaws or perfection?

Action Suggestion:

Stand in front of a mirror and ask God to show you His masterpiece—you! Ask Him to show you what is uniquely you! Begin to thank Him for the masterpiece He made you.

Answer 2: Realize In God's Eyes You Are A Masterpiece

When God created you, in His eyes you were perfect. The Bible says He was focused on your heart (see I Samuel 16:7). In Ephesians 2:10, God tells us we are His masterpiece, created for good works. As you have grown, imperfections have happened with the aging process, but also because you may not have made the best choices for your body. The flaws have come. The mistakes have happened. You have made choices causing the perfection to disappear physically.

A story is told of an Eastern village that through the centuries was known for its exquisite pottery. Especially striking were its high as tables, wide as chairs urns. They were admired around the globe for their strong form and delicate beauty. Legend has it that when each urn was apparently finished, there was one final step. The artist broke it and then put it back together with gold filigree. An ordinary urn was then transformed into a priceless work of art. What seemed finished wasn't, until it was broken.

You are like that broken urn. God sees past the flaws and still sees His Masterpiece. We need to ask God to forgive us for abusing our bodies, and start to focus on taking care of the body He gave us.

I believe when we are abusive to our bodies, whether it's eating, drinking, negative thoughts, gossip or bad language, we really don't love ourselves the way God wants us to. In Matthew 22:39 we read, "Love your neighbor as yourself." Do you believe it's possible to love yourself the way God intended if you aren't taking care of your masterpiece?

Ask Yourself:

What does God see when He looks at me?

Does He see I am His masterpiece?

Does He focus on my flaws?

Action Suggestion:

Stand in front of a mirror and thank God for the body He gave you. Tell yourself that you love you because God made you perfect in His eyes. Ask Him to show you His image in you!

Answer 3: Love the Body God Gave You

Let's look at some scriptures telling us to love ourselves:

> Luke 10:27 is Jesus answering a question of a lawyer when He says, "You shall love the Lord your God with all our heart, soul and strength, and, your neighbor as yourself."

> Matthew 19:19, Matthew 22:39 and Mark 12:31 tell us, "You shall love your neighbor as yourself."

> Romans 13:9 ends by saying, "You shall love your neighbor as yourself."

> Galatians 5:14 says, "For all the law is fulfilled in one word, even in this: 'You shall love your neighbor as yourself.'"

> James 2:8 says, if you really want to fulfill the royal law according to the scripture, "You shall love your neighbor as yourself."

Yes, the first emphasis in all of these scriptures is on loving our neighbor. However, it is so important to realize how big this love needs to be. This love is supposed to be equivalent to the love we have for ourselves. The question we each want to ask ourselves then becomes, "How much do I love myself?" God is telling us to love others as we love ourselves.

Let's look at the flip side of this concept as well. If we are critical of ourselves, what is our relationship with others going to look like? How are we going to follow the other instructions Jesus left for us as His disciples if we cannot relate to others the way God has commanded?

It has to begin by loving the body God gave you and treating it with respect. The way you care for your body gives you and God a clear picture of how much you love yourself.

Ask Yourself:

What am I showing God by the way I am caring for the body He gave me?

Do I cherish and respect myself, His masterpiece, as much as He does?

If you answered no, ask God to show you how to change this characteristic in your life starting today!

Action Suggestion:

Ask God to forgive you for abusing the body He gave you. Tell Him you are sorry for not cherishing your masterpiece. Start out each day by thanking Him for the body He has given you and asking Him to help you begin to cherish and respect His masterpiece!

Answer 4: Admit You Are Made in the Image of God

So God created man in His image; in the image of God He created him; male and female He created them. (Genesis 1:27 NKJV)

We are made in the image of God! This is so exciting! Do you realize how absolutely amazing you are? Nothing else in all of God's creation is made in His image. This body God created for you is a treasure, it's not trash! It's a mansion, not a shack!

I want to share a story about a painting that was taken to an auction and sold for a few thousand dollars. The person who purchased it decided to have it appraised and discovered there was a thumbprint on the painting. It was the thumbprint of the artist! When he found out the thumbprint belonged to a famous artist, the value of the painting went into the millions of dollars.

God created you in His image and put His thumbprint on you! He also created you with a very special purpose! In 1 Corinthians 6:19 it says, "Do you not know that your body is the temple of the Holy Spirit who is in you, whom you have from God, and you are not your own" (NKJV). Since God has called your body the temple of the Holy Spirit, would you be willing to stop and think before putting foods in it which can be harmful?

This *Masterpiece* God has given you is tough, yet delicate. You can hurt it and it can heal. However, when you continually eat unhealthy foods, you overwork it and can destroy it. Your body is the only one you have. It's the only one God is going to give you. He didn't intend for you to abuse it.

God didn't put us on this earth to live to eat; we are to eat to live.

Your masterpiece is more than flesh and blood. You are a three-part being – body, soul and spirit (see 1 Thessalonians 5:23). If you aren't taking care of the flesh are you truly being your best for God?

Ask Yourself:

> *How is knowing I was made in His image going to affect the way I live from now on?*

> *How will it affect what I allow to go in my body?*

> *Am I taking care of my body so I can be my best for God?*

Action Suggestion:

Look in the mirror and ask God to show you His thumbprint on you! Thank Him for making you in His image as the temple of the Holy Spirit. Ask Him to show you ways to improve the way you care for this temple.

Chapter 2

DOES GOD REALLY CARE WHAT I EAT?

¹²You say, "I am allowed to do anything"—but not everything is good for you. And even though "I am allowed to do anything," I must not become a slave to anything. ¹³You say, "Food was made for the stomach, and the stomach for food." (This is true, though someday God will do away with both of them.).... They were made for the Lord, and the Lord cares about our bodies. ¹⁴And God will raise us from the dead by his power, just as he raised our Lord from the dead. ¹⁹Don't you realize that your body is the temple of the Holy Spirit, who lives in you and was given to you by God? You do not belong to yourself, ²⁰for God bought you with a high price. So you must honor God with your body. (1 Corinthians 6:12-15, 19-20 NLT)

I am often asked if God really cares about what we eat. After all, He is watching over and supervising the whole universe and everyone and everything in it. Why would He be concerned with something as seemingly insignificant as what we eat on a daily basis? The answers to this question may surprise you as you see just how important God says what you put into your body and how you treat it, is to Him. You are God's masterpiece and He expects you to treat it like one including what you eat.

Answer 1: Understand You Were Bought With a Price

> *God bought you with a high price. So you must honor God with Your body*. (1 Corinthians 6:0 NLT)

Have you ever purchased something having a high price? How do you treat it? Do you just put anything in it? Did you put it in places where you knew it might get broken? Did you protect it from obvious danger? Why?

When my mother died in August 2011, I inherited something of hers I had admired for years and she wanted me to have it. I cherish and take very good care of this item. Every time I look at it, I think about her. Sometimes I smile. Sometimes I think about how much I miss her and wish I could share with her about this book and other things going on in my life.

This item has a high price in two ways. I know its monetary value, yet it's also a gift with a loving high price. My mom had to die for me to inherit it. Yet this material item doesn't compare with the high price God paid through the death of His son for your sins. It doesn't compare with the price you are paying when you don't take care of your body.

We sing a song in our worship service, "What Is It Worth to Your Soul?" The song wants to know if you are willing to give up worldly things to spend eternity with God. The same thought can be asked, "What are you willing to surrender in order to have a healthy body and take care of it for God?"

1 Corinthians 6:20 says you were bought with a high price. In other words God paid a very high price to make you His. Do you know what that high price was?

> *For why man's Son came not, that it should be ministered to him, but that he should minister, and give his life again-buying for many [and give his life redemption, or again-buying, for many]*. (Mark 10:45 WYC)

God sent His own Son, Jesus to rescue and save us. He paid the price with love. "He gave himself as a payment to free all people" (1 Timothy 2:6 NCV).

Didn't you realize that your body is a sacred place, the place of the Holy Spirit? Don't you see that you can't live however you please, squandering what God paid such a high price for? The physical part of you is not some piece of property belonging to the spiritual part of you. God owns the whole works. So let people see God in and through your body. (1 Corinthians 6:20 MSG)

The Message Bible translation of this verse brings out several key points as we consider whether God really cares about what we eat and put into our bodies.

Your body is a sacred place. It is the place of the Holy Spirit. You therefore need to be selective in what you place in that holy place.

You can't live however you please: squandering and being wasteful with what God paid such a high price for. There are certain things you can and cannot do with something so highly valued by the Creator.

The physical part of you is not some piece of property belonging to the spiritual part of you. You are a spirit, with a soul, housed in a body made of flesh. What you do with your body directly affects the soul and the spirit.

God owns the whole works. He does not just own your spirit.

Others see God in and through your body. Everything you do is a witness to others. People see the truth about God more through your actions than through your words.

Clay Jars and Vessels of Honor

For God Who said, Let light shine out of darkness, has shone in our hearts so as [to beam forth] the Light for the illumination of the knowledge of the majesty and glory of God [as it is manifest in the Person and is revealed] in the face of Jesus Christ (the Messiah). ⁷ However, we possess this precious treasure [the divine Light of the Gospel] in [frail, human] vessels of earth, that the grandeur and exceeding greatness of the power may be shown to be from God and not from ourselves. (2 Corinthians 4:6-7 AMP)

2 Corinthians 4:6-7 says we carry a precious treasure in our frail, human vessels. God's majesty and glory are revealed in and through us to those all around us. If we keep ourselves from what would harm or disfigure God's masterpiece then we are a vessel for honorable use, useful to the Master who created us, and a witness of His love and power to others. Isn't that what we all really want to happen?

> *Therefore, if anyone cleanses himself from what is dishonorable, he will be a vessel for honorable use, set apart as holy, useful to the master of the house, ready for every good work.* (2 Timothy 2:21)

Ask Yourself:

> *Does God care what I eat?*

> *Am I treating my body in a way worthy of the high price God paid for me?*

> *What do others learn about God when they see the way I treat my body?*

Action Suggestion:

As you consider the high price God paid for you, what action can you take starting now to put a higher value on your Temple?

Begin to put together a plan for how you are going to change your eating and health habits based on the value God has placed on you. Refer to the Strategic Daily Plan at the end of the book for some ideas for doing this.

Answer 2: Realize You Are No Longer Your Own

> *You were bought with a price [purchased with a preciousness and paid for, made His own]. So then, honor God and bring glory to Him in your body.* (1 Corinthians 6:20 AMP)

Have you ever borrowed anything from someone? How did you treat that item? Why did you treat it the way you did? What was your motivation?

We need to apply this mindset to our bodies as well. We are no longer our own. We belong to God. He owns the whole works. God has loaned us this physical body to house our spirit and our soul.

"Today God lent me a soul; tomorrow I must return it prepared for eternity." -Rebekah Sunderraj

My life belongs to God. My heart is His. These hands and the talent that fuels them are His possession. Read the Parable of the Talents in Matthew 25:14-30. Think about who gave the talents to the three people in this parable (see verse 14). Consider how the owner of the talents decided how much to give each of these people (see verse 15). What did the owner of the talents expect his people to do with what he had given them (see verse 19)? Jesus told His disciples that the owner in this parable represented God.

Look carefully at how the owner responded to the people who not only returned the talents but produced an increase with what they had been given (see verses 21-23). When you read how the owner responded to the person who did nothing with his talent (see verses 24-28) you see how important it is we use the talents God has given us to produce fruit in our own lives and in the lives of those around us.

God has blessed me to be on this earth as long as I have. All of us are given talents and it's up to us to nurture and grow them. God has blessed me with the opportunity to teach women and young ladies in our Bible classes, retreats, and Ladies' Days. He has also blessed me as I have been a leader in a Direct Sales company for over thirty years. Now He has combined all I have learned to have me coach people from pain to peace and to share my experiences in this book. Even though the past was painful, it's made me who I am and helped me realize how grateful I am to God for my past. I am blessed because God is now using my testimony to minister to others and help them on their journey with Him.

"Get into and maintain excellent physical condition. Practicing 'extreme self-care,' or caring meticulously for your mind, spirit, and body, is a natural by-product of a godly self–concept. When you neglect the wise habits of good health...you become drained, run down, or fatigued... and get stuck in the negative. You may also make daily choices based on expediency-choice, driven by a short-term paycheck rather than a long-term gain. Without maximum energy, you give less to the important people and causes in your life."[1]

By taking care of the body God has loaned you, you can use the talents He has placed within you and reach your full potential as a vessel of honor.

Ask Yourself:

What might happen if I pay better attention to this master-piece He has loaned me?

Might I think differently about how I take care of it?

Am I using my talents to produce a return on what God has given me?

Action Suggestion:

Think of ways you can take better care of the body God has loaned you. Be very specific. Read James 1:5. Pray and ask God for wisdom to help you discover ways you can take better care of yourself. Make a list in your journal of your God-given talents. Begin thinking and praying about how these talents can be used to produce good fruit in your everyday life.

Answer 3: Remember Whose You Are

For you are all children of God through faith in Christ Jesus. (Galatians 3:26 NLT)

In Genesis 1:27 we read that God created man, male and female in His own image. That means we have His nature and His spiritual DNA within us by His design. 1 Timothy 6:15 says He is the King of kings and

---

1 Newberry, Tommy. "The 4:8 Principle" *Practice Extreme Self Care* Tyndale Publishing, 2007. p. 71. (See his list of essential self-care factors in the devotional section for this chapter.)

Lord of lords. Galatians 3:36 says we are all children of God through faith in Christ Jesus. Why is this so important to us?

What does that mean to you personally? If you were a child of an earthly king, what kinds of privileges and opportunities would your father, the king, give you? In Luke 11:13 Jesus asked, "If you then, evil as you are, know how to give good gifts [gifts that are to their advantage] to your children, how much more will your heavenly Father give the Holy Spirit to those who ask *and* continue to ask Him!" (AMP).

"You are a child of the highest King, a privileged member of the household who should never lack for anything that the Father wants you to have. Yet we live as though we are the neediest of creatures. Have we set our desires on the wrong things? Or that we simply haven't learned to apply the promises of God to our lives? Learn to live as a beloved child, and expect His abundance in your life."[2]

What a challenge and honor you and I have been given to reflect the King of kings to others here on this earth. When we see the magnitude of this responsibility, we need to realize how everything we do sends out either a positive or a negative message about our Father in heaven. By remembering Whose we are and Who we represent on a daily basis we can make better choices and begin to fulfill the purpose God has given us here on this earth.

> **"Deciding the value you place on yourself is another choice you have to make. Many people allow this decision to be made for them by their dominant capabilities, media, and other people." (Tommy Newberry)**

As I read the quote from Tommy Newberry, I realized I had not placed value on myself through the years I was fat or after I lost my weight. It's really hard to put real value on yourself when you are constantly made fun of and made to feel you are worthless. For example, when you are always called names such as "Twiggy," Ella (short for elephant), "Big Un" and many other such degrading names, you begin to believe what others are saying about you.

---

2   Tiegreen, Christ. *Wonders of the Cross* Tyndale Publishing, 2009.

When my Algebra II teacher told me it would be better for me to go to the study hall, come back into the classroom to take the test, and then go back to the study hall, I began to believe I was fat and stupid. When a teacher wouldn't let me help color a huge Santa on the wall because I wasn't good at coloring, it just made the things people were saying about me seem true.

I found myself comparing myself to the thin girls. I found myself wishing I could be like others and asking, "Why am I the fat girl?" I don't think I ever wished I was someone else, I just wished I wasn't me. I found myself looking through the Sears catalog and picking out clothes on every page hoping someday I could fit into them. You see, my mom had to make all my clothes because there weren't clothes at the stores to fit me.

Even though I attended college, made the Dean and President's list (I am smart), was picked to be the club Belle for one of the guys' social clubs, and married a man who thinks I'm beautiful, I still at times didn't feel smart enough or good enough. The words people said to me continued to come back and haunt me.

"Do you see yourself as a child of Almighty God? **Remember whose you really are.** You are an original masterpiece. There has never been and there will never be anyone just like you, and God has not made anyone else in the world out of better clay than he used to make you. Your life here on earth is your special, unrepeatable opportunity to fulfill God's vision for your life. Recognize the true you is not your flesh and bones. You are a spiritual being living in a temporary human existence-a dress rehearsal for eternity."[3]

So while you are here on the earth it is your responsibility to take good care of the flesh and bones God has given you as the temple of the Holy Spirit. When you do there will be an abundance of blessings in your life that will allow you to bless others within your sphere of influence. Isn't that what serving God is all about?

Ask Yourself:

Is it possible I am missing out on God's blessings by not taking care of myself?

Do I see myself as a child of almighty God?

---

3 "The 4:8 Principle" by Tommy Newberry, p. 43.

Am I truly living as a beloved child of the King of kings?

Action Suggestion:

Think about who or what you have let determine the value you place on yourself. Begin to discover what it means to be a child of God. As you read about the privileges you have as a child of the King, write them down in your journal and ask the Holy Spirit to reveal God's purpose for your life in His kingdom as His prince or princess. Here are a few verses to get you started. Declare each one of these truths over yourself!

Romans 8:16 says you are _____

1 John 5:1 says you are _____

John 16:27 says you are _____

1 Peter 2:4 says you are _____

Answer 4: Admit Your Disobedience Is Sin

Adam and Eve were created by God and placed in a beautiful garden filled with "every tree that is pleasant to the sight or to be desired, good, suitable, and pleasant for food" (Genesis 2:9). Then God told Adam, "I have given you every plant yielding seed that is on the face of the land and every tree with seed in its fruit; you shall have them for food (Genesis 1:29 AMP). "You may freely eat of every tree of the garden; but of the tree of the knowledge of good and evil and blessing and calamity you shall not eat" (Genesis 2:16-17 AMP).

Adam and Eve were created by God as His children. He placed them in a beautiful garden giving them everything they needed to live a fruitful and healthy life. He told them what they could eat and what they could not eat. Do you think it mattered to God what they ate? All Adam and Eve had to do was obey this one commandment about what not to eat. As a matter of fact, God was very clear in telling them what would happen if they ate what He told them not to, "For in the day that you eat of it you shall surely die" (Genesis 2:17 AMP).

God explained to Adam and Eve there were benefits of obedience and consequences of disobedience. Many people wonder why God even gave man a choice in the first place. God so loved His children that He wanted them to freely choose to love Him back. 2 John 6 says, "And what this love consists in is this: that we live *and* walk in accordance with *and* guided by His commandments (His orders, ordinances, precepts, teaching). This is the commandment, as you have heard from the beginning, that you continue to walk in love [guided by it and following it]" (AMP). In other words, when you love someone you choose to obey them.

What could possibly make Adam and Eve choose to disobey their loving heavenly Father?

> *The serpent was the shrewdest of all the wild animals the LORD God had made. One day he asked the woman, "Did God really say you must not eat the fruit from any of the trees in the garden?"*
>
> *"Of course we may eat fruit from the trees in the garden," the woman replied. "It's only the fruit from the tree in the middle of the garden that we are not allowed to eat. God said, 'You must not eat it or even touch it; if you do, you will die.'"*
>
> *"You won't die!" the serpent replied to the woman. "God knows that your eyes will be opened as soon as you eat it, and you will be like God, knowing both good and evil."*
>
> *The woman was convinced.* ***She saw that the tree was beautiful and its fruit looked delicious, and she wanted the wisdom it would give her.*** *So she took some of the fruit and ate it. Then she gave some to her husband, who was with her, and he ate it, too.* (Genesis 3:1-7 NLT emphasis added)

What did Satan tempt Adam and Eve with? What does Satan tempt you and me with today? What was the first sin in the Bible? "She took some of the fruit and ate it," the Bible tells us which was in direct disobedience to God's command to Adam. So is eating something God says is not good for our bodies in direct disobedience to Him? What does eating what we know God would not approve of show about our love for Him? When you look at it that way, does it change your attitude toward the food you eat?

God's Benefit Package

God is very clear in His Word the benefits He gives to His children when they obey Him. He is also very clear concerning the consequences of disobedience.

> *Do you not know that if you continually surrender yourselves to anyone to do his will, you are the slaves of him whom you obey, whether that be to sin, which leads to death, or to obedience which leads to righteousness (right doing and right standing with God)? But thank God, though you were once slaves of sin, you have become obedient with all your heart to the standard of teaching in which you were instructed and to which you were committed. And having been set free from sin, you have become the servants of righteousness (of conformity to the divine will in thought, purpose, and action). I am speaking in familiar human terms because of your natural limitations. For as you yielded your bodily members [and faculties] as servants to impurity and ever increasing lawlessness, so now yield your bodily members [and faculties] once for all as servants to righteousness (right being and doing) [which leads] to sanctification. For when you were slaves of sin, you were free in regard to righteousness. But then what benefit (return) did you get from the things of which you are now ashamed? [None] for the end of those things is death. But now since you have been set free from sin and have become the slaves of God, you have your present reward in holiness and its end is eternal life. For the wages which sin pays is death, but the [bountiful] free gift of God is eternal life through (in union with) Jesus Christ our Lord. (Romans 6:16-23 AMP)*

- Disobedience makes us unfit to do anything good (see Titus 1:16).
- Disobedience keeps us from entering His rest (see Hebrews 4:6).
- Disobedience may set an example for others to fail to enter His rest as well (see Hebrews 4:11).

So brace up your minds; be sober (circumspect, morally alert); set your hope wholly and unchangeably on the grace (divine favor) that is coming to you when Jesus Christ (the Messiah) is revealed. [Live] as children of obedience [to God]; do not conform yourselves to the evil desires [that governed you] in your former ignorance [when you did not know the requirements of the Gospel]. But as the One Who called you is holy, you yourselves also be holy in all your conduct and manner of living. For it is written, You shall be holy, for I am holy. And if you call upon Him as [your] Father Who judges each one impartially according to what he does, [then] you should conduct yourselves with true reverence throughout the time of your temporary residence [on the earth, whether long or short]. You must know (recognize) that you were redeemed (ransomed) from the useless (fruitless) way of living inherited by tradition from [your] forefathers, not with corruptible things [such as] silver and gold, But [you were purchased] with the precious blood of Christ (the Messiah), like that of a [sacrificial] lamb without blemish or spot. (1 Peter 1:13-19 AMP)

Ask Yourself:

If I am not taking care of this body, this temple God gave me am I disobeying Him?

Do I really want to continue to be a disobedient child?

Action Suggestion:

Read Romans 6:16-23 and highlight all the benefits of obedience listed in these verses. Then write them in your journal. Read the verses that talk about the consequences of disobedience and list those in your journal as well. Ask God for wisdom to remember the benefits of obedience. Make a conscious choice to choose obedience to God in everything you do including what you eat and how you treat your body.

Chapter 3

WHY DID GOD MAKE ME THIS WAY?

As I look back over my life, I think one of the most pertinent questions I asked and people now ask me is why did God make me this way? I had to realize it was not God's fault I was fat. It was not His fault I didn't like who I was. It was not His fault I didn't like what I saw in the mirror. I learned I had to take 100 percent responsibility for being fat. One of the ways God helped me come to these conclusions and begin to do something about it was to show me how and why He made me the way He did. I believe the answers I found through prayer will help you discover who you really are.

Answer 1: Acknowledge You Are Fearfully and Wonderfully Made

I praise you, for I am fearfully and wonderfully made. Wonderful are your works; my soul knows it very well. My frame was not hidden from you, when I was being made in secret, intricately woven in the depths of the earth. Your eyes saw my unformed substance; in your book were written, every one of them, the days that were formed for me, when as yet there was none of them. (Psalm 139:13-16)

Psalm 139:15 says God, the author of life, has intricately woven each of us individually. We are not "cookie-cutter" creations. He has made each one of us wonderfully unique by His own hand. We are fearfully and wonderfully made! There are some very expressive words used in this Psalm to describe God's process of creating us. To understand how to care for what He has given us, we must understand and then acknowledge just how fearfully and wonderfully we have been made.

You are fearfully and wonderfully made! In other words you are awesome, admirable, and created by His hand in a wonderful manner. Intricately woven means you are a complex, elaborately detailed, and very complicated person with many interrelated parts or facets. Have you ever admired a delicate piece of jewelry, twisted with decorative strands of gold and silver for its intricacy? I have a friend whose father owned a jewelry store and also fixed watches. Her father had to be specially trained to know what he was doing when working on a watch. A watch is made by human hands and is so intricate and tiny a jeweler has to use a magnifying glass to be sure all the parts are put together correctly so the watch will work properly.

Designed by the Master, our bodies are made of intricate parts which when taken care of properly work together. Just as the parts in a watch must be precise to work properly, God created the parts in our body to be precise with the heart pumping a certain amount of blood, the heart beating a certain number of times in a minute, and the blood flowing throughout the body at just the right speed. Every part of the body must be precise to make it work properly. When you don't take care of your watch, it can quit. Many times all it takes is a new battery to get it running properly again. The same is true with the body. Sometimes all it needs is a combination of the proper foods, the right amount of exercise and rest, and it will begin working properly again.

Think about how marvelous, wonderful, intricate, and complex the details of the human body are.

Intricacies of the Human Body

Interesting facts about the human body:
1. The average red blood cell lives for 120 days. There are 2.5 trillion red blood cells in your body at any moment. To maintain this number, about two and a half million new ones need to be produced every second by your bone marrow. A red blood cell can circumnavigate your body in under 20 seconds. We give birth to 100 billion red cells every day.
2. Considering all the tissues and cells in your body, 25 million new cells are being produced each second. That's a little more than the population of Australia–every second!

Why Did God Make Me This Way?

3. Nerve Impulses travel at over 400 km/hr (240 miles/hr).

4. Our heart beats around 100,000 times every day. Our blood is on a 60,000-mile journey. Give a tennis ball a good, hard squeeze and you're using about the same amount of force your heart uses to pump blood out to the body. The human heart creates enough pressure when it pumps blood, that it could squirt blood 30 feet. The aorta, the largest artery in the body, is almost the diameter of a garden hose. Capillaries, on the other hand, are so small that it takes ten of them to equal the thickness of a human hair. Your body has about 5.6 liters (6 quarts) of blood. These 5.6 liters of blood circulates through the body three times every minute. The heart pumps about 1 million barrels of blood during an average lifetime–that's enough to fill more than 3 super tankers.

5. Our eyes can distinguish up to one million color surfaces and take in more information than the largest telescope known to man. It is believed that the main purpose of eyebrows is to keep sweat out of the eyes. If you could save all the times your eyes blink in one life time and use them all at once you would see blackness for 1.2 years! Your eyeballs are three and a half percent salt. Our eyes never grow.

6. Our lungs inhale over two million liters of air every day, without even thinking. A person can expect to breathe in about 40 pounds of dust over his/her lifetime. The surface area of a human lung is equal to that of a tennis court.

7. We exercise at least 30 muscles when we smile. The human body has fewer muscles in it than a caterpillar. You sit on the biggest muscle in your body, the gluteus maximus a.k.a. the butt. Each of the two cheeky muscles tips the scales at about two pounds (not including the overlying fat layer). The tiniest muscle, the stapedius of the middle ear, is just one-fifth of an inch long.

8. We are about 70 percent water. We make one liter of saliva a day. People are the only creatures in the world who cry tears.

9. Our nose is our personal air-conditioning system: it warms cold air, cools hot air and filters impurities. A sneeze generates a wind of 166 km/hr. (100 miles/hr.), and a cough moves out at 100 km/hr. (60 miles/hr.). It's impossible to sneeze with your eyes open. When you sneeze, all your bodily functions stop–even your heart.

Our nose and ears never stop growing. You can only smell 1/20th as well as a dog. You breathe in about 7 quarts of air every minute.

10. In one square inch of our hand we have nine feet of blood vessels, 600 pain sensors, 9000 nerve endings, 36 heat sensors and 75 pressure sensors. When we touch something, we send a message to our brain at 124 mph. There are more living organisms on the skin of a single human being than there are human beings on the surface of the earth. One square inch of human skin contains 625 sweat glands. Humans shed about 600,000 particles of skin every hour–about 1.5 pounds a year. By 70 years of age, an average person will have lost 105 pounds of skin. Every month you grow a brand new outer layer of skin, "a new you!"

11. We have copper, zinc, cobalt, calcium, manganese, phosphates, nickel and silicon in our bodies. Your body contains enough iron to make a spike strong enough to hold your weight. The amount of carbon in the human body is enough to fill about 9,000 "lead" pencils.

12. From the age of thirty, humans gradually begin to shrink in size.

13. Most people have lost fifty per cent of their taste buds by the time they reach the age of sixty. The life span of a taste bud is ten days.

14. Babies start dreaming even before they're born and acquire fingerprints at the age of three months.

15. The human body can function without a brain.

16. Humans are the only primates that don't have pigment in the palms of their hands.

17. 10% of human dry weight comes from bacteria. There are more bacteria in your mouth than the human population of the United States and Canada combined. Every square inch of the human body has an average of 32 million bacteria on it.

18. The average human head weighs about 10 pounds. The average human brain weighs three pounds.

19. The DNA helix measures 80 billionths of an inch wide.

20. Human teeth are almost as hard as rocks.[4]

What happens when we don't take care of any part of this intricate body God has given us?

---

4   www.com/Intricacies+Of+Human+Body

What might be causing some of the parts not to work correctly?

Ask Yourself:

How has God intricately created my body as His masterpiece?

In what ways am I fearfully and wonderfully made?

Do I truly acknowledge just how marvelously God has put me together?

Action Suggestion:

Use Psalm 139:14 to give thanks to God for making you so wonderfully complex, so intricate, and so amazing! Thank God for His workmanship and how marvelous it is that He has made you the way He did!

Answer 2: Acknowledge God Knows All About You

Before I formed you in the womb I knew [and] approved of you [as My chosen instrument], and before you were born I separated and set you apart, consecrating you; [and] I appointed you as a prophet to the nations. (Jeremiah 1:5 AMP)

God knew you before He formed you in your mother's womb and approved of you as His chosen instrument. That means God had something in mind for you to accomplish here on this earth even before you were born. God intricately designed you to accomplish that specific purpose. God separated and set you apart before you were born to do a very important and unique job for Him in His kingdom. In Jeremiah 1:5 God told Jeremiah He had called him to be a prophet to the nations. It is important you understand just how important you are to God and that He knows what you need to accomplish your specific purpose here on the earth.

Psalm 139:1 says, "O Lord, you have examined my heart and know everything about me" (NLT). God is all-seeing, all-knowing, all-powerful, and everywhere present. God knows us, God is with us, and His greatest gift is to allow us to know Him. You don't need a name tag. You aren't just a number in a computer. You don't even have to wait on hold to talk to Him!

> *You know when I sit down or stand up. You know my thoughts even when I'm far away. You see me when I travel and when I rest at home. You know everything I do. You know what I am going to say even before I say it, LORD.* (Psalm 139:2-4 NLT)

Psalm 139:2-4 says God also knows what you do, where you go, and what you think. God knows **all** there is to know about you. He even knows what you don't want others to know. This is such a personal passage showing God's continual, active presence wherever you go – day or night. He knows and understands you better than anyone else ever will. He loves you as though you were the only one to love! I believe these verses are saying, "You are special to God and He wants to be a part of your life."

As I was dealing with weight issues in my own life, realizing God wanted to be an active part in my life became a turning point for me. When I was working with my business coach, Sean, I realized I had a lot of questions I had asked God over the years, yet I had never taken the time to search the scriptures for answers. The questions were coming from a heart which was not joyful. They were coming from a blaming heart instead of a grateful heart. As I studied, Psalm 139:5 became a key verse for me. "You go before me and follow me. You place your hand of blessing on my head" (NLT).

God knows you and He knows what you need. By laying His hand gently on your head He is giving you reassurance of His presence in your life no matter where you are or what you do. Think about how good it feels to have someone lay a loving hand on your head. In January 2014, my second grandson was born. He had some issues and was taken to NICU. One of the pictures I have of my son is with his hand on his baby's head. It was his way of showing his love and reassuring the baby. I feel this way when I visualize God's hand of blessing on my head.

Ask Yourself:

> *How does it make me feel to know God knows where I am and what I do?*

What has God chosen me to do for Him in His kingdom?

What special ability has He equipped me with to accomplish His purpose?

Action Suggestion:

If you can't answer the questions about what God has chosen you to do, pray and ask Him for wisdom to help you find your why, your purpose, and your mission in life. Study the scriptures and allow the Holy Spirit to work in you. Record your thoughts in your journal. How has God specifically equipped you to do the job? Think of your journal as your own personal conversation with God.

Thank God that He knows all about you and loves you anyway! Tell Him you want Him to be an active part in your life from today on! You can also contact me and have me coach you. I will guide you as you discover your core strengths, what makes you feel important, and your purpose on this earth. My contact information is at the end of this book.

Answer 3: Acknowledge You Cannot Hide from God

> *I can never escape from your Spirit! I can never get away from your presence! [8] If I go up to heaven, you are there; if I go down to the grave, you are there. [9] If I ride the wings of the morning, if I dwell by the farthest oceans, [10] even there your hand will guide me, and your strength will support me. [11] I could ask the darkness to hide me and the light around me to become night—[12] but even in darkness I cannot hide from you. To you the night shines as bright as day. Darkness and light are the same to you.* (Psalm 139:7-12 NLT)

It is important that you understand there is no place you can be hidden from God. He knows where you go and what you do. Have you ever wanted to hide your sins and your guilt from everyone including God? You might be able to hide certain things from others. However, God knows everything. It's not because He is trying to catch you at something, it's because

He cares and loves you just as a parent loves a child. When you were a child did you believe your mother had eyes in the back of her head like I did?

When we read the story of Adam and Eve in the Garden of Eden, we may think to ourselves how foolish they were to think they could hide from God (see Genesis 3:8). When God called out for Adam in Genesis 3:9, do we really think God did not know where Adam was? God knew exactly where Adam and Eve were hiding. He also knew why they were hiding. God wanted them to acknowledge they could not hide from Him and to confess to Him what they had done.

Don't we sometimes do the very same thing? We are ashamed or embarrassed by something we have done or said and want to hide it from everyone, including God. It is very important that we acknowledge the fact we cannot hide anything from God. This will help us stop and think before we say or do something we know He wouldn't approve.

Even though people around us normally don't know what is going on with us until we speak or act, God knows our thoughts as well. There are many places in the Bible that talk about being careful of what we focus our thoughts on because what we think will often become our words and actions.

Philippians 4:8 gives us a list of positive things to think about. Psalm 94:11 says, "The LORD knows the thoughts of man." Isaiah 55:8 says, "'My thoughts are nothing like your thoughts,' says the LORD" (NLT). We want to focus on God's thoughts, especially what He thinks about us!

How precious are your thoughts about me O God. They cannot be numbered! I can't even count them; they outnumber the grains of sand! And when I wake up, you are still with me! (Psalm 139:17-18 NLT)

Psalm 139:10 tells us why God is so intent on knowing where we are and what we are doing. "Even there," wherever "there" might be, the Psalmist writes, "God's hand will guide me, and His strength will support me." Isn't that what we really want God to do? Don't we want Him to be there to guide and support us every step of the way?

*Lean on, trust in, and be confident in the Lord with **all** your heart and mind and do not rely on your own insight or under-standing. In **all** your ways **know, recognize, and acknowledge***

Him, and He will direct and make straight and plain your paths. (Proverbs 3:5-6 AMP emphasis added)

By acknowledging you cannot hide anything or go anywhere without God, it will allow you to access the promise of Proverbs 3:6. Why not get this truth set in your mind and heart today and start acknowledging and welcoming His presence in your life.

Ask Yourself:

What have I tried to hide from God?

Has it worked? How come?

Do I want Him to direct and make straight my paths?

What do I need to do today to receive this guidance and support from God?

Action Suggestion:

Reread Psalm 139:7-18. Acknowledge God's presence in your life and thank Him that you do not have to hide anything from Him. Tell God today that you want to lean on, trust in, and be confident in Him with all your heart and mind, and ask Him to guide and direct your path. Openly share with Him in your Conversation with God section what you have tried to hide. Ask and receive His forgiveness. Begin each day acknowledging and welcoming His presence in your life.

Answer 4: Acknowledge God Has a Plan for Your Life

Search me, O God, and know my heart; test me and know my anxious thoughts. Point out anything in me that offends you, and lead me along the path of everlasting life. (Psalm 139:23-24 NLT)

David knows God can access his thoughts. He has already acknowledged in the previous verses of Psalm 139 that God knows all about us, knows what we are doing and where we are. We have to come to a place where we have acknowledged God knows everything about us, and we cannot hide anything from Him. Having come to that conclusion, David now asks God to search his heart for any sin in his life, and to point out that sin! He even goes so far as to ask God to reveal anything that offends God and asks God to lead him along the path of everlasting life.

Do a study of David's life. He went from a shepherd boy to a king with a lot of trials and tribulations in between. He even committed some very serious sins, but one of the amazing things about David is God referred to him in a very special way. God said, "I have found David, son of Jesse, a man after my own heart. He will do everything I want him to do" (Acts 13:22 NLT). David wrote the Psalms so we could learn what he had discovered about how to please God. David was willing to write about his adventures and misadventures so we could learn from his mistakes as well as his victories. I believe God gave us the record of David's life so we could see that this great king was not perfect, yet he deeply desired to fulfill God's plan for his life.

In 1 Chronicles 28:9 we read what David then told his son, Solomon who would become the next king. "And you, Solomon my son, know the God of your father [have personal knowledge of Him, be acquainted with, and understand Him; appreciate, heed, and cherish Him] and serve Him with a blameless heart and a willing mind. For the Lord searches all hearts *and* minds and understands all the wanderings of the thoughts" (AMP).

Combined with what we have learned about David, the two verses in Psalm 139 open up a whole area we need to explore if we are going to please God with our lives here on earth and show Him we want to walk that path to eternal life with Him. Like David we have to be willing to have God shine His light into those dark areas in our hearts and expose anything that does not belong there.

These are hard questions, but by answering them we can begin to acknowledge that God not only fearfully and wonderfully formed us, but also that He knows us from the inside out. We cannot hide anything from Him and we have to be willing to allow Him to expose anything that does not belong in our lives. Then, even when we miss the mark and do something we know does not please God, we can pick ourselves up and continue on down the path God has set before us.

Do you want God to point out your sin?

Do you want God to search you from the inside out?

Do you want to know what thoughts offend God?

Do you want God to lead you on a path of everlasting life?

Remember, it is sin to know what you ought to do and then not do it. (James 4:17 NLT)

Ask Yourself:

> *Am I willing to make verses 23 and 24 my prayer?*

> *Is God ever offended by the choices I make that do not take good care of the masterpiece He created?*

> *Am I willing to invite God to search my heart and reveal to me what He finds?*

> *Am I willing to change or do away with anything that offends God?*

Action Suggestion:

Read Psalm 139 several times this week and write down what pops out at you. Before you eat, think about whether the food you are thinking of consuming will nurture or hurt your masterpiece. Ask God to remind you of what you have learned every day.

I'm Special

(From the children's book, "I'm Special, I'm Me" by Sarah Massini)
I'm special. In all the world there's nobody like me.
Since the beginning of time, there has never been another person like me.
Nobody has my smile. Nobody has my eyes, my nose, my hair,
my hands, my voice. I'm special.
No one can be found who has my handwriting.
Nobody anywhere has my tastes for food or music or art.
No one sees things just as I do.
In all of time there's been no one who laughs like me, no one who
cries like me. And what makes me laugh and cry will never provoke
identical laughter and tears from anybody else, ever.
No one reacts to any situation just as I would react. I'm special.
I'm the only one in all of creation who has my set of abilities.
Oh there will always be somebody who is better at one of the things
I'm good at, but no one in the universe can reach the quality of my
combination of talents, ideas, abilities and feelings. Like a room full
of musical instruments, some may excel alone, but none can match
the symphony sound when all are played together.
I'm a symphony.
Through all of eternity no one will ever look, talk,
walk, think or do like me.
I'm special, I'm rare.
And in all rarity there is great value.
Because of my great rare value, I need not attempt to imitate others.
I will accept—yes, celebrate my differences.
I'm special. And I'm beginning to realize it's no accident that I'm
special. I'm beginning to realize that God made me special for a very special
purpose. He must have a job for me that no one else can do
as well as I. Out of all the billions of applicants only one is qualified,
only one has the right combination of what it takes.
That one is me. Because... I'm special.

Chapter 4

How Can I Keep From Failing at Every Diet I Try?

———⧼⧽———

*For His divine power has bestowed upon us **all things** that [are requisite and suited] to life and godliness, through the [full, personal] knowledge of Him Who called us by and to His own glory and excellence (virtue). By means of these He has bestowed on us His precious and exceedingly great promises, so that through them **you may escape** [by flight] from the moral decay (rottenness and corruption) that is in the world because of covetousness (lust and greed), and become sharers (partakers) of the divine nature.* (2 Peter 1:3-4 AMP)

"Why do I fail at every diet I try?" is the cry of so many women I talk to as a Certified Grief Coach. Billions are spent each year on weight loss programs supposedly designed to help you get the weight off quickly. The problem with "diets" is they are designed to treat the symptoms, not the cause. We need to understand there is a price to pay for everything we put in our bodies. As I focused on helping women take care of themselves physically to be their best spiritually, I started thinking about the challenges I had when I was overweight. I believe the answers I found concerning dieting will be of great value as you move forward to become all that God has designed you to be.

Answer 1: Understand He Has Given You What You Need

Today we live in a microwave society that wants a quick answer for every question they ask. The internet has made it easy to look up things online and often find a quick answer to a question. However, when it comes to losing (or releasing) weight and then keeping it off, there is no quick fix or quick answer. One thing I have learned is there is a consequence—good or bad—to everything we do. If we touch a hot stove we are going to get burned. If we take good care of our bodies we will be healthy. We need to realize there is a price to pay for everything we put in our bodies.

Do you know every little decision you make each and every day will make a difference and grow to an amazing final result?

"The food you eat today is walking and talking tomorrow."
– Jack LaLanne

We know from previous lessons that God designed our bodies to function in a certain way. They were designed to need a certain kind of fuel. The nutritional approach is not new. The founder of medicine, Hippocrates, in 390 B.C. said, "Let food be your medicine and medicine be your food." Thomas Edison, inventor of the light bulb, said, "The doctor of the future will give no medicine but will interest his patients in the care of the human frame, diet, and the cause and prevention of disease." Instead of thinking of our body as a machine that needs fixing, we need to see it as an intricate, complex, divinely assembled group of systems designed by God to take us safely through life here on this earth. All we really need to do is supply it with the right kind of fuel.

The evidence has been staring each of us in the face for decades: eating healthy will help us look better, feel better, give us more energy, prevent disease, and add years to our lives. The problem with most diets is they list the foods we need to stop eating and they are usually foods we want to eat. We like those foods. Which approach is better—telling us what we can't eat or what we can eat? Many people begin to feel they live a "yo-yo" life where they lose the weight, gain it back, lose the weight, and often gain back even more. Now that's a problem! Obviously conventional approaches to dieting that give us a "do not eat" list are not really effective.

Another problem I have discovered is when most people start a weight loss program, it's all about reaching a certain number on the scale, wearing a certain size, and how fast can you do it. However the problem is once a person has achieved their goal weight or their dress size they go right back to their old way of eating and the vicious cycle begins all over again.

I came to realize it's not about the number on the scale or the dress size. It's about taking care of myself physically to be my best spiritually. It's about understanding, loving, and cherishing this amazing creation God gave me. It became easier and easier to say no to the foods I knew would harm my body and to focus on foods to fuel my body and keep me healthy. And, what's even more exciting and amazing, I eat foods I thought were "no- no's"—foods I love but thought I could never eat! I found that being focused on losing weight was a negative mindset because when you lose something it usually means you want to find it. Instead I began to focus on taking care of the masterpiece God gave me and eating the way God intended me to eat.

Throughout the rest of these lessons, we will talk about eating healthy and eating to live instead of living to eat, because when you decide to eat healthy the rest of your life, you can release the weight and keep it off! If you choose not to take care of yourself and not eat the way God intended you are headed for the yo-yo cycle.

What message are you sending to yourself, your family, and others when you are living a yo-yo lifestyle? What message are you sending God? Are you telling Him His creation isn't important and you don't care about the gift He has given you? God has equipped us with everything we need, from the inside out, to escape corruption and partake of the divine nature. Learn to work with God's design and you will experience amazing results!

"Reality is that we are sons and daughters of the living God. We have His spiritual genetics within us. We haven't simply been taught a better way, we have the Spirit of the true way living within us."[5]

---

5   (*Beloved Children* by Chris Tiegreen "Wonders of Wholeness," Tyndale, 2009, February 10)

Ask Yourself:

Am I willing to do what is necessary to have a healthy masterpiece?

Am I ready to make the right decisions every day?

Am I ready to have a lifestyle of healthy eating instead of a quick fix diet?

Action Suggestions:

I invite you to pray every day and ask God for wisdom on your journey. Ask Him to help you when you know there are going to be foods available you know aren't the best for you to eat. Journal your prayers to Him. Write down what you eat, why you eat, and when you eat. Ask God to help you stop when you feel full! Use the Strategic Daily Plan at the end of the book to help guide your new eating habits. Look at this as a lifestyle change, not another diet.

Answer 2: Know God Will Help When You Think You Can't Bear it

*For **no temptation (no trial regarded as enticing to sin), [no matter how it comes or where it leads]** has overtaken you and laid hold on you that is not common to man [that is, **no temptation or trial has come to you that is beyond human resistance and that is not adjusted and adapted and belonging to human experience, and such as man can bear**]. But God is faithful [to His Word and to His compassionate nature], and **He [can be trusted] not to let you be tempted and tried and assayed beyond your ability and strength of resistance and power to endure**, but with the temptation **He will [always] also provide** the way out (the means of escape to a landing place), that **you may be capable** and strong and powerful to bear up under it patiently.* (1 Corinthians 10:13 AMP)

Notice in the verse it says, "God will provide a way out." When a temptation comes, we can't overcome it alone. We must have God's help. Maybe we need to spend more time seeking God and get our eyes off of the temptation. God wants us to ask Him for help!

People often tell me they have a hard time with this because the temptations around them are so great. God is aware and has promised us we will not be subjected to any temptation that we cannot endure. If we would just ask Him, He will show us a way out so we can endure no matter what the temptation.

The story of Daniel (1:8-16) in the Old Testament gives us an example of how God will not allow us to be tempted beyond what we can handle and how He will show us a way out. He will even use our obedience to His commands to promote us to a position of influence among those who need to know about Him.

> But **Daniel was determined not to defile himself by eating the food and wine** given to them by the king. He asked the chief of staff for permission not to eat these unacceptable foods. [9] **Now God had given the chief of staff both respect and affection for Daniel.** [10] But he responded, "I am afraid of my lord the king, who has ordered that you eat this food and wine. If you become pale and thin compared to the other youths your age, I am afraid the king will have me beheaded."
>
> [11] Daniel spoke with the attendant who had been appointed by the chief of staff to look after Daniel, Hananiah, Mishael, and Azariah. [12] **"Please test us for ten days on a diet of vegetables and water,"** Daniel said. [13] "At the end of the ten days, see how we look compared to the other young men who are eating the king's food. Then make your decision in light of what you see." [14] The attendant agreed to Daniel's suggestion and tested them for ten days. [15] **At the end of the ten days, Daniel and his three friends looked healthier and better nourished than the young men who had been eating the food assigned by the king.** [16] So after that, the attendant fed them only vegetables instead of the food and wine provided for the others. (Daniel 1:8-16 NLT emphasis added)

What a powerful testimony Daniel's life is of God's protection and provision when we are determined not to defile ourselves with what we eat and drink. Several other translations of verse 9 say God gave Daniel favor with the chief of staff. Interesting that Daniel earned this high court official's respect by doing what God had instructed him to do in the area of eating and drinking. If you read the rest of Daniel's story you will find Daniel was promoted to a very high position by King Darius which resulted in an amazing declaration by this "heathen" king.

> *Then King Darius wrote to all the peoples, nations, and languages that dwell in all the earth: "Peace be multiplied to you. [26]* ***I make a decree, that in all my royal dominion people are to tremble and fear before the God of Daniel,*** *for he is the living God, enduring forever; his kingdom shall never be destroyed, and his dominion shall be to the end. [27] He delivers and rescues; he works signs and wonders in heaven and on earth, he who has saved Daniel from the power of the lions."* (Daniel 6:25-27 emphasis added)

I have an acronym for you to use when you are being tempted. We are going to spell "weight" a slightly different way. It has to do with becoming aware of why you are eating what you are eating.

W–Why
A–Am
I–I
E–Eating
T–This?

Ask Yourself:

What if I asked myself this question when I am tempted?

What if I begin to eat only when I am really hungry?

What if I choose to eat the foods God intended for me to eat?

Could I be enthused about feeling better and sleeping better?

Could I be enthused about having more energy?

What if others began to notice the difference in me?

What if I choose to find out what God says about taking care of my Masterpiece?

Action Suggestions:

Read 1 Corinthians 10:13 out loud to yourself. It is important that you get this truth deep inside of you and really begin to believe it. The secret to overcoming temptation is to trust God to show you the way out.

> *The temptations in your life are no different from what others experience. And God is faithful. He will not allow the temptation to be more than you can stand. When you are tempted, he will show you a way out so that you can endure.* (1 Corinthians 10:13 NLT)

Implement the "what if" listed questions above and talk to God about the temptations you have been facing. Ask for wisdom in overcoming them. Thank God for His promise to always provide you a way of out! Use the "I Did" and "I Didn't" Journal sample below to get you started.

MY DAILY "I DID" and "I DIDN'T" JOURNAL

This Journal is designed to help you stay focused on your accomplishments for the day.

Examples of "I Did."
*I did eat a healthy lunch (write down what you ate)
*I did enjoy the healthy food I ate.
*I did have a potluck at work today; however, I took small amounts of food.
*I did keep my mouth shut instead of saying some words that are offensive.

Examples of "I Didn't."
*I didn't eat the cookie offered to me at break time today.
*I didn't eat burger and fries today.
*I didn't eat the desserts at the potluck at work today.

The goal is to find three "I Did" and three "I Didn't" per day.

If you gave in to the temptation during the day, write down why you think it happened and what could you do to keep it from happening again.

Answer 3: Realize Gluttony Does Not Honor God

> *So, whether you eat or drink, or whatever you do, do all to the glory of God.* (1 Corinthians 10:31)

We are clearly told in this verse we are to honor God in all that we do, including what we eat and drink. The Apostle Paul told his young disciple in 2 Timothy 1:7, "For God did not give us a spirit of timidity (of cowardice, of craven and cringing and fawning fear), but [He has given us a spirit] of power and of love and of calm *and* well-balanced mind *and* discipline *and* self-control" (AMP). Gluttony or self-indulgence is the opposite of self-control.

Gluttony is defined as excessive eating, the act or practice of eating and drinking to excess or indulging in an activity to excess; voracious. Gluttony also refers to a greedy or excessive indulgence in anything

(Wikipedia Encyclopedia). The Bible has a lot to say about gluttony. Ezekiel 16:49 says one of the sins of Sodom and Gomorrah was over indulgence in food. Proverbs 23:19-21 advises us, "Do not associate with winebibbers; be not among them nor among gluttonous eaters of meat, for the drunkard and the glutton shall come to poverty, and drowsiness shall clothe a man with rags" (AMP). Proverbs 28:7 says, "A companion of gluttons and the carousing, self-indulgent, and extravagant shames his father" (AMP).

Our bodies are the temple of the Holy Spirit. We are to be an example to others. We are to honor and glorify God with our bodies. It is up to each of us to make the decision to exercise self-discipline and self-control and realize God has given us all we need to be able to escape the corruption in the world caused by evil desires. We do, however, play a part in the development of that self-control.

> [5] *For this very reason, adding your diligence [to the divine promises], employ every effort in exercising your faith to develop virtue (excellence, resolution, Christian energy), and in [exercising] virtue [develop] knowledge (intelligence), and in [exercising] knowledge [develop] self-control, and in [exercising] self-control [develop] steadfastness (patience, endurance), and in [exercising] steadfastness [develop] godliness (piety), and in [exercising] godliness [develop] brotherly affection, and in [exercising] brotherly affection [develop] Christian love.*

> [8] *For as these qualities are yours and increasingly abound in you, they will keep [you] from being idle or unfruitful unto the [full personal] knowledge of our Lord Jesus Christ (the Messiah, the Anointed One). [9] For whoever lacks these qualities is blind, [spiritually] shortsighted, seeing only what is near to him, and has become oblivious [to the fact] that he was cleansed from his old sins. [10] Because of this, brethren, be all the more solicitous and eager to make sure (to ratify, to strengthen, to make steadfast) your calling and election; for if you do this, you will never stumble or fall. (2 Peter 1:5-10 AMP)*

Let's look at the progressive list we have been given in this passage of scripture:

- Add your diligence to the divine promises (1 Timothy 4:14-15)
- Employ every effort in exercising your faith to develop virtue, excellence, resolution, and Christian energy (Colossians 3:1-14)
- In exercising virtue develop your knowledge (2 Peter 3:18, Proverbs 1:7)
- In exercising knowledge develop your self-control (1 Peter 5:8)
- In exercising self-control develop your patience, endurance (Romans 12:12)
- In exercising steadfastness develop your godliness (1 Timothy 4:12)
- In exercising godliness develop your brotherly affection (Colossians 3:12)
- In exercising brotherly affection develop your Christian love (1 John 4:7-12)

Read again 2 Peter 1:3-4.

You cannot just pray and ask God to give you self-control and self-discipline. This passage of scripture clearly shows us we have to follow God's instructions and go through the process in order to access what we need to achieve our victory. We are an active participant in this process. This also shows us why quick fix diets do not work. There are steps that must be followed. You cannot skip any of them either. This is not meant to discourage you but encourage you to stick to it knowing the end result is lasting not temporary. You can stop the yo-yo weight loss cycle by doing things God's way. He has told you He has given you all you need to move forward and achieve the victory. He expects you to use what He has given you to honor Him!

Ask Yourself:

What does self-discipline or self-control mean to me personally?

Am I showing self-control with my eating?

Am I associating with those who encourage me to give in to gluttony?

Am I ready and willing to go through God's process to win the victory?

Do I truly want to honor God with what I eat and drink?

Action Suggestions:

What changes do you want to make in your lifestyle to make sure everything you are doing, including eating or drinking, honors God? Ask God to help you come up with a list and then ask Him to honor His promise to show you the way out of every temptation that comes your way. If you are associating with those who encourage you to behave in a gluttonous way, perhaps it is time to separate yourself from them until you can be a positive witness to them instead of letting them influence your behavior. Pray daily for God's wisdom and favor and you will find you can overcome every temptation.

Go back over the progressive list given in 2 Peter 1:5-10 and start looking up the additional scriptures given there to help you get started on your road to victory.

Answer 4: Enhance Your Health with Moderation

*Let your **moderation be known** unto all men.*
(Philippians 4:5 KJV)

Moderation is a word that you'll often hear when you're trying to lose or release weight and live a healthier lifestyle. The more you read and learn about healthy habits, the more this word comes up. We're told to eat in moderation, drink in moderation, and even exercise in moderation. I think we all have our own ideas about what moderation really means. We know it means avoiding extremes, but it can mean different things to different people. It's important for you to think about what moderation really means for you.

We can start with a dictionary definition of moderation which says, "avoiding extremes of behavior or expression, observing reasonable limits, temperate, and never to excess. It is an action of limiting, controlling or restricting something so that it becomes or remains moderate" (Merriam Webster's Collegiate Dictionary).

The Bible uses the word temperance or the word self-control when it describes moderation. However, no matter what word we use, it is something we have to learn to do. Self-control means we learn to control ourselves. We are not God's puppets. He wants us to learn to control ourselves out of love and respect for Him and how He created us as His masterpiece.

> *Whereby are given unto us exceeding great and precious promises: that by these ye might be partakers of the divine nature, having escaped the corruption that is in the world through lust. ⁵ And beside this, giving all diligence, add to your faith virtue; and to virtue knowledge; ⁶ And to knowledge **temperance**; and to **temperance** patience; and to patience godliness;* (2 Peter 1:4-6 KJV)

> *⁵ For this very reason, adding your diligence [to the divine promises], employ every effort in exercising your faith to develop virtue (excellence, resolution, Christian energy), and in [exercising] virtue [develop] knowledge (intelligence), and in [exercising] knowledge [develop] **self-control**, and in [exercising] **self-control** [develop] steadfastness (patience, endurance), and in [exercising] steadfastness [develop] godliness (piety), and in [exercising] godliness [develop] brotherly affection, and in [exercising] brotherly affection [develop] Christian love.* (2 Peter 1:5-6 AMP)

As we have studied these scriptures the one thing that stands out is when God tells us to do something, it is for our own good and He has given us what we need to obey Him. He also has given us the Holy Spirit to guide us if we will seek His help.

> *And everyone who competes for the prize **is temperate in all things**. Now they do it to obtain a perishable crown, but we for an imperishable crown.* (1 Corinthians 9:25 NKJV)

What is the prize spoken of in this scripture that we are competing for?

Is it worth being temperate in all things to attain it?

Proverbs 25:16 warns us to eat even things that are good for us in moderation. "If you have found honey, eat only enough for you, lest you have your fill of it and vomit it."

The opposite of eating and drinking in moderation is self-indulgence. In Matthew 23:25 Jesus criticized the Pharisees for their self-indulgence saying, "Woe to you, scribes and Pharisees, hypocrites! For you clean the outside of the cup and the plate, but inside they are full of greed and self-indulgence." Let us not be grouped with those Jesus considers self-indulgent. Learn the lesson of moderation!

Ask Yourself:

> *Who draws the line between excess and moderation in my life?*

> *Who is my "moderation guide?"*

> *Where do I discover the answers to my questions even about the food I eat?*

> *Is the prize I am trying to attain worth being temperate in all things, even in the food I eat?*

> *Do I want to be my best for Him?*

Action Suggestions:

Here are a couple of suggestions for beginning to implement moderation into your eating. When you eat – pay attention – savor the first bite (it's the best,) enjoy it, and take your time. Then pay attention to the chewing and really taste your food. Prepare your mind before eating, especially in a situation where there will be a lot of food – food fests, pot lucks, and holiday dinners. Think about what you have learned about gluttony and moderation. Think about honoring God in all you do. If you need to take a break and leave the room in order to "coach" yourself, take a trip to the restroom and talk to yourself in the mirror about treating your masterpiece the way God wants you to. Continue to journal the revelation God gives you and daily ask the Holy Spirit to be your guide.

Chapter 5

WHY DO I TURN TO FOOD FOR COMFORT?

A s we continue on our journey of discovery concerning the masterpiece God has given us, I want you to begin to look at food differently. I want you to see food as something to fuel your body. God didn't put us on this earth to live to eat – we are to eat to live. I want you to learn how to be in control of what you eat and not allow food to control you. Below are some questions to consider as we begin this next chapter.

Why do I use food as a crutch?

Why do I turn to food to comfort me?

Why do I turn to food whether I'm happy or sad?

Answer 1: Discover the Mindset behind Your Choices

In order to break the control food has over you, you will want to discover the mindset behind the choices you make when you eat. It's about *why, when, and what* you eat.

Confrontational Food–Perhaps your parents were one of those who told you if you eat the food on your plate, you would be rewarded with dessert. There is a seed planted in your mind that dessert is a reward for eating foods that are "good" for you. Did you ever tell yourself if you eat a salad for lunch you can have dessert with dinner? I can remember not wanting to eat cooked spinach. I didn't like the taste, looks or smell of it! I thought it was disgusting. It's my parent's fault I eat the way I do, right?

Cover Up Food–This is the food you eat to cover up pain. It is similar to comfort food, however, I believe it goes deeper. It's so deep, you may not even be aware of the real issue. Just as I wasn't aware I was trying to cover up the fat girl hiding in me, you may not know what you are covering up or you may know and choose to cover it up! Maybe you have had the death of a loved one and today was a particularly rough one so you tried to dull the pain by eating a special treat. Did it really dull the pain or did it cause more in the long run?

Convenient Food–This is the food you quickly grab and eat. It's mindless, it's careless, and it's extremely bad for your health. It's the burgers, fries, hot dogs, donuts, and the drive through food. You are running late, didn't have time for breakfast so you just went through the drive through at the donut place and picked up a coffee and a donut to hold you until lunch, right? You'll eat healthier at lunch so that makes it alright, right?

Celebration Food–This is the food you were rewarded with when you ate the foods your parents begged you to eat as a child. Remember being promised dessert if you ate your vegetables? So you grew up thinking vegetables were the "bad" food and desserts were the reward for eating the bad food. You were given a belief that sweet, sugary foods were the reward for "winning." You got a good report card or evaluation at work so you went out to dinner to celebrate and ate anything and everything you wanted. You earned it, right?

Comfort Food–This is the food you eat when you are sad about something. Unlike cover up food which is hiding pain, comfort food is eaten when you know what's going on and believe eating will comfort you. It's when you had a rough day at work and weren't treated the way you thought you should be treated. It's when a friend, spouse, or family member disappointed you. Have you ever had one of those days when people were rude and even mean to you so you went home and ate a quart of ice cream to make yourself feel better? How did you feel the next morning? Was it really worth it?

Conquer Food–This is when you look at food as a "win"–something to prove to yourself. When I was fat and told I shouldn't eat certain foods or I needed to go on a diet; it seemed I was even more determined to prove I could have those foods. No one was going to tell me I couldn't eat what I wanted to eat. By the time I was a senior in high school, I weighed about 210 pounds–that's a lot for a 5'4" female with small bones. My parents tried to get me to lose weight, but I resisted–I liked food and every time they pushed me about my weight, I would eat more. I was determined to prove I could eat what I wanted and still lose weight. Ever try it? How did it go for you?

Ask Yourself:

Confrontational Food–*It's my parent's fault I eat the way I do, right?*

Cover Up Food–*Did it really dull the pain or did it cause more in the long run?*

Convenient Food–*Did I eat healthier at lunch after I had convenient food for breakfast?*

Celebration Food–*I earned it, right?*

Comfort Food – *When I have had one of those days when people were rude and even mean my comfort food made me feel better, right? How did I feel the next morning? Was it really worth it?*

Conquer Food–*I was determined to prove I could eat what I wanted and still lose weight. How did it go for me?*

Action Suggestion:

As you read through the descriptions of the different mindsets connected with the food choices you make, did you see some answers to your questions concerning why food controls you sometimes? Now that you have begun to discover the mindsets behind your choices, I invite you to be open to what God would have you do to overcome these negative influences. Remember He has promised to give you a way out and has given you everything you need to live a godly, healthy, and productive life. In your conversations with God, talk to Him openly about what you are discovering. He is only a prayer away. Continue to use the "I Did" and "I Didn't" format in your journal to track eating patterns you might not have seen before based on what you learned about the mindsets behind your eating choices.

Answer 2: Face Your Circumstances

I had a friend share that when his dad was dying, he would sit down at the table and eat unhealthy foods. He said he was like a child out of control. It was as though he had to prove something. What my friend realized was his dad couldn't conquer his illness, however; when he sat down to eat, he could have a win. Have you ever felt you could never achieve what you wanted in life or weren't worthy enough to have what you wanted, so you compensated by eating whatever you wanted? Have you experienced circumstances that overwhelm you to the point you give up on trying to deal with them and turned to food for relief? Ever seen that commercial that asks how do you spell relief? Are you one that spells it – F O O D? The problem here is the circumstances don't go away and now you've made yourself overweight and unhealthy.

God has given you everything you need to make it through any circumstance and has promised to never tempt you beyond what you have the capability to overcome. Many times in the Bible, God did not take His people out of what they considered a negative circumstance. Rather, He took them safely through it, using it to help them become stronger. Instead of asking God to take you out of your current circumstance, ask Him to help you walk through it to the end. Then God will use you and that circumstance to help others as well.

When I was invited to go with several of the ladies I worked with to a weight loss meeting, I had to face the fact that I needed help to lose weight and keep it off. I kept thinking I should be able to do this myself, but it was time I faced the reality of my situation. As I joined the group and learned practical safe ways to lose weight; I realized this was one way God was using to help me not only face my situation, but move forward toward victory. There were times I would feel sorry for myself because I didn't get to eat like I wanted to. I faced the fact that I had issues. I discovered it's about taking care of myself physically to be my best spiritually. I learned it's about loving and cherishing this amazing creation God gave me and wanting to honor Him with the way I ate and drank. It became easier and easier to say no to the foods I knew would harm my body and to focus on foods to fuel my body and keep me healthy. Now I use what I have learned to help others deal with this issue of weight loss.

Look at the chart below and see how risky it is to not face the truth about what you are doing to your body because you refuse to face your circumstances head on.

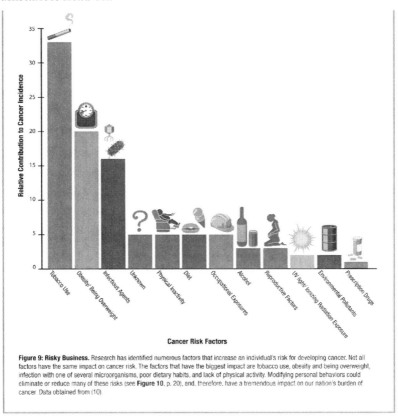

Figure 9: Risky Business. Research has identified numerous factors that increase an individual's risk for developing cancer. Not all factors have the same impact on cancer risk. The factors that have the biggest impact are tobacco use, obesity and being overweight, infection with one of several microorganisms, poor dietary habits, and lack of physical activity. Modifying personal behaviors could eliminate or reduce many of these risks (see Figure 10, p. 20), and, therefore, have a tremendous impact on our nation's burden of cancer. Data obtained from (10).

Information provided by AACR Cancer Progress Report 2013|
www.cancerprogressreport.org

Just as a car is designed to use certain products (gasoline, oil, etc.) so it runs smoothly, your body is designed to run smoothly on certain foods. When you don't give a car what is needed to run smoothly, it won't go. It is similar with your body. Unlike a car, your body will run when given the wrong fuel. However, it doesn't run at full capacity on the wrong fuel and the parts begin to break down. You are fatigued, have headaches, indigestion issues, heart problems, diabetes, etc. when you consistently fill your body with the wrong kind of fuel.

"The recent 'EPIC' study published in the Archives of Internal Medicine studied 23,000 people's adherence to 4 simple behaviors, (not smoking, exercising 3.5 hours a week, eating a healthy diet [fruits, vegetables, whole grains, nuts, seeds, and limited amounts of meat], and maintaining a healthy weight [BM<30]). In those adhering to these behaviors, 93% of diabetes, 81% of heart attacks, 50% of strokes, and 36% of all cancers were prevented." (*Lifestyle Journal of Medicine: Treating the Causes of Disease* by Mark A. Hyman, M.D.; Dean Ornish, M.D.; Michael Roizen, M.D.)

When you are careless in your eating habits, you may begin to "care less" about everything else in your life as well. Care about what you eat because everything you put in your mouth will have a consequence. You decide whether it will be a beneficial or detrimental consequence by the food and drink choices you make. It is very important that you learn about the types of fuel you should and should not use in the masterpiece God has given you.

"The future of medical care must be to transform the general lifestyle guidance (eat a healthy diet, exercise regularly). Many physicians already try to provide their patients with individually tailored lifestyle prescriptions for both prevention and treatment of chronic diseases. Lifestyle is the best medicine when applied correctly." ("Diabetes Reversal and Blood Sugar Control" Elevation Health Publications, North Richland Hills, TX © 2013)

The more you learn about the type of fuel your body needs the better choices you will make about the food you eat. Take the time to learn about the foods that benefit and strengthen your heart, muscles, and brain. Your body will reward you by staying healthy and strong. It is equally important to learn what not to put in your body.

Evidence is mounting that sugar is a primary contributing factor not only in obesity and diabetes, but other chronic and lethal diseases. There's really no doubt anymore that sugar is indeed toxic to your body, and it's only a matter of time before it will be commonly accepted as a causative factor in most cancer, in the same way that now we accept without question that smoking and alcohol abuse are direct causes of lung cancer and cirrhosis of the liver, respectively.

I have developed a Strategic Daily Plan provided at the end of this book to give you a way to start making right choices for the fuel your body needs. Eating sensibly, drinking lots of water, and regular exercise will reap wonderful benefits. You will enjoy life more when you are not constantly trying to repair the damage done to your masterpiece by the food choices you make on a daily basis. Consistently choosing wisely based on diligently seeking to know and understand how your body works will strengthen your body from the inside out. Stop spelling relief from your circumstances F O O D, and ask God to give you the right way to deal with them.

Ask Yourself:

Am I using food to deal with circumstances I don't want to face?

Am I damaging the masterpiece God has given me by the food choices I am making on a daily basis?

Is this really the way I want to continue living?

Action Suggestion:

It is vitally important to your health to begin to make better food choices. The Bible says people perish for lack of knowledge (Hosea 4:6). Science has proven this is true when it comes to the way we treat our bodies. Take the time to learn more about how the intricacies of your body work and the kind of fuel that will make it run more smoothly and efficiently. It will be time well spent. Ask God to continue to direct your path as you thank Him for the food He provides for you at every meal. Continue to use the "I Did" and "I Didn't" format in your journal to show you where you are not making healthy choices in the fuel you are selecting. Be honest with yourself if you find you have been spelling relief F O O D.

Answer 3: Find the Stuff beneath the Stuff

What I know to be true about someone who wants to lose weight is you must first get to the stuff beneath the stuff–the "meat" of the real issue for your weight problem. If you want to find a way to release the weight and keep it off for life, it's important you get to the core of the problem causing the weight issue. It is like trying to put a band-aid on a deep wound that is infected under the skin. The band-aid on top covers up the wound but it does nothing to get rid of the poison infecting the body from the inside. Until the wound is opened up and the infection is exposed and dealt with, there can be no healing. As a matter of fact, it could cause serious damage in the future if not dealt with properly now. Digging for the root cause of your food issues may be uncomfortable but it will pay long term benefits.

What if you and a friend ate out one evening and something in the food caused food poisoning. The poisoning causes you to have a horrible pain in your stomach and you throw up to get rid of the poison. Your friend however, holds it in. What will happen? The poison will spread and cause even more serious problems.

Another visual I use to explain the importance of getting to the "meat" of the issue is to compare it to holding a beach ball under water. When you let go it will explode out of the water. Not facing the real issues going on in your life will be like having food poisoning and keeping it stuffed in your body or like the beach ball being held under the water. Eventually it will burst through, possibly causing even more problems. Let's dig a little deeper into the reasons you might use food and expose the stuff beneath the stuff.

"A friend suggested we see a nutritionist. I was skeptical," writes Dr. Cheryl Townsley, N.D. "I knew a lot about food. He calmly answered every question related to my physical problems. He introduced me to the concept that stress can impact physical health. The more I studied and worked on my own health, the more I realized unresolved emotions lay at the root of nearly all disease states I encountered. I began to see that we truly are a triune being. " ("Discovering Wholeness – The Spirit, Soul and Body Connection." LFH Publishing, Littleton, CO. © 2000 by Dr. Cheryl Townsley, N.D.)

Confrontational Food–Even if your parents planted the seed in you as a child that dessert is a reward, what have you discovered happens when you continue to hold onto this idea? Would you agree God wouldn't want you eating things that are not good for your body even if you look at them as a reward for eating other things that are good for you? Is our God a god of compromise? Would you agree He wants you to take care of the beautiful creation, your masterpiece, in the best possible way so you can be your best not only for you, but for others and for Him? The body you are living in is the only body you will be given. Would you agree God would want you to focus on Him instead of always turning to food as your reward? Besides, the Bible warns us God expects us to grow up out of our childish ways and become a healthy productive adult (1 Corinthians 13:11).

Cover-up Food–Have you ever known someone who lost weight, was looking great and yet put the weight back on? When this happens, there is usually a deeper issue going on in their life and they turn to food thinking they can "cover up" the pain. The problem is, by doing so they bring more pain in their life because they have now put the weight back on and their health is suffering. I had never dealt with how I was treated by others when I was fat – the name calling, the embarrassment I was to my family, the way I was made to feel stupid by my teachers, and how unworthy society thought I was. Yes, these were things no one should have to deal with; yet, I did. So in order to overcome, I had to look at the cost of letting those memories continue and decide to stop using them as an excuse to eat those cover up foods. I had to let those memories go and let God help me deal with the grief and pain. Psalm 147:3 says God will heal the brokenhearted.

Convenient Food–This is one of the biggest problems in today's fast-paced society. The food you quickly grab and eat carelessly is extremely bad for your health. They are loaded with the things which cause heart disease, diabetes, cancer, etc. Your body is the temple of the Holy Spirit (1 Corinthians 6:19.) Is this really the way you should treat it? Just like a car is designed to use certain products so it runs smoothly, your body is designed to run smoothly on certain foods. Your "convenience" food causes many "inconveniences" in the long run due to the damage they can do to your body (Proverbs 14:12). If the truth be told, you are probably using a fast-paced life as an excuse to eat what you want and not exercise, instead of taking the time to learn ways to do what is really important in the long run. Track your day and you will find you do have time for what's important to you.

Celebration Food–You were led to believe sweets were the answer or "reward" when you accomplished something. What happens with this mindset? It causes you to look at food as a reward–"I deserve this piece of pie because I worked hard today." Or, "I deserve chips and dip because I walked three miles today." You can find reasons or excuses to reward yourself–it's easy to do (Proverbs 14:15). Isn't it time you focused on the real reward, the one God has for you when you follow His plan and fulfill His purpose? Who do you really want to reward you when you accomplish great things? (see Jeremiah 17:10)

Comfort Food–Just as some people choose to drown their sorrows in alcohol, you choose to drown your sorrows in food. The problem with comfort food is once you have eaten it, you beat yourself up mentally for allowing food to be in control. It's a vicious cycle. You eat to comfort yourself, then you are disappointed in yourself for losing self-control, then you gain weight because you didn't have the self-control to say no to the food. Then the clothes are tight and the comfort food becomes "uncomfortable food." The process will start again and again until you deal with the stuff beneath the stuff. Who do you really want to be your Comforter? (see 2 Corinthians 1:3-4).

Conquer Food–Even though I got to a number on the scale and in a dress size I liked, I still struggled with my head talk. I was determined I would never put the weight back on. I never wanted to go through the pain and grief of name calling and feeling unworthy again. Yet, it seemed the fat girl wouldn't leave. I had kept the weight off for over forty years, but still struggled with the fat girl living in me. I still felt I wasn't good enough or smart enough. I had a college education, had taught school, was married to a wonderful man, raised two amazing children, and a leader in a direct sales company. Yet, I always thought the other person could do better than me. I had to deal with the fat girl issue within me before I could conquer the control food had over me (see Proverbs 23:7).

"It is not a mystery where energy comes from. It is not a mystery where good health comes from. We want to be hearers as well as doers of what is right and walk in health." ("Diabetes Reversal and Blood Sugar Control," Elevation Health Publications, North Richland Hills, TX ©2013 Elevation Health)

Ask Yourself:

Am I focusing on food or God for my reward?

Am I allowing childish ways to prevent me from becoming a productive adult?

Am I settling for short-term convenience instead of long-term health?

Am I constantly finding excuses to reward myself with food?

Am I stuck in a vicious cycle of weight gain and loss because I resort to comfort food instead of the comfort God offers me?

Have I allowed food to control me?

Am I ready to take back control?

Action Suggestion:

As you have read about the ways that could make you a slave to food, use your conversations with God to reveal the stuff beneath the stuff that you personally need to deal with. Ask Him to be your comforter and give you the reward of a healthy body and a sound well-balanced mind. Continue to use the "I Did" and "I Didn't" format in your journal to help you pinpoint which of the "C's" you are dealing with in your eating.

Imagine what life would be like living at your God-given health potential.

Answer 4: Learn to Break Food's Control

Confrontational Food–Do you really believe God wants such chaos in our minds during a time of fueling our bodies? When you pray and thank God for the food He has provided, thank Him for how unique and intricately He has made you (Psalm 139:14). Thank Him for providing food that will help the growth of your body. Remember you are teaching your children and setting an example by the way you eat. As you exemplify how important taking care of your body is others will learn by your example. Don't bribe yourself or your children with unhealthy food. Eat healthy food because you know it is the right fuel for the temple God has provided for you.

Cover-up Food–What if instead of drowning your sorrows in food, you turn to God? Psalm 121:2 says, "Where does my help come from? My help comes from the Lord." When you cover up your pain with food, it's like digging a hole and going deeper and deeper. You feel you can never climb out. When you turn instead to God you will find His peace–a peace food or any other source cannot give you. Then you can pull yourself out of the hole and love yourself again–never having to eat "Cover-up" food to try to hide your pain.

Convenient Food–If there's a lot going on and you feel you have to eat convenient food, what if you choose a restaurant with healthier choices? More and more restaurants are offering healthier choices, even in the fast-food industry. Remember your children are watching your eating habits so be conscious of what are you teaching them. What may seem convenient today will bring major inconveniences in your future when you are forced to deal with the consequences of your choices. Focus on long-term gain instead of short-term gratification.

Celebration Food–If you feel you have to reward yourself, what if you reward yourself with healthy food choices or relaxed with a book and a hot bubble bath? What if you look yourself in the mirror and congratulated yourself with a "high five"? How about sitting down and writing about what you did and be grateful for the victories you attained today? Look for ways you could be an encouragement in helping others achieve and have accomplishments by the example you set.

Comfort Food–In Galatians 5:22-23, we read about the fruit of the Spirit and how one of the segments is self-control. What if instead of drowning your sorrows and disappointments in comfort food, you choose to nurture and use the self-control you have through the Holy Spirit? What if you allow God to comfort and heal you (see Exodus 15:26) and allow Him to be your peace (see Ephesians 2:14)? Comfort food will lose its control over you when the inner wound has been healed by the Great Physician.

Conquer Food–When you sit down to eat, this is the one place you can win. You are in control of what is going in your mouth. Instead of being careless in your eating, begin to really care about what you allow to enter your masterpiece. Care about what you eat and drink and you can win while eating. Instead of feeling you have to be a "conqueror" with your food, choose to conquer the deeper issues going on in your life and realize how special you are to God. In His eyes you are His masterpiece and He loves you and wants to help you become all He designed you to be.

You can choose to take control of your eating instead of letting food control you. Learn how to face what is going on in your life instead of turning to food for the answer. Get rid of the stuff beneath the stuff and release the weight forever.

TV commercials and media marketing try to tell you that living life to the fullest means eating and drinking whatever you want. The Bible says when you know the truth, the truth will set you free (John 8:32). To stop letting food control you and take control of your life, you must know the truth about what God says about you, your body, and His purpose for you!

As we continue our journey to discover how to best care for the masterpiece God has given us through the next half of this book, we will explore and reveal both biblical and scientific truths to help you live the healthy productive life God designed for you to live. Below is one of those scientific, medically backed truths that will set your body free to become healthy and strong.

The Truth about Low Energy and Fatigue

Low energy combined with fatigue is the number one complaint heard by doctors today. One of the biggest causes of and cure for this complaint is in understanding body function, proper nutrition, and the appropriate forms of exercise. We can cooperate with the way our bodies are designed to operate and our energy level and health will soar. It's important to understand how to get the right fuel down to the cellular level because every cell in our body has to convert nutrients into energy in order to help do things like: grow hair, pump blood through arteries, and send nerve signals to the brain or move muscles. We need a steady diet of nutritional foods that our bodies can convert into sustained energy in order to have energy throughout the day.

High Energy, Dietary Recommendations:

1. Reduce or eliminate refined carbohydrates; eat whole fruits and brown rice rather than white.
2. Taper off caffeine, avoid sodas even diet sodas, and avoid alcohol.
3. Eliminate hydrogenated corn and safflower oils, margarine, and fried foods.
4. Eat more omega-3 fats like cold water fish, sardines, raw nuts and seeds, avocado, and use olive oil.
5. Snack on foods high in minerals such as nuts, sunflower seeds, and pumpkin seeds. Carry healthy bars, nuts or other snacks with you so you are not tempted to eat junk food when hungry.
6. Eat three meals a day with protein at every meal.
7. Eat five to nine servings of fresh fruits and vegetables daily
8. Drink at least eight glasses of water daily. Our bodies are 70 percent water. Your bones need water. You need water to heal the ligaments, joints and hips. (http://www.nhlbi.nih.gov/health/health-topics/topics/sdd/howmuch.html)

Ask Yourself:

Am I ready to take control of my eating instead of letting food control me?

Am I willing to face my circumstances instead of turning to food for the answers?

Am I willing to get rid of the stuff beneath the stuff so I can release the weight forever?

Am I willing to take the time to find out what kind of fuel my masterpiece needs to run efficiently?

Action Suggestion:

God has given you everything you need to live a long and healthy life. He has also given you the freedom of choice. You can make the right choices if you will seek the knowledge you need to take control of the food you eat. Take the time to find out what foods benefit and strengthen your body. Find ways to prepare foods you know you need in a way that makes them appealing to you. Use your conversation time with God to ask His help in staying true to your eating plan. Continue to use the "I Did" and "I Didn't" format in your journal in writing out your eating plan. Post your plan on your refrigerator and thank God at every meal for the healthy food He has made available to you. Know that God is 100 percent for your success!

Scientific Truth: Extra or excessive weight puts stress on the neuro-musculoskeletal system as it can push down on one's lungs and other vital structures. A 10 percent weight gain predicts an approximate 32 percent increase in sleep apnea and just about guarantees a six-fold increase in the odds of developing moderate to severe sleep breathing disorders. (http://bit.ly/1dsquBB)

Chapter 6

WHY ME?

As a certified grief coach, I am taught to guide and help people go from pain to peace. As a person who was once very overweight (over 200 lbs), I dealt with a lot of things which I allowed to cause me grief – the way I was treated by people – even some of my school teachers. The things people said to me, the name calling and being made fun of caused me intense hurt. I pretended it didn't bother me. I would laugh and joke with them. However, it hurt deeply and caused me a lot of grief. I seemed to be a happy, well-adjusted kid, yet deep down I wished I could look like other kids. I wished I would be liked for me. I chose to let all this affect my self-worth, my self-confidence, and my self-esteem. Fortunately, I received help through a grief coach. Now with God's help, I get to share what I learned with others so they too can learn how to understand and answer the "Why Me?" question.

Answer 1: Learn to Focus on Your Inner Self

I started losing weight my senior year in high school. By the time I graduated, I had lost about forty pounds and over the summer I continued to lose. By the time I went to college in the fall, I had lost most of the weight I wanted to lose. It was fun to be able to buy clothes instead of my mom making all of them because there were no clothes in the stores to fit me. It was also fun to have the guys wanting to go out with me. My sophomore year in college I was the belle of one of the guy's social clubs. I continued to enjoy college, kept my weight off, and in my senior year started dating the man I would marry. He thought I was beautiful and to this day tells me how great I look. However, even with his compliments and the compliments of others, I wouldn't let go of the fat girl inside of me. I wouldn't let go of the things others had said to me when I was fat. I allowed my weight issues to cause me grief just as I had when I was younger and overweight. The head talk and limiting beliefs I had created were ridiculous!

Because of holding on to the fat girl in my past, I would not allow myself to be the best I could be. I realized I was missing out on things in my life. It was as though I was still overweight. When I looked in the mirror I was still seeing the fat girl, not someone who had released the weight and kept it off for over forty years. I had accomplished something very few people achieve and yet I was allowing my weight issues to still control me.

I found it was not only affecting me, it affected my children, too. I would look in the mirror and say to my husband, "Does this make me look fat?" Not realizing what I was doing, my daughter learned to look in the mirror and be critical and ask the same question, "Does this make me look fat?" My daughter has never had an ounce of fat on her body. She's a young woman, about 5'1" and weighs about ninety-eight pounds! My issues around weight also affected my son! Have any of you ever beat yourself up after eating foods you knew weren't the best for you? You splurged, ate too much at dinner, had extra dessert, and then tried to justify your actions or beat yourself up? I would say things like, "Why did I eat that? I shouldn't have eaten that?" On and on I would go and drive people crazy by not letting it go! I found out last year, my son drives his wife crazy with regretting and trying to justify when he eats too much. He's not overweight either, yet my insecurities caused my children grief! I have wonderful, successful children, yet they now have crazy head talk because of their mother! I realized I had so much grief surrounding my weight that I was also causing others grief.

I was so focused on the outer self and how I looked; I forgot to focus on my inner self! The head talk was unreal! Fortunately, I received help through a grief coach and was able to release my past and get rid of the hurt and grief.

One of the things that really helped me begin the upward move toward improving my self-confidence and self-esteem was discovering how much I am worth to God. Remember we talked earlier about the value God has placed on us? Well, studying how much God says I am worth increased my own self-worth. Here are some of the scriptures that helped me grow in my life and may be helpful to you as well.

Proverbs 31:30 says, "Charm is deceptive, and beauty does not last; but a woman who fears the LORD will be greatly praised" (NLT).

Jesus said in Matthew 10:29-31, "Are not two sparrows sold for a penny? Yet not one of them will fall to the ground outside your Father's care. And even the very hairs of your head are all numbered. So don't be afraid; you are worth more than many sparrows" (NIV).

1 Peter 3:3-4 clearly defines the difference between the inner and the outer self and what is worth more to God. "Let not yours be the [merely] external adorning with [elaborate] interweaving *and* knotting of the hair, the wearing of jewelry, or changes of clothes; But let it be the inward adorning *and* beauty of the hidden person of the heart, with the incorruptible *and* unfading charm of a gentle and peaceful spirit, which [is not anxious or wrought up, but] is very precious in the sight of God" (AMP).

I realized there are others like me who are dealing with grief due to weight issues and I wanted to be there for them. Instead of asking, "Why me?" I asked God, "How can I use what I've learned from my experiences to help others?" My mission now is to inspire and encourage women to cherish their bodies as God's Masterpiece. I want to help others take care of themselves physically so they can be their best spiritually! As I have studied more about how amazing our masterpiece is, I am even more convinced we can move from pain to peace. We all can get rid of what's causing us to not release weight and move to a place where we cherish our masterpiece and release the weight – a new thought process! It's not why me, but, how can God use me is what I now ask!

Ask Yourself:

> *Am I letting what others have said about my outer self cause me grief?*

> *Am I allowing society's standard for the perfect size affect my self-esteem?*

Has the hurt inflicted on me by others lowered my self-confidence?

Do I want to do something about this?

Action Suggestion:

As you continue to journal all that you are learning about your amazing masterpiece and God's purpose for your life, begin to think of people in your life that could benefit from what you have learned. Start making a list and look for ways to share your amazing discoveries with them. The more you pour out what God is giving you, the more He will give you. Ask Him to guide you every day to someone you can help from what you have been through and learned. Continue to use the "I Did" and "I Didn't" format in your journal and add a section on whom you helped today from what you have learned.

Answer 2: Discover Your Weight Grief

Did you know weight issues usually point to another deeper issue? Fix the other deeper issue and you can fix the weight issue.

What about you, what grief are you dealing with because of your weight?
Is it low self-worth?
Depression?
No Self-confidence?
Is your health suffering?

Are you experiencing high blood pressure, diabetes, heart issues, or back issues?
Is it hard to walk because you are out of breath?
Is it hard to exercise?

What are you dealing with because you haven't been willing to make the right choices about taking care of your masterpiece?

These are some very tough questions I encourage you to answer. I invite you to be very honest with yourself and discover your own personal weight grief. To overcome the influence grief is having on your life, it's so very important to deal with it.

Here are some more very pointed questions that will help you pinpoint your specific area of weight grief.

Are you embarrassed when you buy clothes?

Do you feel family members are embarrassed concerning you?

Are you treated differently by others – do you feel they judge you?

Are you able to get on the floor and play with your children or grandchildren?

Is your weight causing you to miss out on enjoying life?

Have you gone through a crisis in your life and you chose to turn to food for comfort?

I have a friend who was having problems in her marriage and she decided to lose weight to make her husband happy. He divorced her anyway. After the divorce she turned to food for comfort and gained all her weight back and more. Her grief over a divorce was now causing a second grief – her weight issue.

Psalm 6:7 is a Prayer of Faith in a Time of Distress where David writes, "My eye wastes away because of grief...." In Psalm 31:9 David is sharing how God is a fortress while in adversity. He says, "Have mercy on me, O Lord, for I am in trouble; my eye wastes away with grief..." David was in a deep grief – it was accompanied by uncontrollable crying. I had this kind of grief when I was overweight. It doesn't feel good.

Have you ever had such deep grief – the kind where your have uncontrollable crying?

Internal Emotional Response to Loss or a Problem: I want to share something here about emotional response to a loss. This usually means the loss or death of a person. However, when it came to my weight issues, I realized I allowed the fat girl to lurk behind me. It was as though I was carrying her on my back everywhere I went and she was a heavy load.

Why Me?

Did I grieve her loss? I began to examine this and discovered this may be why many people gain their weight back – being overweight was safe. However, I didn't want the weight back. I never wanted to go through the pain of being treated the way I was treated. Yet something wouldn't allow me to let go of my past until a grief coach helped me understand what was going on so I could release the fat girl. I'm sharing this to make you aware that you may have allowed your overweight girl back in your life.

The Different Stages of Grief

Sometimes when you are dealing with grief, whether it is the loss of a loved one, weight issues or any other form of grief, you will go through different emotional stages. Let's look at five for this lesson:

Depression can many times cause you to eat more and more and start you on a vicious cycle. You are depressed due to either your weight or another grief in your life and to compensate, you eat to comfort yourself and then you are depressed because you didn't use self-control.

Denial is when you try to convince yourself you are not that overweight. You say to yourself, "I look okay and I feel good. At least I'm not as heavy as _____." You may even try to convince yourself it's not your weight that is causing your health problems; it's just your body getting older or some other excuse. Maybe you even feel you were born that way so there is really nothing you can do about it! You are in denial and you are choosing to pretend it's not a problem!

Anger manifests when you ask those why questions like, "How come I'm fat? Why can my friend eat anything she wants and never gain weight?" I had these thoughts when I was growing up. I had a friend who really could eat anything she wanted and never gained weight. I felt it just wasn't fair! How come I got that "fat" gene? I'll be honest; I was jealous and envious of people like this – which depressed me and caused me to eat. But what I didn't realize was my friend had her own issues and things she wished she didn't have in her life. She was dealing with her own level of grief. My anger kept me prisoner causing a vicious cycle of grief in my life!

Bargaining can be with yourself. I'll just eat this one cookie tonight and be good tomorrow and no one will know. But this starts the process of guilt, justifying, and beating yourself up because you didn't remain true to yourself. I'm a person who does everything possible to keep commitments. I want to be a woman of my word. However, it amazes me how I would break commitments to myself! One bite won't hurt me, I would tell myself. I've even had others say that to me when I choose not to have dessert or other foods at a potluck. Why will we not break our commitment to others, but we do with ourselves? I believe there is an important lesson in integrity here about being true to ourselves and having self-control, which is one of the segments in the fruit of the Spirit.

Another way of bargaining might be with God where you say, "This is the way God made me and if He wanted me to be thin, He would have made it where I could eat anything and not gain weight." What if God is saying, "I want you to learn self-control in this area so you will also have self-control in other areas?" He might be saying to you, "Eat the healthy foods I have put on this earth for you and you will be thin. It's a choice you have to make."

Acceptance is deciding to accept you have a weight issue and you choose to make wise choices when eating. You have accepted the fact God wants you to nurture what He has given you. Learn all you can about how to take care and feed your masterpiece. Use your self-control to win over temptation, and show Him He is more important in your life than food! Make the decision to dig deeper and find what other issues are going on in your life. Include God in this process by asking for His help, His wisdom, and His guidance as you choose to focus on eating the way He intended you to eat.

Ask Yourself:

Am I using the acronym suggested when I am being tempted to eat for the wrong reasons?

W – Why
A – Am
I – I
E – Eating
T – This?

What emotion am I dealing with that is leading me to eat the way I do?

Action Suggestion:

Reread each of the stages of grief. Zero in on the one you think is most prevalent in your life right now. In your conversation with God, tell Him what you have discovered about your weight grief. Ask Him to help you move through that emotional phase and head toward acceptance. God is compassionate, understands your grief, and wants to help you through yours no matter what the underlying cause. Continue to use the "I Did" and "I Didn't" format in your journal and especially ask yourself why you are eating what you are eating.

Answer 3: Let God Heal Your Broken Heart

Let's look at some scriptures about grief and how God can help you during these stages.

Hebrews 12:1-2: "Therefore, since we are surrounded by so great a cloud of witnesses, let us also lay aside every weight, and sin which clings so closely, and let us run with endurance the race set before us...**looking to Jesus,** the founder and perfecter of our faith, who for the joy set before Him, endured the cross, despising the shame, and is seated at the right hand of the throne of God." There are many things that can keep us from effectively running our race. Food and weight loss can be obstacles along this path. The comforting thought from this scripture is when you fix your eyes on Jesus you can keep your focus in the right place. By doing so, you can be aware of what you are doing to your body and will want to make the changes so you can be your best for God.

2 Timothy 2:3-5 and 7 also gives us insight along these same lines. Notice we are referred to as soldiers of Jesus Christ and competitors in the race. We need to honor and please our commander-in-chief and seek to win the race. To this end we must follow orders and do things according to the rules laid down by God. Also notice verse 7 tells us if we think these things over, God will give us full insight and understanding in everything. What an amazing promise!

> *Take [with me] your share of the hardships and suffering [which you are called to endure] as a good (first-class) soldier of Christ Jesus. No soldier when in service gets entangled in the*

*enterprises of [civilian] life; **his aim is to satisfy and please the one who enlisted him**. And if anyone enters competitive games, he is not crowned unless he competes lawfully (fairly, **according to the rules laid down**). Think over these things I am saying [understand them and grasp their application], for the **Lord will grant you full insight and understanding in everything.*** (AMP emphasis added)

Galatians 5:22-24: "The fruit of the Spirit is love, joy, peace, patience, kindness, goodness, faithfulness, gentleness, self-control; against such things there is no law. And those who belong to Jesus have crucified the flesh with its passions and desires." One of the segments of the fruit of the Spirit is self-control – that means taking control of yourself – not letting others control what you do and not letting food control you. In 2 Timothy 1:7 it says, "God has not given us a spirit of fear, but of power and love and self-control" (NKJV). God has given you the power of self-control. When you aren't using this power of self-control, what are you doing? You are letting someone or something else take control. Let's take it back – let's show God we appreciate this gift of self-control and use it!

In verse 24 it says you need to be willing to crucify or give up the passions and desires you have for your flesh. Would you agree when you are focused on food and don't control what you eat those are passions and desires of the flesh? Are you willing to give up the passion for unhealthy food and create a passion for what God intended you to eat?

Ephesians 5:10: "Try to discern what is pleasing to the Lord." Do you feel focusing on taking care of your masterpiece is pleasing God? I do. I believe it shows Him gratitude for the masterpiece He has given you and me. I believe it shows Him we are willing to do what it takes to take care of it so it will last a long time and we can share about Him and serve others. There are so many areas in life where we want to ask ourselves if we are pleasing God. Most of the time how we take care of our masterpiece is ignored when it comes to looking for ways to please God.

Lamentations 3:22-23: "The steadfast love of the Lord never ceases, his mercies never come to an end; they are new every morning, great is your faithfulness. 'The Lord is my portion,' says my soul, 'therefore I will hope in Him.'" This is one of my favorite scriptures. It tells me God has new blessings for me every day. I want to encourage you to open your eyes to see them every morning. His compassion never fails. He loves you and He is here for you, right now at this moment. Wouldn't it be a shame to miss out on God's blessings because you choose not to take care of yourself and don't have the energy, the knees, the hips, and the health to enjoy those blessings? Each day when you get up, God has special blessings just for you. I pray you will take care of yourself so you can enjoy them! I also believe this scripture shows He will help you through this process of eating the way He intended you to eat when you ask Him for His help. I truly believe I'm where I am because of asking for His help and searching the scriptures for answers to all of my questions.

Psalm 34:18: "The Lord is near to the brokenhearted and saves the crushed in spirit." The Lord is near to those who have a broken heart. Not only that but He wants to help heal your broken heart and the grief you have. Psalm 147:3 says, "He heals the brokenhearted and binds up their wounds." In Isaiah 61:1 we learn that God so desired to heal our broken hearts, He sent His Son Jesus to us.

> *The Spirit of the Lord GOD is upon me, because the LORD has anointed me to bring good news to the poor; he has sent me to bind up the brokenhearted, to proclaim liberty to the captives, and the opening of the prison to those who are bound.*

Remember His blessings are new every morning. He cares about you. He wants to help you heal. He wants you to pay attention to the masterpiece He gave you. Love it, nourish it, and protect it because it's the only masterpiece you get. Why treat it like a piece of junk?

Ask Yourself:

Am I letting someone or something else take control of my eating?

Am I using the gift of self-control He has given me?

Am I being kind to the masterpiece He has given me?

Am I showing love to Him by loving my masterpiece?

Am I willing to give up the passion for unhealthy food and create a passion for what God intended me to eat?

Action Suggestion:

Use these scriptures to help you focus on your masterpiece. Write them in your journal and use them in your prayer time today as you ask God to help heal your broken heart and your grief. Thank Him that His blessings are new every morning. Continue to use the "I Did" and "I Didn't" format in your journal to focus on the areas where you are not exercising self-control over the way you treat the masterpiece God has given you. Check out any area where you are not experiencing peace and search for the root cause of the chaos in your life. Especially if you are suffering from a broken heart, seek His healing in your life so you can move up and out of your grief into a productive life for Him.

Answer 4: Be Anxious for Nothing

In Matthew 6:25-34 Jesus talked about the fruitlessness of worry. He also talks about an unhealthy focus on food, drink, and the clothes we wear. He is not telling us to disregard them; He is saying there is a right way and a wrong way to focus in life.

Therefore I tell you, stop being perpetually uneasy (anxious and worried) about your life, what you shall eat or what you shall drink; or about your body, what you shall put on. Is not life greater [in quality] than food, and the body [far above and more excellent] than clothing? Look at the birds of the air; they neither sow nor reap nor gather into barns, and yet your heavenly Father keeps feeding them. Are you not worth much more than they? And who of you by worrying and being anxious can add one unit of measure (cubit) to his stature or to the span of his life? And why should you be anxious about clothes? Consider the lilies of the field and learn thoroughly how they grow; they neither toil nor spin. Yet I tell you, even Solomon in all his magnificence (excellence, dignity, and grace) was not arrayed like one of these. But if God so clothes the grass of the field, which today is alive and green and tomorrow is tossed into the furnace, will He not much more surely clothe you, O you of little faith? Therefore do not worry and be anxious, saying, What are we going to have to eat? or, What are we going to have to drink? or, What are we going to have to wear? **For the Gentiles (heathen) wish for and crave and diligently seek all these things,** *and your heavenly Father knows well that you need them all.* **But seek (aim at and strive after) first of all His kingdom and His righteousness (His way of doing and being right), and then all these things taken together will be given you besides.** *So do not worry or be anxious about tomorrow, for tomorrow will have worries and anxieties of its own. Sufficient for each day is its own trouble.* (AMP emphasis added)

Jesus is inferring here that by worrying over food and drink and clothing we are showing the world that we are not God's people or we do not trust Him to provide for our needs. Worrying dishonors God. It is a sin! Focusing on food and drink in an unhealthy way dishonors God. The right way is discovering His way of doing things and when we do we have nothing to worry or be anxious about!

Philippians 4:6-7 says, "Do not be anxious about anything, but in everything by prayer and supplication with thanksgiving let your requests be made know to God. And the peace of God, which surpasses all understanding, will guard your hearts and your minds in Christ Jesus."

Be anxious for nothing! When God says nothing does He really mean **nothing**? The answer is yes because the next verse says in **everything**, pray and let your requests be made known to God. When God says nothing and everything He means exactly what He says.

There is another verse I often think of that goes with this one using these words **nothing** and **everything**. In Jeremiah 32:17, the prophet says he knows God made everything and "Nothing is too hard for You (God)" (NIV). I also remember what the angel told Mary in Luke 1:37 when he said she was going to give birth to the Son of God, "Nothing is impossible with God" (NIV).

As I think about the forty years I allowed my head talk and my limiting beliefs to control my life, I realized I was not living with faith. In

Matthew 21:22 we are told to "pray believing," but I didn't believe God would really help me. At that time, I didn't believe my weight issues were important to God. Why would He take the time to concern Himself with my weakness with food? He had more important things to take care of like sick and dying people, troubled families, etc. However, the more I studied the scriptures and read how I am fearfully and wonderfully made and He knew me before I was born, the more I realized my grief surrounding my weight was important to Him. I realized "nothing was impossible" for Him and He could help me release the fat girl and the limiting beliefs I had about myself. It was now up to me to allow Him to work in my life.

Philippians 4:8-9 goes on to tell us how to learn not to be anxious about anything. We are to pray and make our requests known to Him and we are to redirect our thinking.

> *Finally, brothers, whatever is true, whatever is honorable, whatever is just, whatever is pure, whatever is lovely, whatever is commendable, if there is any excellence, if there is anything worthy of praise, think about these things. What you have learned and received and heard and seen in me—practice these things, and the God of peace will be with you.*

As I let the words of Philippians 4:8 sink in, I began to realize how my focus was more on the next meal and what I would have to eat! I was also focused on what people thought about how I looked, and did they think I was fat. Wow, definitely not commendable or worthy of praise. What about you? Do you focus on joyful happy things in your life, or are you more concerned about the next meal and how yummy you can make it?

Remember, you are God's masterpiece and He wants you to take care of it. He has given you scriptures to show you how important you are to Him and how He cares for you. He is telling you to think about His truth, about what is honorable and commendable, and to praise Him even in the way you think. Then He tells you to practice what you have learned. When you do, He gives you His peace instead of the anxiousness and the worry you bring upon yourself!

The *Message Bible* puts this passage into a very practical format for us:

Don't fret or worry. **Instead of worrying, pray.** *Let petitions and praises shape your worries into prayers, letting God know your concerns. Before you know it, a sense of God's wholeness, everything coming together for good, will come and settle you down.* **It's wonderful what happens when Christ displaces worry at the center of your life.** *Summing it all up, friends, I'd say you'll do best by filling your minds and meditating on things true, noble, reputable, authentic, compelling, gracious—**the best, not the worst; the beautiful, not the ugly; things to praise, not things to curse.** Put into practice what you learned from me, what you heard and saw and realized. Do that, and God, who makes everything work together, will work you into his most excellent harmonies.* (Philippians 4:6-9 emphasis added)

Realize God knows your grief and your sorrow. In Isaiah 53:3 we read, "He was despised and rejected by men; a man of sorrows, and acquainted with grief." This scripture is referring to Jesus and more than anyone, He can feel your grief and anguish. God knows you want to take better care of your masterpiece. Allow yourself to reach out and get the help you need instead of being weighed down in your grief.

When I first began coaching with my business coach, I allowed my limiting beliefs to take over so much that I told him I didn't believe I was making a difference in the lives of others and I wanted to quit. I was so focused on tangible things and winning, I forgot what was really important. I found my insecurities were spilling over into my business and my leadership. Even though I appeared to be happy and joyful, my limiting beliefs were constantly playing in my head and keeping me from being what God intended me to be and from sharing Christ with others. My limiting beliefs soon became fears–fear of failure, fear of success, fear of the phone, and ultimately the fear I wasn't good enough. A scripture that encouraged me was Psalm 34:4, "I sought the Lord...and He delivered me from my fears." Once I changed my limiting beliefs and my fears to empowering beliefs, I was able to release the "fat girl" and begin to share about being God's masterpiece with others.

Ask Yourself:

What am I anxious about?

Am I making my requests known to God or am I trying to handle everything on my own?

Do I really believe nothing is impossible for God?

If I do, am I showing Him I believe by my prayers and actions?

Do I seek His way of doing things?

Am I willing to put into practice what I have learned?

Action Suggestion:

Continue to journal and be aware of what you eat and why you eat using the "I Did" and "I Didn't" format. Continue to cherish and respect your masterpiece and record your victories and challenges. Be true to yourself – be accountable to yourself – remember this is the only body you get – love it, cherish it, respect it just as you would a newborn baby, a family member or your best friend. Allow yourself to reach out and get the help you need instead of being weighed down in your grief (see the information about contacting a grief coach below). Let your worries become prayers knowing with God nothing is impossible. Redirect your thinking by filling your mind with *the best, not the worst; the beautiful, not the ugly; things to praise, not things to curse.* Do that, and God, who makes everything work together, will work you into His most excellent peace!

What is a coach?

A coach is someone who stays with you through a difficult time in your life. She will be there for you and empower you to once again find joy in your life. She is someone who will listen and guide you while keeping all you share confidential. She will help you travel from heartbreak to happiness. The purpose of a coach is to listen with compassion without any rescuing or "fixing," and create a safe, non-judgmental space. To contact me and check out my website go to: www.themastersmasterpiece.com

Scientific Truth: According to WebMD, "The health problems associated with obesity are numerous. Obesity is not just a cosmetic problem. It's a health hazard. Someone who is 40% overweight is twice as likely to die prematurely as is a normal-weight person. Obesity has been linked to several serious medical conditions, including heart disease and stroke, high blood pressure, diabetes, cancer, gallbladder disease and gallstones, osteoarthritis, gout, and breathing problems such as sleep apnea (when a person stops breathing for a short episodes during sleep) and asthma." (http://www.webmd.com/cholesterol-management/obesity-health-risks)

Chapter 7

AM I DISRESPECTING GOD WHEN I EAT UNHEALTHY?

⸻ ◦⧉◦ ⸻

During the writing of this book, my second grandson was born. I have shared how I believe every baby is one of God's masterpieces. We have talked about the intricacies of the body and how God designed our bodies to heal itself. Without going into lots of details, my grandson had some serious issues when he was born. He was immediately taken to the NICU in another hospital where he received the best of care. With the help of a ventilator, nutrition, IV medications specific for his needs, and many prayers, he was able to go home sooner than the doctors expected.

As I think about how intricate his little organs are and how he knew to breath, move, cry, and open his eyes, I once again stand in awe of our amazing God. I am so thankful for the doctors and nurses who took the time to study and learn so they could help babies like my grandson. I also know God created our bodies to heal, heard the prayers of thousands of people, and allowed his little body to heal.

As you think about your own body and how intricate it is, realize God created you and He wants you to take care of and cherish your amazing masterpiece. No matter what age you are—a newborn or very elderly, it's important to appreciate how your body works, and cherish and take care of it.

Answer 1: Cherish Your Masterpiece

For no one ever hated his own flesh, but nourishes and cherishes it, just as Christ does the church. (Ephesians 5:29)

When you love something you cherish it. When you learn to love your body, you will cherish and nourish it. When I read about how God loves and provides all we need to prosper on this earth, it tells me it's really important to cherish and take care of my body. Cherish means to protect and care for lovingly, to hold something dear, and to treat it with affection and tenderness. Think about holding a new born baby or something you really cherish and write it down in your journal. I cherish pictures, memories, hugs from my children and my grandchildren, along with time with my family and my friends.

I have a friend who is a member of a direct sales company and had the privilege of helping a young lady get ready for a "Miss Fabulous" pageant. She sent me an email on November 10, 2012 I would like to share with you.

> *I had the privilege of being a part of the Miss Fabulous Pageant. This is an event that was started in 2011 by a young teen who had won a local pageant and one of her friends, who had a disability, told her she would never be able to be in a pageant. The young teen who had won the local pageant wanted ALL girls to feel special and beautiful. So she came up with the idea of a pageant for disabled young women like her friend and called it "Miss Fabulous." Several women got together to help the girls with hair and makeup and someone brought jewelry so the girls would have some bling.*

My friend helped pamper some of these young women for the pageant and received a letter from one of the girls afterwards. When my friend called to find out about the young girl who wrote the letter, she found out the young woman had died recently. How does this fit with our lesson? It fits with the word "cherish." This young lady felt cared for, cherished, and loved so much by my friend on the day of the pageant that she wrote the letter. My friend cherishes this letter so much that she has made a collage with it and pictures of the young lady.

> *He makes the whole body fit together perfectly. As each part does its own special work, it helps the other parts grow, so that the whole body is healthy and growing and full of love.* (Ephesians 4:16 NLT)

Part of cherishing your masterpiece is understanding your whole person. Remember we said earlier that you are a spirit and a soul housed in a physical body. In order to be the best spiritually and not allow your emotions to rule your spirit, you want to transform your mindset and focus on doing things the way God designed, especially when it comes to our bodies.

"Learning to live blessed is a process. Getting the power to have good success is kind of like getting a Ferrari. It really helps to know how to drive!" (Dr. Cheryl Townsley, N.D. from her book Discovering Wholeness – The Spirit, Soul and Body Connection, LFH Publishing, Littleton, CO ©2000.)

To really understand your whole person, you need to identify the grief that impacts your sense of wellbeing, uncover the sources of anger that you may not have yet dealt with, deal with the rejection you have felt from others, choose sensible exercise that will best meet your lifestyle, determine to eat healthier by learning what is beneficial to the body you have been given, and discover optimal health by caring for your spirit, soul, and body.

You support your soul by filling your mind with positive and up-lifting thoughts. That is why Philippians 4:8 gives us a list of things to focus our minds on. We feed and nurture our spirits by studying and reading the Word of God on a daily basis. We support our physical body through good nutrition and exercise. The soul must be fed with beauty, music, joy, relationships, and purpose. The spirit must be fed on God's truth which we glean from His Word and spending time with Him. The body must be nurtured and fed through the food we eat, the water we drink, and even the air we breathe.

Many people in today's busy fast-paced world spend more time, energy, and money on insuring their car and their house than they do on their own health. Funny thing is the car and the house are replaceable, but you only get one body. The World Health Organization has said, "Ignorance and complacency are the two most serious threats to our health."[6] Ignorance and complacency generally disappear when we are faced with a crisis in our health. Wouldn't it be better to be proactive and do something now to prevent a health disaster?

Cherishing your masterpiece means you will do anything to protect it. In order to avoid a crisis in the physical realm, you want to become a conscious competent. That means you find out the right way to do things and then you begin to do them on a consistent basis. In other words, cherishing your body and treating it with respect becomes "second nature." Developing good habits takes a commitment of approximately twenty-one days.

James 1:22-25 gives us some great advice when it comes to reaping good fruit in our health and developing good habits in everything we do in life.

> *Do not merely listen to the word, and so deceive yourselves. Do what it says. Anyone who listens to the word but does not do what it says is like someone who looks at his face in a mirror and, after looking at himself, goes away and immediately forgets what he looks like. But whoever looks intently into the perfect law that gives freedom, and continues in it—**not forgetting what they have heard, but doing it**—they will be blessed in what they do.* (NIV emphasis added)

Those around us will know if we truly cherish the body God has given us. Our actions will clearly display just how much we value His gift. Not only will we look and act differently, it is going to be obvious God is blessing us! Let us not be like those described in Titus 1:16 who claim to know and love God yet deny it by their very actions. Our lifestyle must reflect how much we cherish the masterpiece God has given us.

---

6   http://www.iom.edu/-/media/Files/Activity%20Files/ Environment/EnvironmentalHealthRT/Smith.pdf

Ask Yourself:

Is the condition of my body limiting my achievements?

Have I spent more time insuring my car and house than I have cherishing my body as the masterpiece God designed it to be?

Does the way I treat my body tell others I cherish it as much as God does?

Action Suggestion:

Don't allow ignorance and complacency let a health crisis happen in your life. Diligently study the Word of God to feed your spirit, think on the things listed in Philippians 4:8 to strengthen your soul, and study the intricacies of your body so you know the right fuel for it. Then be a doer, using what you learn from God's Word and cherishing the body He gave you. He has given you everything you need to stay healthy and prosperous. He has promised to give you wisdom (James 1:5.) Record in your journal the things you are seeking to learn about the amazing body God has given you and be prepared to share them with others. Enjoy the benefits of a healthy mind, body, and spirit.

Answer 2: Respect God, Your Creator

Do your best to present yourself to God as one approved, a worker who has no need to be ashamed, rightly handling the word of truth. (2 Timothy 2:15)

What does respect mean to you? According to the dictionary, it means a feeling of deep admiration for someone or something elicited by their abilities, qualities or achievements; to admire deeply, to regard, esteem, honor, and revere. I want you to think of someone you really respect. Why do you respect them? As I think of the people in my life who have impacted me, there are many I have much respect and admiration for. There are also people I don't know, yet I've heard about their lives and it causes me to have a deep respect for them.

My mother comes to mind as someone I admired deeply and wanted to show her honor. I was blessed to have my mom live to be eighty-seven years old. My mom was involved with my life as a child. She was my Brownie and Girl Scout Leader and there are still, to this day, women who will talk about the fun times we had at our Girl Scout events. My mom taught me about God and we attended worship and Bible classes three times a week at our local congregation. She mentored many young girls and grown women over the years. My dad died in January 1989 so my mom was a widow for twenty-two years. My dad had been a preacher for the last eighteen years of his life and my mom was definitely the best preacher's wife ever. Even though she was no longer a preacher's wife, she continued to serve God. In June 2011, she became ill. Five and a half weeks later she died. I had the honor of taking care of her during those weeks and saw how others also loved, respected, and honored her. Young and old came to pay their respects, get one more hug, and one more bit of wisdom from her. We kept a journal of the people who came to visit during that time and I have over 600 signatures from those five and half weeks.

Another person I think of when I think of the word respect is my friend Sue. I first met Sue when I moved to Tennessee and was looking for a leader to mentor me in the Direct Sales business I was in. Sue accepted me with open arms and poured belief into me. She always showed love for everyone, no matter their life circumstance. Because of her loving, caring heart, she is respected by everyone who knows her. I have been blessed by her for over twenty-five years. She still continues to mentor and pour belief into me.

I also have much respect for my husband, Ken, a minister of the gospel of Christ. He is the kind of man who never makes it about him. When he stands in the pulpit to preach, it is always about the Word of God. He knows he will be held accountable for what he preaches and he has such a respect for God's Word. His children love and respect him; even our oldest grandson tells him he is his favorite. Our life isn't perfect. We are human like everyone else. However, when I focus on his life's work and why I fell in love with him, it is easy to admire and respect him.

When you respect someone, how do you treat them? How do you talk about them even when they are not right there with you? If they ask you to do something are you more than willing to comply? Isn't that one of the ways you show them your respect? If they give you a gift or are willing to give you their time, how do you treat the gift and time? Do you pay close attention to what they say to you? Do you value their opinion and their instructions? Do you trust their advice?

How much do you know about the One who created you? Perhaps you already know He has often been called Jehovah. But did you know He also revealed Himself by using other descriptions of His nature? Jehovah-Elohim means the Lord our Creator (Genesis 2:4), Jehovah El-Elyon means the Most High God (Genesis 14:22), Jehovah-Jireh means the Lord our Provider (Genesis 22:14), Jehovah-Rapha means the Lord our Healer (Exodus 15:26), and Jehovah-Shalom means the Lord our Peace (Judges 6:24) just to name a few.

Isn't our Creator worthy of our respect? Psalm 139:14 says we are fearfully and wonderfully made. Jeremiah 1:5 says God knew us before we were even formed in the womb. God has given us a masterpiece to care for and He has given us instructions on how to care for it. He has even made sure we have everything available to thrive and prosper. David was a mere shepherd boy and was considered the least among his handsome and strong brothers, yet God chose him to become the king over His people. David knew that God was responsible for any success he achieved in life and he wrote songs to praise his Creator. Read Psalms 33:1, 34:1, 48:1, 100:4, 105:2, 150:2 and 6.

David also knew it would take more than words to properly show respect for his Creator. He found ways to serve God whether he was working in the field watching over the sheep or a soldier in the king's army. Even as a great and powerful king, David wanted to show honor and respect to God. We can learn from David how to praise and worship our Creator, and we can learn to show Him respect by caring for the masterpiece He has given us.

Hebrews 12:9 says, "Moreover, we have had earthly fathers who disciplined us and we yielded [to them] *and* respected [them for training us]. Shall we not much more cheerfully submit to the Father of spirits and so [truly] live?" (AMP).

Proverbs 13:13 says, "Whoever despises the word *and* counsel [of God] brings destruction upon himself, but he who [reverently] fears *and* respects the commandment [of God] is rewarded" (AMP).

1 Corinthians 10:31 reminds us to show our respect for our Creator, "So then, whether you eat or drink, or whatever you may do, do all for the honor *and* glory of God" (AMP).

Colossians 3:17 also says, "And whatever you do [no matter what it is] in word or deed, do everything in the name of the Lord Jesus *and* in [dependence upon] His Person, giving praise to God the Father through Him" (AMP).

Many people feel resistance when we suggest that part of overall health includes scheduling time to get alone with God and spending time studying and reading His Word. They use some of the same excuses for not doing this as they do for not eating right. They are too busy, it has not worked in the past, no matter what they do or say nothing changes anyway. However, just like in our natural relationships with one another, our relationship with God must be nurtured in order to grow and reach its full potential. God created us because He desired a relationship with us. We can never become all we are destined to be without a close and very personal relationship with our Creator. How can we know what God likes and dislikes if we don't get to know Him? How can we learn what pleases and displeases God without spending time studying His instructions to us? How can we understand His great love for us if we don't read the letters He has written to us?

"All Scripture is inspired by God," the Apostle Paul told Timothy, "and is useful to teach us what is true and to make us realize what is wrong in our lives. It corrects us when we are wrong and teaches us to do what is right" (2 Timothy 3:16 NLT).

"For the word of God is living and active," Paul wrote in Hebrews, "sharper than any two-edged sword, piercing to the division of soul and of spirit, of joints and of marrow, and discerning the thoughts and intentions of the heart" (Hebrews 4:12).

"I have hidden your word in my heart," David writes, "that I might not sin against you" (Psalm 119:11 NLT).

I'm inclined to ask, "God, why can't people see they are being disrespectful to You when they allow food to control them? How can I help them see the truth?"

"As I began to pursue health and understanding of who I really was, I came face to face with God," says Dr. Cheryl Townsley, N.D. "I believed I had to be perfect and someday God might say, 'Good job.' God had another plan. He did not want a robot...He wanted a daughter's love, my love. I began to see the complexity and yet simplicity of being alive. How could I ever hope to get healthier if I ignored any part of me? I couldn't."[7]

I came to the same conclusion. I had to seek to be whole and that meant dealing with my whole person; body, soul, and spirit. I had to start by getting to know my Creator. When I did, I came to respect Him even more for all that He has done in and through me.

Ask Yourself:

How do I treat someone I respect?

How do I talk about them?

If they ask me to do something am I willing to comply?

Do I pay close attention to what they say?

Do I value their opinion and their instructions?

Do I trust their advice?

Am I being disrespectful to God when I allow food to control me?

Action Suggestion:

Are you scheduling time alone with God to study and read His Word? Take time to nurture your relationship with God. He created you and desires a relationship with you. Get to know what God likes and dislikes, and what pleases and displeases Him. Read the letters He has written to you and talk them over with Him during you conversations with Him. Record in your journal what you learn about God during your time alone with Him. Start each day praising and thanking Him for creating you as His special masterpiece.

---

7   "Discovering Wholeness – The Spirit, Soul and Body Connection." LFH Publishing, Littleton, CO. © 2000 by Dr. Cheryl Townsley, N.D.

Scientific Truth: "Being overweight contributes significantly to lower back pain! For those overweight individuals with lower back problems, Kapandji in *The Physiology of the Joints* says that for every one pound of extra weight a person is carrying, this equates to ten pounds of extra pressure on the discs in the lower lumbar spine. That's all, just one pound! This can be explained to an overweight person by pointing out that the forty pounds of extra weight they are carrying is 400 pounds of extra pressure on the discs in their lower spine. This is dangerous for their discs and also retards recovery and progress. Kapandji is considered the foremost spine researcher and authority in the world. (*Fat Burning Fitness*, ©2014 Elevation Health Publications, North Richland Hills, TX 76182)

Answer 3: Develop a Healthy Self-Respect

God took so much love and care in creating your body, would you say He cherishes and respects it? So do you respect your body as much as God does?

When you think of the things you cherish is your body one of them?

Does it seem strange to talk about cherishing your own body?

Does it seem strange to talk about respecting your own body?

When you hold a newborn baby in your arms do you think about how you want to take care of them and how you want to keep them safe? I remember when my first grandson was a baby; his parents took great care to prepare just the right foods for him. They cherished his body so much they wanted to be sure he had what he needed to grow and mature.

What about us now as grown adults? Have we gotten away from wanting to be sure we put the right foods into our bodies to make sure we grow and mature correctly? Do we think because we've grown up we've arrived and it doesn't matter what is put into this body? Even though we are grown up it doesn't mean our heart, lungs, kidneys, and all our other inner parts don't need to be taken care of.

Remember, Psalm 139:13 from the English Standard version says, "You formed my inward parts; you knitted me together in my mother's womb." The Life Application Bible says, "You made all the delicate, inner parts of my body." God made the delicate, inner parts and intricately created you! How are you treating those delicate, inner parts? Are you treating them like a treasure or trash? Do you really truly believe it's important to take care of your body, your masterpiece or do you feel you can feed it whatever you desire and whatever happens, happens? Which attitude shows the kind of respect God would expect us to show the masterpiece He has created for us?

What is God's definition of self-respect? Does it mean we are being selfish when we respect ourselves?

Selfish means self-seeking, egotistical, and self-centered. It is true that God is to be at the center of our lives, and He expects us to respect everything He has provided for us, including our bodies. How can we truly be self-controlled when it comes to eating properly if we do not have any self-respect? Another word we could use here is self-worth. How much does God say we are worth? Self-esteem is also part of the overall definition of self-respect. We cannot be confident in anything we do if we do not have the right level of self-esteem. Notice what the scriptures below say about how we are to present ourselves to others.

> *So that you may **bear yourselves becomingly and be correct and honorable and command the respect of the outside world**, being dependent on nobody [self-supporting] and having need of nothing.* (1 Thessalonians 4:12 AMP emphasis added)

> *[The] women likewise must be **worthy of respect** and serious, not gossipers, but temperate and self-controlled, [thoroughly] trustworthy in all things.* (1 Timothy 3:11 AMP emphasis added) In this scripture, Timothy is sharing the qualifications for the wife of a deacon; however, would you agree this can apply to all women?

I personally struggled a lot with self-esteem issues. I kept remembering the degrading names people called me. I remembered how I embarrassed my family, especially my brother and sister. I kept thinking about how, because I was fat, people thought I was stupid. People would tell me that I had a pretty face and just imagine how pretty I would be when I lost the weight. People can be cruel to fat people. I felt I was treated differently and it hurt!

As I was being coached, I remember being told, "hurting people hurt people." However, I realized it wasn't that people were hurting and wanted to hurt me. It was because I didn't fit the "norm." I wasn't slim and trim. I was fat. I looked different and it wasn't popular to be friends with someone who didn't fit the norm.

I now realize because I looked different, it caused people to feel uncomfortable. Have you ever been around people who have a disability and you aren't sure how to act around them or what to say? Even though a person with a disability is a human just like you and me, their "differences" make us feel uncomfortable. When we focus on how God created them and in His eyes they are one of His masterpieces, we will see them with different eyes. When I was fat, if those who were cruel to me could have seen I was one of God's masterpieces, they would have treated me differently.

I feel it's important at this part of my story to share that not everyone was cruel to me. I had some wonderful friends–girls and guys–and I still stay in touch with some of them even though we live far from each other. However, the sad thing is how I allowed the negative words and actions of others affect me more than the positive things in my life. Insecure people who want to be popular with the "in crowd" try to make themselves look better by making fun of others, and treating them differently trying to prove they are cool. When someone looks different, it makes people feel uncomfortable, and because they are uncomfortable, they strike out by speaking hurtful words and treating them differently.

After I released the fat girl, I also knew it was important to forgive those who were cruel. There is something much more important to me and that's my eternity with God. He is willing to forgive me and has asked His children to forgive as He forgives. If you have been hurt by others, I encourage you to release the hurt and forgive those who have hurt you. I also encourage you to find a coach or someone who can guide you from pain to peace.

Self-esteem and self-respect cause you to look at things from a different perspective. Remember when we were all encouraged to look at a situation through the eyes of Jesus and before we reacted to it ask ourselves,

What Would Jesus Do? What if we tried to look at ourselves from God's perspective? What does God see when He looks at you and me?

It dawned on me one day that God knew all about me. He knew about my strengths and my weaknesses. He saw my flaws and how imperfect I was, but He still gave me an opportunity to become His child through Jesus His Son. As a matter of fact, the adoption papers had already been signed. All I had to do was agree to the terms in Acts 2:38 and I would be called a child of the Most High God. The cool thing about adoption is many times the people who adopt you know all about you. They know your background and who your natural parents were, and yet they chose to adopt you. When we obey God's commandments, He still wants to adopt us even though He knows all about us and our weaknesses and sins. God chose to adopt you, too.

Ephesians 1:5 says, "For He foreordained us (destined us, **planned in love for us) to be adopted** (revealed) as His own children through Jesus Christ, in accordance with the purpose of His will [because it pleased Him and was His kind intent]" (AMP emphasis added).

Romans 8:15-17 says, "For [the Spirit which] you have now received [is] not a spirit of slavery to put you once more in bondage to fear, but **you have received the Spirit of adoption** [the Spirit producing sonship] in [the bliss of] which we cry, Abba (Father)! Father! The Spirit Himself [thus] testifies together with our own spirit, [assuring us] that **we are children of God.** And if we are [His] children, then we are [His] heirs also: heirs of God and fellow heirs with Christ [sharing His inheritance with Him]" (AMP emphasis added).

That should boost your self-esteem a little to know that God adopted you fully knowing who and what you were. Doesn't it seem right to respect yourself and treat the body He has given you with respect?

As I close this lesson, my prayer is you will respect your body as much as God does and you will want to take better care of it. My mission is to inspire you to cherish and respect the body God gave you as your Masterpiece and to guide your thoughts about yourself so you will want to take care of yourself physically to be your best spiritually.

Ask Yourself:

When I think of the things I respect and cherish, is my body one of them?

Does it seem strange to talk about cherishing my own body?

Does it seem strange to talk about respecting my own body?

Have I let the words and actions of others damage my self-esteem?

How does it make me feel to know God chose to adopt me?

How is this going to change the way I treat my body?

Action Suggestion:

In order to develop a healthy self-respect, it's important to see yourself from God's perspective. Reread the scriptures in this chapter and write them out in your own words in your journal. Then use them to thank God for how He has chosen and esteemed you. Allow Him to minister to you in this area of self-respect and self-esteem. Continue to look for ways you can reach out and help others. Realize you are on a mission for the King of kings as His ambassador, as His child. Ask Him to use you in at least one person's life each and every day. Continue to use the "I Did" and "I Didn't" format to reveal areas where you are not respecting your body the way God does.

Scientific Truth: When you are sleep deprived, you are more likely to overeat and crave sugar and carbohydrates. "When your body is under the stress response, whether acute or chronic, your cortisol and insulin levels rise. These two hormones tend to track each other, so when your cortisol is consistently elevated under a chronic low-level stress response, you may experience difficulty losing weight or building muscle. Additionally, if your cortisol is chronically elevated, you'll tend to gain weight around your midsection, which is a major contributing factor to developing diabetes, heart disease, and metabolic syndrome," says Dr. Mercola in his article, *Stress: It Should Never Be Ignored!* (http://articles.mercola.com/sites/articles/archive/2012/06/14)

Answer 4: Develop a Healthy Respect for Food

> "If you really want something you will find a way; if you don't you will find an excuse." -Jim Rohn

I have to share something I saw on TV recently. It was a dog food commercial talking about how their dog food was gluten free, sugar free, corn free, soy free, etc. and how important it is to feed your dog healthy food so you have a healthy, energetic dog with a beautiful shiny coat. As I watched the commercial, I couldn't believe how much importance people put on what they feed their dog and yet they will put whatever food they choose in their own body!

There are very few healthy food commercials for us. How many food commercials brag about being gluten free, sugar free, etc.? The commercials are about how they can make their food look the best and be the most tempting to get you in their restaurant or get you to buy it at the store. Take note of how many food commercials you see during a one hour program. Notice what they are advertising and how they are enticing you to eat their product. How do you feel while you are watching those commercials? Does it make you hungry? Are you tempted to get up and go to the kitchen for a snack no matter what time of day it is?

Did you know there are good times and bad times to eat? It is not always just about what you eat or how much you eat; sometimes it is about when you eat! I heard one nutrition coach describe her former self as a "nibbler or a grazer." She would eat a sensible meal and then nibble all night right up until it was time to go to bed. She didn't realize how much she was consuming or how hard she was making it on her body to digest that food so close to bedtime. If you are constantly snacking you will never burn fat; snacking hinders your progress for burning fat.

Fat-Burning Hint: Pace yourself between meals. Have four to six hours between each meal. Go to sleep on an empty stomach and you will wake up energized, rested, and rejuvenated because the metabolic process requires good digestion. If you go to sleep on an empty stomach, instead of your body having to work at digestion all night, it goes to work healing and repairing the cells that were broken down during the day. If you have a lot of food in your stomach or you go to sleep an hour after eating a lot of food, especially carbohydrates, sugars, and popcorn, it causes your insulin to go up which makes you feel groggy in the morning. Give yourself an eleven- or twelve-hour window of time with no food. When you get up in the morning you are going to be hungry and you will be amazed at how great you feel. This is a simple way to give your body a chance to heal. (*Fat Burning Fitness*, ©2014 Elevation Health Publications, North Richland Hills, TX 76182)

A root that has healthy nourishment produces good fruit. This is a basic law of nature.

When you think about how God made your delicate inner parts, does this make you want to treat your body, your masterpiece differently? Does it make you think about what you are doing to your heart, lungs, kidneys, liver, and all your other parts by the food you put in your body? How about the way food affects your brain function? Is mental clarity a good reason to eat healthier? Giving your body the right fuel can help you sharpen your focus and help you think more clearly. You can increase your creativity and your stress tolerance.

The best reason of all is that life and good health are gifts from God and what we do with that health and how we steward our life is our gift back to God. In order to do this we have to learn all we can about the food we are considering putting in our bodies. Gaining a healthy respect for the food we eat begins by acquiring knowledge and then putting what we learn into practice in our lives.

Health Trivia: Beets and beet greens are both powerful cleansers and builders of the blood. Apples have calcium, magnesium, phosphorus, vitamin C, beta-carotene, and pectin.

Remember we are to eat to live not live to eat because food is the fuel our body needs to run all those delicate inner parts smoothly. A car is manufactured to last hundreds of thousands of miles. However, if we don't properly maintain it, it will die early. If we don't care for our bodies, we can take ourselves out early, too. We were built to go the distance. Science actually confirms that most cells in our body were constructed to last 125 years (SierraSciences.com).

Wisdom will multiply your days and add years to your life. If you become wise, you will be the one to benefit. If you scorn wisdom, you will be the one to suffer. (Proverbs 9:11-12 NLT)

Doing what we are *supposed to do* versus what we *want to do* will always bring us success, especially in the area of caring for the masterpiece God has given us. Regaining and maintaining our health should begin with the mindset that our bodies will function best when the "owner's manual" is followed exactly as instructed. Logically speaking, the One who created us is the One we should seek knowledge from if we want to live a long and healthy life. This means having the obedience and discipline to live the healthy lifestyle we were created to live. Conversely, it can also be said that it is foolish to think we can abuse our bodies with poor nutrition, lack of exercise, and destructive thoughts and still live a productive and healthy life.

Think about it this way. If we were to call an authorized technician to ask for help with installing or repairing our computer, he would begin by asking us some very basic questions:

Did you carefully follow the basic instructions?

Did you try to by-pass any of the steps listed in the manual?

Did you try to make it do something it was not designed to do?

Do you realize if you do not follow the instructions in the owner's manual your warranty may be made invalid?

The man considered wisest of them all once said, "Live wisely and wisdom will permeate your life; mock life and life will mock you" (Proverbs 9:12 MSG). Without a basic understanding of the instructions given by our Creator, life is just one health crisis after another. We are all creatures of habit, for better or worse. Bad habits create a poor quality of life. Good habits create an outstanding quality of life. If we do what we are designed to do, then success is the logical outcome. This concept spans every aspect of blessing, joy, and well-being in our lives.

Basically, we are all slaves to our habits. Why not be a slave to the good habits that can unconsciously and effortlessly lead us to obtaining good health and long life? It has been said if we don't plan for success then we plan to fail. When our plan for success lines up with how we were engineered and designed, we will discover health and success! Greater blessings will be poured upon us than can be contained! Planning for success means knowing and then implementing habits that will bring health through the way we treat our physical bodies.

Planning for success involves obtaining the knowledge we need about the food we eat so we can cooperate with the Creator's design. There are many resources available to help us become more knowledgeable about the benefits and dangers of the food available for us to purchase and eat. One very good way to become more aware of what we are putting into this marvelous masterpiece God has designed for us is to become a label reader. It's important to check more than the calories and the fat content on these labels. Find out what is packed inside the food you are considering putting into your body.

For example do you know that there are many ingredients listed on food labels that are really just other forms of sugar? One so-called healthy breakfast bar included eight different names for sugar on their ingredients list. Watch out for high fructose corn syrup, sucrose, dextrose, glycerin, maltodextrin, and any other form of corn syrup.

1 Thessalonians 5:21 says, "But examine everything carefully; hold fast to that which is good" (NASB). The Amplified Bible adds, "But test *and* prove all things [until you can recognize] what is good; [to that] hold fast." We can take this advice and apply it to our physical life as well.

Scientific Truth: "Eating carbohydrates for breakfast will promote fat storage, making weight loss more difficult despite exercise. Avoiding fructose and other grain carbohydrates is a critical element of a successful weight-loss strategy." (*Fat Burning Fitness*, ©2014 Elevation Health Publications, North Richland Hills, TX 76182). Instead see my recipe for a great homemade healthy breakfast smoothie at the end of this chapter.

I believe when we are abusive to our bodies whether it's eating, drinking or thinking negative thoughts we really don't love ourselves the way God wants. Do you cherish and respect yourself, His masterpiece, as much as He does?

Are we tempting God or daring Him when we continue to eat foods we know are harmful? Studies show the foods we eat can cause diabetes, heart disease, strokes, etc. Yet we are so controlled by the food we ignore the signs. It is as though we think, "This won't happen to me." We continue to eat unhealthy foods, ignoring what can happen with an attitude of "I'll eat what I want" and play Russian roulette with our health! Jesus said, "On the other hand, it is written also, You shall not tempt, test thoroughly, *or* try exceedingly the Lord your God" (Matthew 4:7 AMP).

Get proper hydration: You can treat your water with lemon/lime and liquid sea salt which has iodine and supports your thyroid (one of the glands responsible for your metabolic rate). Slow, consistent saturation all day long is the most effective way to hydrate your body. Use water, not sports drinks, to properly hydrate your body. (*Fat Burning Fitness*, ©2014 Elevation Health Publications, North Richland Hills, TX 76182)

Ask Yourself:

Does my plan for success line up with how I was engineered and designed?

Am I a slave to the good habits that lead to good health and long life?

Do I respect my body and the food I put in it enough to start reading labels and becoming more conscious of what I am putting in my masterpiece?

Am I tempting God or daring Him when I continue to eat knowing the foods are harming me?

Am I willing to change my eating habits based on what I have learned?

Action Suggestion:

Write in your journal your plan for success. Research how your body is designed to function and the types of fuels it needs to give you a long and healthy life. Post the list of dos and don'ts on your refrigerator and have it handy when you go shopping for your groceries. Become a label reader! Be sure to thank God for creating you and paying attention to every little detail of your inner parts. Thank Him for providing the type of fuel your body needs to run smoothly and efficiently for a long time! Remember your health affects every part of your life so do what you can today so you can enjoy a healthier tomorrow! Look for recipes like the one below.

Homemade Healthy Smoothie
Frozen Fruit: choice of 2 or 3 of the following
1/2 cup Frozen Pineapple,
Blueberries, Strawberries or Mangos
1 small avocado (a good fat)
4 Tbsp Hemp Powder (gives 15 grams of protein)
1 Tbsp Coconut Oil (a good fat)
1/2 tsp vanilla
1 Tbsp Raw Honey
Raw Kale
Raw Baby Spinach
Chia Seeds (helps you feel full)

This smoothie is really like eating soft serve ice cream! I recommend putting this in a blender and put about four ounces of unsweetened Almond or Coconut milk in first–add more as needed. This is your smoothie, add what you want–just be sure you keep it healthy!

You could also substitute other foods instead of fruit and make it for lunch or supper. A tablespoon of almond or cashew butter or tahini is yummy. When choosing a protein meal replacement, be sure to watch for sugar or artificial sweetener. I have found milk products cause eye fatigue for me, so I stay away from any product which has whey or casein.

Chapter 8

HOW CAN I STAY IN CONTROL?

God gave us a spirit not of fear but of power and love and self-control. (2 Timothy 1:7)

One thing I have learned as I have walked with God these many years is that if He tells us to do something then we are able to do it. If it says we have self-control and can live a life reflecting that power, then there is way we can accomplish it. Galatians 5:16-18 is the beginning of understanding how to overcome this lack of self-control and begin to live the life God designed us to live.

But I say, walk by the Spirit, and you will not gratify the desires of the flesh. [17] For the desires of the flesh are against the Spirit, and the desires of the Spirit are against the flesh, for these are opposed to each other, to keep you from doing the things you want to do. (Galatians 5:16-17)

We are told in this passage to let the Holy Spirit guide our lives. The Amplified Bible says, "But I say, walk *and* live [habitually] in the [Holy] Spirit [responsive to *and* controlled *and* guided by the Spirit]; then you will certainly not gratify the cravings *and* desires of the flesh (of human nature without God)" (Galatians 5:16). We are to walk and live guided and controlled by God's Holy Spirit. That is the only way we can keep from giving into the cravings and desires of the flesh.

This passage also says the desires of flesh are against the Spirit. They are directly opposed to one another. Not only opposed, but the two forces are constantly fighting each other! So how are we to walk and live controlled by God's Holy Spirit and not our own fleshly desires? We start by learning how to display the fruit of the Spirit in our everyday lives.

Answer 1: Display the Fruit of the Spirit

> *But the fruit of the Spirit is love, joy, peace, patience, kindness, goodness, faithfulness, gentleness, self-control; against such things there is no law. And those who belong to Christ Jesus have crucified the flesh with its passions and desires. If we live by the Spirit, let us also keep in step with the Spirit.*
> (Galatians 5:22-25)

Galatians 5:22-23 lists for us the fruit of the Spirit: love, joy, peace, patience, kindness, goodness, faithfulness, gentleness, and self-control. So how can we start giving control over to the Holy Spirit? First we have to allow God's Spirit to dwell within us.

> *Do you not know that your body is a temple of the Holy Spirit within you, whom you have from God? You are not your own.*
> (I Corinthians 6:19)

The Holy Spirit of God will not enter our temple unless we first follow God's commandment in Acts 2:38, "Repent and be baptized every one of you in the name of Jesus Christ for the forgiveness of your sins, and you will receive the gift of the Holy Spirit." We also read in Acts 5:32, "And we are witnesses to these things, and so is the Holy Spirit, whom God has given to those who obey Him." This is such an exciting scripture. When we do something so simple as confess Jesus as our Lord, obey God's command to be baptized, then God will give us the amazing gift of the Holy Spirit. We don't have to ask the Spirit to enter us; He is immediately given to us as soon as we are baptized!

The description for the fruit of the Spirit isn't about productivity, it's about character. It's about reflecting God's character in our lives. These are traits of what He already looks like. The fruit of the Spirit is supposed to come forth from us because the Spirit comes forth from us. It's not about us striving to be this; it's about displaying what we have been given. The Fruit of the Spirit is already love, joy, peace, patience, kindness, goodness, faithfulness, gentleness, and self-control because that is the way our Creator is. His DNA is within us and is allowed to shine forth from our lives when we submit our thoughts, desires, and actions to the guidance of His Holy Spirit. We just have to live and display these traits in all that we say and do.

You see, the works of the flesh get in the way. It wants to do evil and keep us from displaying the fruit of the Spirit. It's not that we need patience, it's we want to magnify God in us. It's not about trying to improve our character; it's about focusing on the virtue of the Holy Spirit! When we focus on allowing the fruit of the Spirit to shine forth and commit our daily life to God, we won't have to say I need patience or I need joy in my life. Instead we want to seek a closer relationship with God, the Creator of our Masterpiece.

> *But the fruit of the [Holy] Spirit [the work which His presence within accomplishes]* is love, joy (gladness), peace, patience (an even temper, forbearance), kindness, goodness (benevolence), faithfulness, gentleness (meekness, humility), self-control (self-restraint, continence). (Galatians 5:22-23 AMP emphasis added)

We are given this fruit primarily to find out if our fellowship with the Spirit is deep enough. Here is a brief description of what each segment of the fruit of the Spirit represents.

Love – God's unconditional love (1 John 3:16)
Joy – Deeper than happiness, gladness (John 15:11)
Peace — Security, safety, and tranquility (John 14:27)
Patience – Endurance, steadfastness, forbearance, and an even temper (James 1:4)
Kindness – Compassion and thoughtfulness (Romans 11:22)
Goodness – Uprightness of heart and life, benevolence (Romans 15:14)
Faithfulness – Covenant keeping (Psalm 119:90 and Proverbs 11:3)

Gentleness – Strength under godly control, meekness, humility (Philippians 4:5)
Self-control – Mastery of desires and passions, self-restraint (Proverbs 25:28)

We don't want our insufficiencies to lead us to search for more fruit, but instead to be in search of the fruitful One. In His arms, under His leadership, and given over to His influence, the fruit will come! We will become mature and can let the world know the fallen flesh doesn't have to rule. We can let the world know there is an alternative lifestyle and it is life in the Spirit of God. Our job is to get self out of the way and let Him shine. To help us with this, Galatians 5:19-21 gives us a list of the desires of the flesh we need to watch out for.

> *Now the works of the flesh are evident: sexual immorality, impurity, sensuality, [20] idolatry, sorcery, enmity, strife, jealousy, fits of anger, rivalries, dissensions, divisions, [21] envy, drunkenness, orgies, and things like these. I warn you, as I warned you before, that those who do such things will not inherit the kingdom of God.* (Galatians 5:19-21)

What does all of this have to do with caring for the masterpiece God has given us? The fruit of the Spirit is kindness; so along with being kind to others, how about being kind to your masterpiece? Another segment is love; so along with showing love to others, how about showing love to your masterpiece? What about peace? You can only attain true peace when you are doing things the way God has instructed you to do them. That includes your use of food. Patience means you also have to follow the procedure and not try to get a quick fix. Fads and quick weight loss diets are never the answer. God always rewards faithfulness. There are many stories in the Bible of those who benefited from remaining faithful to doing things God's way.

Paul was one of the most spiritually mature human beings that ever walked planet earth, and yet he had a continual, agonizing struggle with his own flesh. God used Paul to plant churches all over the known world and to write nearly three quarters of the New Testament, yet here he is confessing that he struggles with his flesh.

*For I do not understand my own actions. For I do not do what I want, but I do the very thing I hate. Now if I do what I do not want, I agree with the law, that it is good. So now it is no longer I who do it, but sin that dwells within me. For I know that nothing good dwells in me, that is, in my flesh. **For I have the desire to do what is right, but not the ability to carry it out.** For I do not do the good I want, but the evil I do not want is what I keep on doing. Now if I do what I do not want, it is no longer I who do it, but sin that dwells within me. So I find it to be a law that when I want to do right, evil lies close at hand.* (Romans 7:15-21 emphasis added)

God puts within us a life that will manifest His character the more we seek, believe, and persist in our relationship with Him. Paul's life reflects his constant pursuit of a relationship with God and his desire to reflect God's character in all that he said and did.

Knowing we have been given the gift of the Holy Spirit, and knowing we don't have to ask for any of these characteristics because they have been given to us when we obey God; would you agree it would benefit us to do everything in our power to nurture these segments of the fruit of the Spirit? The more I study and realize it's my responsibility to nurture the fruit, the more I want to be sure I nurture to full potential!

Ask Yourself:

Am I being kind to the masterpiece He has given me?

Am I showing love to Him by loving my masterpiece?

Am I displaying God's faithfulness by faithfully caring for my body?

What am I showing the world about the character of God through the way I am treating my masterpiece?

Action Suggestion:

Further study the fruit of the Spirit by looking up each of the suggested scriptures. As you gain understanding of each of these character traits of God, begin to watch for them to manifest in your own life. Ask God to show you how to protect your masterpiece from the desires and works of the flesh and to guide you in the manifestation of the fruit of His Spirit in your life. In your conversations with God ask Him to reveal any area where you have bad fruit and how to deal with it. Continue to use the "I Did" and "I Didn't" format in your journal to help you pinpoint areas where you need to deal with bad fruit.

Answer 2: Commit Your Daily Life to God

> *For we are God's [own] handiwork (His workmanship), recreated in Christ Jesus, [born anew] that we may do those good works which God predestined (planned beforehand) for us [taking paths which He prepared ahead of time], that we should walk in them [living the good life which He prearranged and made ready for us to live].* (Ephesians 2:10 AMP)

What a powerful scripture to begin this section on the fruit of the Spirit and mastering self-control. What has God continually impressed upon us about how and why He created us? We are His own handiwork! He created us to do good works! He has prepared a path of good works for us to accomplish if we will just follow His plan!

As you read the verses prior to this amazing truth presented to us by our Creator, see how God deals with the excuses people have for not walking in the Spirit and living the godly life He has prepared for us.

> *And you were dead in the trespasses and sins [2] in which you once walked, following the course of this world, following the prince of the power of the air, the spirit that is now at work in the sons of disobedience— [3] among whom we all once lived in the passions of our flesh, carrying out the desires of the body and the mind, and were by nature children of wrath, like the rest of mankind.* (Ephesians 2:1-3)

Can you see how well our Heavenly Father knows us? He has been watching us since before we were born! He knows what we have and have not done. The next set of verses starts out with "But God."

> *But God is so rich in mercy, and he loved us so much, that even though we were dead because of our sins, he gave us life when he raised Christ from the dead. (It is only by God's grace that you have been saved!) For he raised us from the dead along with Christ and seated us with him in the heavenly realms because we are united with Christ Jesus.* (Ephesians 2:4-6 NLT)

This phrase "But God" is used many times in the Bible to show us just how much we need His presence in our lives. In Genesis 8:1 it says, "But God remembered Noah... and the flood waters receded." In Genesis 19:29 it says, "But God listened to Abraham's request and kept Lot safe" (see also 2 Peter 2:7). Genesis 50:20 says Joseph told his jealous brothers, "You intended to harm me but God intended it all for good" (see also Acts 7:9). The Apostle Paul in Acts 26:22 tells us, "But God has protected me so I can testify to everyone." Romans 5:7-8 says, "Rarely will anyone die even for a righteous man, but God demonstrates His own love for us that while we were yet sinners Christ died for us."

> *So God can point to us in all future ages as examples of the incredible wealth of his grace and kindness toward us, as shown in all he has done for us who are united with Christ Jesus. God saved you by his grace when you believed. And you can't take credit for this; it is a gift from God. Salvation is not a reward for the good things we have done, so none of us can boast about it.* (Ephesians 2:7-9 NLT)

God saved you by His grace when you believed. Why did He do it? It was to show the immeasurable, exceeding, incredible wealth of His grace and kindness toward you. You cannot get this grace by your works. It's a gift from God so you can't personally boast. You need to always give God the glory for whatever you accomplish in this life. There is no limit to what the grace of God can do when unleashed in your life and accepted by faith. How much of that grace is available to you? There is a limitless supply. You may be convinced that you are not worthy of God's grace. That's the good news because if you were worthy, you wouldn't need it. If you could earn it, it wouldn't be grace any longer. Grace is receiving God's Riches At Christ's Expense. It cost you nothing to receive it, but it cost Him everything to give it. It is a gift more powerful than all of man's effort, intellect, and wisdom and it's yours as a gift from God.

2 Corinthians 9:8 says, "And God is able to make all grace (every favor and earthly blessing) come to you in abundance, so that you may always *and* under all circumstances *and* whatever the need be self-sufficient [possessing enough to require no aid or support and furnished in abundance for every good work and charitable donation]" (AMP).

Here is a formula for a powerful, victorious life. **God gives you His grace in abundance which gives you whatever you need no matter what the circumstance you are facing in life!** Did you catch those words—all grace, always and under all circumstances? Did you see why He is giving you this grace? So you can do every good work! Ephesians 2:10 also says you were created to do good works to glorify Him. What do you think those good works are?

The main thing you and I are called to do is to let the Holy Spirit shine through us so we glorify God in everything we say and do. The world needs to see the evidence of the Christ in us no matter what we are doing. Remember our actions speak much louder than our words.

So what does God require of us? Our answer is in Micah 6:8.

He has told you, O man, what is good; and what does the LORD require of you but to do justice, and to love kindness, and to walk humbly with your God? (Micah 6:8)

"Displaying the Spirit is one of our primary functions in this world. Our job is to get self out of the way and let Him shine!" ("Wonders of the Cross" by Chris Tiegreen, January 10, Tyndale Publishing, 2009)

Jesus gave us a description in Matthew 5:14-16 that will help us understand what God desires of our lives here on this earth.

You are the light of the world. A city set on a hill cannot be hidden. Nor do people light a lamp and put it under a basket, but on a stand, and it gives light to all in the house. In the same way, let your light shine before others, so that they may see your good works and give glory to your Father who is in heaven.

In other words, God expects us to influence the world around us. We need to start out each day asking God what His plans are for our day. Our prayers should be to find out what His priorities are so we can set ours accordingly. When we totally commit our day to Him we not only accomplish more but stay on track with everything we do. We can avoid time and energy wasters and resist the traps and temptations the world sets all around us. Instead of being the thermometer that is affected by everything that is happening around us we become the thermostat and set the standard according to God's way of doing things.

The more we commit to Him the more His light shines through us and onto those we are called to influence in the world around us.

Commit your way to the Lord [roll and repose each care of your load on Him]; trust (lean on, rely on, and be confident) also in Him and He will bring it to pass. And He will make your uprightness and right standing with God go forth as the light, and your justice and right as [the shining sun of] the noonday. (Psalm 37:5-6 AMP)

Spending time studying His Word and building your relationship with Him will prepare you to do His good works. When you determine to commit your day to Him, doing everything to please Him and not man, you will see the fruit of the Spirit manifested brightly in your life! God will teach you every day what you need to know to face life's daily trials. As you study the scriptures begin to expect God, through His Spirit, to enlighten you so you can be His light to the world.

All Scripture is inspired by God and is useful to teach us what is true and to make us realize what is wrong in our lives. It corrects us when we are wrong and teaches us to do what is right. God uses it to prepare and equip his people to do every good work. (2 Timothy 3:16-17 NLT)

Whatever you do, work heartily, as for the Lord and not for men. (Colossians 3:23)

Ask Yourself:

Am I totally committed to God in all I say and do?

Am I willing to let His light shine through me to others even if it means I have to change some of my ways?

Am I spending quality time with Him?

Am I seeking to know Him and His ways so I can truly reflect Him to those around me?

Action Suggestion:

As you spend time with God, ask Him to show you how He can express Himself fully through you today and every day. Use Galatians 2:20 as your prayer today, "It is no longer I who live, but Christ lives in me." Commit everything you say and do to Him and watch Him do the miraculous in and through you. Continue to use the "I Did" and "I Didn't" format in your journal to help you pinpoint areas where you did or did not let the light of the Holy Spirit shine through you today.

Answer 3: Get Self Out of the Way

If then you have been raised with Christ, seek the things that are above, where Christ is, seated at the right hand of God. [2] Set your minds on things that are above, not on things that are on earth. [3] For you have died, and your life is hidden with Christ in God. [4] When Christ who is your life appears, then you also will appear with him in glory. [5] Put to death therefore what is earthly in you: sexual immorality, impurity, passion, evil desire, and covetousness, which is idolatry. [6] On account of these the wrath of God is coming. [7] In these you too once walked, when you were living in them. [8] But now you must put them all away: anger, wrath, malice, slander, and obscene talk from your mouth. ⁹ Do not lie to one another, seeing that you have put off the old self with its practices ¹⁰ and have put on the new self, which is being renewed in knowledge after the image of its creator. ¹¹ Here there is not Greek and Jew, circumcised and uncircumcised, barbarian, Scythian, slave, free; but Christ is all, and in all.¹² Put on then, as God's chosen ones, holy and beloved, compassionate hearts, kindness, humility, meekness, and patience, ¹³ bearing with one another and, if one has a complaint against another, forgiving each other; as the Lord has forgiven you, so you also must forgive. ¹⁴ And above all these put on love, which binds everything together in perfect harmony. ¹⁵ And let the peace of Christ rule in your hearts, to which indeed you were called in one body. And be thankful. (Colossians 3:1-15)

Put off the old self and put on the new self is an important part of gaining control of any habit. I know a family who read this scripture everyday together to remind themselves of the importance of this concept in their lives. By reading this scripture each morning before the children went to school and the parents went to work, they were more focused on loving others and how God wanted them to act throughout the day. Can you imagine what our day would be like if we start it out with setting our minds on things that are above? Not only will we be kind to everyone, we will also be kind to ourselves.

Colossians 3:5-9 describes putting off the old self and all of its practices or habits. The Amplified translation says we should "kill, deaden, deprive of power the evil desire lurking in our members" (verse 5). Verse 8 says we need to "rid yourselves completely of all these things" (AMP). Then verse 9 says, "For you have stripped off the old self with its evil practices" (AMP).

Romans 6:6-7 reminds us that this old self was crucified with Christ so that we would no longer be a slave to these fleshly desires. Galatians 2:20 says this as well and adds, "It is no longer I who live but Christ who lives in me." Even though we still live in the flesh we do not have to allow that flesh to control us because of the power God has placed within us through Christ's death and the presence of His Holy Spirit within us.

We know that our old self was crucified with him in order that the body of sin might be brought to nothing, so that we would no longer be enslaved to sin. [7] For one who has died has been set free from sin. (Romans 6:6-7)

I have been crucified with Christ. It is no longer I who live, but Christ who lives in me. And the life I now live in the flesh I live by faith in the Son of God, who loved me and gave himself for me. (Galatians 2:20)

Colossians 3:10 and12 tells us to put on our new self or clothe ourselves with the image of God and behavior that includes compassionate hearts, kindness, humility, meekness, patience, bearing with one another, and forgiving one another. Then it wraps this up by saying in verse 14, "Above all put on and clothe yourself as God's Masterpiece with love which binds everything together in perfect harmony." Galatians 3:27 says, "For as many of you as were baptized into Christ have put on Christ."

It is important that we notice here who is doing the putting off and putting on. Is God doing it? Does He strip us of the old self and then clothe us with the new one? No, we have to do this. We are responsible for the "clothing" we wrap ourselves in. We have to choose every single day how we will present ourselves to those around us. I like what the Amplified translation adds in verses 15-17.

*And let the peace (soul harmony which comes) from Christ rule (**act as umpire continually**) in your hearts [**deciding and settling with finality all questions that arise in your minds**, in that peaceful state] to which as [members of Christ's] one body you were also called [to live]. And be thankful (appreciative), [giving praise to God always]. [16] **Let the word [spoken by] Christ (the Messiah) have its home [in your hearts and minds]** and dwell in you in [all its] richness, as you teach and admonish and train one another in all insight and intelligence and wisdom [in spiritual things, and as you sing] psalms and hymns and spiritual songs, making melody to God with [His] grace in your hearts. [17] **And whatever you do [no matter what it is] in word or deed,** do everything in the name of the Lord*

*Jesus and **in [dependence upon] His Person**, giving praise to
God the Father through Him.* (AMP emphasis added)

He will act as an umpire continually answering the questions that
arise in our minds if we allow His Word to have a home in our hearts and
minds. That is how we can fulfill verse 17 and no matter what we do, in
word or deed, we can do everything as Jesus would do it!

2 Peter 1:3-4 reminds us, "His divine power has granted to us all
things that pertain to life and godliness, through the knowledge of him
who called us to his own glory and excellence, by which he has granted
to us his precious and very great promises, so that through them you may
become partakers of the divine nature, having escaped from the corruption that is in the world because of sinful desire." Then it goes on in verses
5-7 to tell us how to move forward and get the old self out of the way so
the new self can truly reflect the divine nature He has placed within us.

> *For this very reason, make every effort to supplement your faith
> with virtue, and virtue with knowledge, and knowledge with
> self-control, and self-control with steadfastness, and steadfast-
> ness with godliness, and godliness with brotherly affection, and
> brotherly affection with love.*

Then we come to verses 8-9 which explain that the more we grow
in Christ, the more effective and productive we are in life. If we fail to
develop in Christ we are shortsighted, nearsighted or blind, forgetting
we have already been cleansed from that old self.

> *For if these qualities are yours and are increasing, they keep you
> from being ineffective or unfruitful in the knowledge of our Lord
> Jesus Christ. For whoever lacks these qualities is so nearsighted
> that he is blind, having forgotten that he was cleansed from his
> former sins.*

2 Peter 1:10-15 says it is going to take hard work and diligence, but
if we do these things on a daily basis we will not fall. Lots of people are
watching us. We have to choose on a daily basis what example we are
going to be.

Therefore, brothers, be all the more diligent to confirm your calling and election, for if you practice these qualities you will never fall. For in this way there will be richly provided for you an entrance into the eternal kingdom of our Lord and Savior Jesus Christ. Therefore I intend always to remind you of these qualities, though you know them and are established in the truth that you have. I think it right, as long as I am in this body, to stir you up by way of reminder, since I know that the putting off of my body will be soon, as our Lord Jesus Christ made clear to me. And I will make every effort so that after my departure you may be able at any time to recall these things. (2 Peter 1:10-15)

Our calling and election or our job as God's child is to present His character, His divine nature to the world around us. When we put off the old self and put on the new, we begin to look and act like our Heavenly Father. One of the ways to do this is to seek to reflect His great love for one another.

Ask Yourself:

Am I effectively depriving fleshly desires from controlling me?

Am I ridding myself of all those things that reflect the old self?

Have I stripped off the old self especially in my eating habits?

Am I still a slave to these fleshly desires?

Have I put on and clothed myself appropriately as God's Masterpiece?

How do my daily choices reflect God's love?

Action Suggestion:

Sometimes a visual of a spiritual concept helps us get a better feel for what these scriptures mean to us in the natural. Stand in front of the mirror and go through the motions of taking off that old self. Maybe take sticky notes and write the names of those desires you battle with and stick them on a coat you are wearing. Then take it off and strip off all of those fleshly desires and throw those sticky notes away. Maybe even burn them in a fireplace or charcoal grill. Then put the coat back on free of all of those fleshly desires. Record in your journal that this is the day you took that old self off. Ask God to show you how to show His love to those around you today.

Answer 4: Realize It's All About Him

> *And he said to him, "You shall love the Lord your God with all your heart and with all your soul and with all your mind. This is the great and first commandment. And a second is like it: You shall love your neighbor as yourself. On these two commandments depend all the Law and the Prophets."* (Matthew 22:37-40)

Jesus said this is the first and greatest commandment. We are to love God with all our heart, soul, and mind. The second commandment is to love our neighbor as ourselves.

All the rest of God's instructions are based on these two commandments. This is not about who we are striving to be. It's about how we manifest and display Him with our lives. It's all about Him! We have the mind of Christ and we are to display the character of God no matter where we are or who we are with. That is the only way we can manifest Him in our lives.

> **Have this mind among yourselves, which is yours in Christ Jesus,** *who, though he was in the form of God, did not count equality with God a thing to be grasped, but emptied himself, by taking the form of a servant, being born in the likeness of men. And being found in human form, he humbled himself by becoming obedient to the point of death, even death on a cross. Therefore God has highly exalted him and bestowed on him*

the name that is above every name, so that at the name of Jesus every knee should bow, in heaven and on earth and under the earth, and every tongue confess that Jesus Christ is Lord, to the glory of God the Father. (Philippians 2:5-11 emphasis added)

"When we allow the love of God to move in us, we can no longer distinguish between ours and His." -Austin Farrer

So what is this God kind of love that we are to display with our lives? And if we do not take care of our masterpiece showing that we love ourselves, how can we show this God kind of love to others as Jesus has instructed us to do? The Apostle Paul has given us one of his famous lists in Romans 12:9-21. This is a long passage but worth reading and studying regularly. Just as He has promised us, when God gives us a command He provides the instructions and the way to accomplish it.

Let love be genuine. Abhor what is evil; hold fast to what is good. [10] Love one another with brotherly affection. Outdo one another in showing honor. [11] Do not be slothful in zeal, be fervent in spirit, serve the Lord. [12] Rejoice in hope, be patient in tribulation, be constant in prayer. [13] Contribute to the needs of the saints and seek to show hospitality. [14] Bless those who persecute you; bless and do not curse them. [15] Rejoice with those who rejoice, weep with those who weep. [16] Live in harmony with one another. Do not be haughty, but associate with the lowly. Never be wise in your own sight. [17] Repay no one evil for evil, but give thought to do what is honorable in the sight of all. [18] If possible, so far as it depends on you, live peaceably with all. [19] Beloved, never avenge yourselves, but leave it to the wrath of God, for it is written, "Vengeance is mine, I will repay, says the Lord." [20] To the contrary, "if your enemy is hungry, feed him; if he is thirsty, give him something to drink; for by so doing you will heap burning coals on his head." [21] Do not be overcome by evil, but overcome evil with good. (Romans 12:9-21)

If we truly focus on this list, we will be so busy doing things that please God and manifesting His character and nature, we won't have time to even look at those fleshly temptations that cause us to lose control. Take

The Master's Masterpiece

the time to study everything on this list and write your own definition of how you will accomplish this in your life on a daily basis.

- Let your love be genuine means I want to _____
- Abhorring evil means I want to _____
- Loving with brotherly affection means _____
- Outdo showing honor means I look for ways to _____
- Be zealous/work hard/serve the Lord where and when? _____
- Rejoice in hope and be patient in tribulation means _____
- Being constant in prayer means _____
- Helping God's people means I get to _____
- Showing hospitality means I get to _____
- Bless those who curse you where and when? _____
- Rejoice with those who rejoice where and when? _____
- Weep with those who weep means I want to _____
- Live in harmony with whom? _____
- Don't be haughty or too proud to be in the company of ordinary people means _____
- Don't be wise in my own sight and don't think I know it all means _____
- Never pay back evil for evil/do things so others see you are honorable means _____
- Do all you can to live at peace with everyone means _____
- Don't take revenge/let God take care of that means _____
- Feed/clothe/give drink to your enemy means what to you? _____
- Overcome and conquer evil with good means I _____

"You will follow your passions. Our love for the Spirit must run deeper than our love for the world." ("Wonders of the Cross" by Chris Tiegreen devotional, January 8)

What do we offer ourselves to? Is it to the entertainment world, to the philosophies of our generation, to the passions of the flesh or to the pursuit of intellectual interests? Check your day planner and see where you spend the majority of your time and you'll find out where your passions really are focused. Sin can only exercise power over you to the extent you offer it your time and energy. Romans 6:13 says we are not to offer the parts of our bodies to sin as instruments of wickedness, but rather to offer ourselves to God (author paraphrase).

If you want to truly defeat the passions of the flesh you need to offer yourself to God each and every day. He will never lead you astray. A deep love for God is the ultimate defense against the temptation of forbidden fruit.

> *I appeal to you therefore, brethren, and beg of you in view of [all] the mercies of God, to make a decisive dedication of your bodies [presenting all your members and faculties] as a living sacrifice, holy (devoted, consecrated) and well pleasing to God, which is your reasonable (rational, intelligent) service and spiritual worship.² Do not be conformed to this world (this age), [fashioned after and adapted to its external, superficial customs], but be transformed (changed) by the [entire] renewal of your mind [by its new ideals and its new attitude], so that you may prove [for yourselves] what is the good and acceptable and perfect will of God, even the thing which is good and acceptable and perfect [in His sight for you].* (Romans 12:1-2 AMP)

Are you willing to surrender your will and ways to God? You have a choice to make whether to surrender your own self-centered will to God. **The problem is never God's provision – the problem is always our surrender.**

> *For consider your calling, brothers: not many of you were wise according to worldly standards, not many were powerful, not many were of noble birth. But God chose what is foolish in the world to shame the wise; God chose what is weak in the world to shame the strong; God chose what is low and despised in the world, even things that are not, to bring to nothing things that*

are, so that no human being might boast in the presence of God.
(1 Corinthians 1:26-29)

Yes, God chooses the weak, foolish, and despised to be His masterpieces and then to fulfill a specific calling and purpose here on the earth. We can change our inner selves and our behaviors from wrong to right only if we understand that it is all about God.

Robert McGee writes, "What a waste to attempt to change behavior without truly understanding the driving needs that cause such behavior! Yet millions of people spend a lifetime searching for love, acceptance, and success without understanding the need that compels them. We must understand that this hunger for self-worth is God-given and can only be satisfied by Him. Our value is not dependent on our ability to earn the fickle acceptance of people, but rather, its true source is the love and acceptance of God. He created us. He alone knows how to fulfill all of our needs."[8]

Ask Yourself:

Am I willing to surrender my will and ways to God?

Is my love for God deeper than my love for the world?

What do I offer myself to?

Do I truly want to defeat the passions of the flesh?

Do I now know how to do this?

Action Suggestion:

Take the time to go back and read and fill in the list given in Romans 12:9-21. Write your own definition of how you will accomplish this in your life on a daily basis. Give specific examples of situations at home, at work, at church, and in your neighborhood where you can implement

---

8   Robert S. McGee. *The Search for Significance: Seeing Your True Worth Through God's Eyes* (p. 11). Kindle Edition.

the things on this list. Keep a record in your journal of what you do and the results you see in your life. You will be amazed at the progress you will make toward gaining control over what used to tempt you.

Healthy Hint: If not dealt with correctly, stress and lack of rest can drain your body of energy. They cause your blood sugar to go up and start you on an energy rollercoaster ride. Your body is looking for sugar, for artificial stimulation or for that fast food rush. Sugar jacks your serotonin level up, but then the level goes down and crashes. Now the vicious cycle begins as you need more sugar, more comfort foods, more energy drinks to get that endorphin and serotonin release. This rollercoaster ride starts doing serious damage to your body. ("Energizing Nutrition" ©2013 Elevation Health Publications, North Richland Hills, TX 76182)

Chapter 9

HOW CAN I KEEP MY COMMITMENTS?

———— ∞∞∞ ————

"The world can be divided into feelers and doers. Feelers take action and initiative only when they feel like doing so. In other words, they feel their way into acting. If they don't feel like doing something that will advance their goals, they won't do it. If a feeler feels like exercising, he will. If he doesn't feel like exercising, he won't. If a feeler feels like watching television, he will... He is a prisoner of the desire for instant gratification, and naturally will suffer the long-term consequences of this short-term perspective... Doers, on the other hand, act their way into feeling. After determining what needs to be done, doers take action. They just do it. If they don't feel like taking action, they consider that emotion to be a distraction and take action in spite of it. They refuse to let their desire for short-term comfort divert them from their long-term goal." (Tommy Newberry)

Answer 1: Be Willing to Make a Decision

Procrastinate means to put off or postpone doing something that needs doing intentionally and habitually. To make a decision means to make a determination arrived at after consideration; to make a choice or select a course of action.

"Procrastination, which is the delaying of higher priority tasks in favor of lower priority ones, is more responsible for frustration, stress, and under-achievement than any other single factor." (Tommy Newberry)

The prophet Jeremiah was called by God to warn His people about the consequences of their decisions. They had wavered back and forth for many years trying to decide whether or not they wanted to worship and serve God exclusively.

> *Has a nation changed its gods, even though they are no gods? But my people have changed their glory for that which does not profit. [12] Be appalled, O heavens, at this; be shocked, be utterly desolate, declares the LORD, [13] for my people have committed two evils: they have forsaken me, the fountain of living waters, and hewed out cisterns for themselves, broken cisterns that can hold no water. [14] "Is Israel a slave? Is he a home born servant? Why then has he become a prey? [15] The lions have roared against him; they have roared loudly. They have made his land a waste; his cities are in ruins, without inhabitant. [16] Moreover, the men of Memphis and Tahpanhes have shaved the crown of your head. [17] Have you not brought this upon yourself by forsaking the LORD your God, when he led you in the way? [18] And now what do you gain by going to Egypt to drink the waters of the Nile? Or what do you gain by going to Assyria to drink the waters of the Euphrates?[19] Your evil will chastise you, and your apostasy will reprove you. Know and see that it is evil and bitter for you to forsake the LORD your God; the fear of me is not in you, declares the Lord GOD of hosts. (Jeremiah 2:11-19)*

As a certified coach, I am taught to guide and help people go from pain to peace. I want you to look at your hands. They are a part of your body. Now think about this, would your hands intentionally hurt you? Remember Ephesians 5:29 says, "No one hates their flesh, but nourishes and cherishes it." Your hands are used to help others, too. They nurture and care for other people, so why not allow them to take care of you?

Your hands don't want to put bad food into your mouth. It's our mind not paying attention to what we are doing that is causing the problem. It's the mindless eating like when I used to sit and eat a whole bowl of chips and not even realize I was doing it. Instead, prepare yourself before you eat. It's important to prepare your head talk and the rest of your body will follow! This preparation is the decision and commitment you make about what you will and will not allow in the masterpiece God has given you.

I have a feeling you might be wondering, "Diane, can't I splurge once in a while and have something not so good for me?" It's your decision. However, I want to ask you if you would be willing to eat healthy for ninety days? I recommend eating lean protein, vegetables, and one or two pieces of fruit per day. Eat three meals a day and only healthy snacks in between if your stomach is growling so loud others can hear it. No eating three hours before going to bed unless your stomach is growling and it would cause a blood sugar issue. If you want more details about this ninety-day eating plan, check out my strategy plan in the appendix of this book.

I found out, after I had the bad stuff out of my system, I didn't feel bloated and lethargic anymore. If I chose to once again make bad choices with my eating, the bloated and lethargic feeling came back. I really didn't like that feeling. It's about making a decision!

Do you remember the story of Daniel? He was deported to Babylon with three other young men and caught the attention of King Nebuchandnezzar.

> *But Daniel resolved that he would not defile himself with the king's food, or with the wine that he drank. Therefore he asked the chief of the eunuchs to allow him not to defile himself. ⁹ And God gave Daniel favor and compassion in the sight of the chief of the eunuchs, ¹⁰ and the chief of the eunuchs said to Daniel, "I fear my lord the king, who assigned your food and your drink; for why should he see that you were in worse condition than the youths who are of your own age? So you would endanger my head with the king." ¹¹ Then Daniel said to the steward whom the chief of the eunuchs had assigned over Daniel, Hananiah, Mishael, and Azariah, ¹² "Test your servants for ten days; let us be given vegetables to eat and water to drink. ¹³ Then let our appearance and the appearance of the youths who eat the king's food be observed by you, and deal with your servants according to what you see." ¹⁴ So he listened to them in this matter, and*

tested them for ten days. [15] At the end of ten days it was seen that they were better in appearance and fatter in flesh than all the youths who ate the king's food. [16] So the steward took away their food and the wine they were to drink, and gave them vegetables. [17] As for these four youths, God gave them learning and skill in all literature and wisdom, and Daniel had understanding in all visions and dreams. [18] At the end of the time, when the king had commanded that they should be brought in, the chief of the eunuchs brought them in before Nebuchadnezzar. [19] And the king spoke with them, and among all of them none was found like Daniel, Hananiah, Mishael, and Azariah. Therefore they stood before the king. (Daniel 1:8-19)

Daniel and his friends made a crucial decision about what they would and would not allow into their bodies. They decided to follow God's eating plan and the results were amazing. Compare the decisions the people made in Jeremiah's day to the decisions Daniel and his friends made even in the courts of an enemy king.

Do you know what decision means? It means to "cut off." It means cutting the alternatives away – which in the case of eating means not cheating and no excuses (birthdays, weddings, potlucks, etc.) You are stronger than your excuses–God has given you the power of self-control–use it! As a preacher's wife, I attend a lot of potlucks and weddings. When preparing my mind before the meal, I remind myself that ten minutes after eating the food, I won't remember what it tasted like. If I take one bite, it never seems to be enough because I will tell myself, "That was really good, have another bite, then another and another." Another way I prepare my mind is to remind myself that in the past, if I ate something I shouldn't or I ate too much, then the head talk and chastising would begin again for getting out of control. It's really fun to get in the car after an event and say to my husband, "I did it. I ate foods that were good for me. I didn't eat the desserts, I didn't eat the fried foods, etc." It is such an amazing feeling to have that kind of victory!

Your decisions influence others as it says in Romans 14:13, "Rather decide never to put a stumbling block or hindrance in the way of a brother." And in Romans 14:22, "Your personal convictions [on such matters]—exercise [them] as in God's presence, keeping them to yourself [striving only to know the truth and obey His will]. Blessed (happy, to be envied) is he who has no reason to judge himself for what he approves [**who does not convict himself by what he chooses to do**]" (AMP).

Everything we give to God requires a decision whether it is our bodies as a living sacrifice or our offerings. 2 Corinthians 9:7 says we should choose to do it out of love, "You must each decide in your heart how much to give. And don't give reluctantly or in response to pressure. For God loves a person who gives cheerfully" (NLT).

God has given us the ability to make a decision and choose the way we will do things.

Joshua 24:14-15 says, "Now therefore fear the LORD and serve him in sincerity and in faithfulness. Put away the gods that your fathers served beyond the River and in Egypt, and serve the LORD. ¹⁵ And if it is evil in your eyes to serve the LORD, choose this day whom you will serve, whether the gods your fathers served in the region beyond the River, or the gods of the Amorites in whose land you dwell. But as for me and my house, we will serve the LORD."

Ecclesiastes 10:2 says, "A wise person chooses the right road; a fool takes the wrong one" (NLT).

In Psalm 119:30 David says, "I have chosen to be faithful; I have determined to live by your regulations" (NLT).

Ask Yourself:

Am I willing to take the ninety-day healthy eating plan?

Am I willing to make that decision?

Have I determined to live by God's rules?

Will I be wise and choose the right road?

Will I cheerfully give my body as a living sacrifice to God?

Action Suggestion:

Read again these two passages and compare the choices the people from the time of Jeremiah made with those of Daniel and his friends. Carefully consider the consequences each group experienced because of their choices. Tell God you are ready to make a decision to start doing things His way like Daniel and his friends. Determine to do it cheerfully knowing that is what will please the Creator of your masterpiece. Record your daily decisions in your journal. Keep track of the blessing you experience as a result of each of those decisions. Thank God daily for His guidance and presence in your life.

Answer 2: Be Willing to Live with Integrity

> *The integrity of the upright guides them, but the crookedness of the treacherous destroys them.* (Proverbs 11:3)

This answer is about being accountable and living with integrity! It's about making a decision and a commitment and then keeping your promises! Let's start by defining these important words. Being accountable means you are willing to be held responsible for your own actions and decisions. So many times we hear things like, "The devil made me do it!" "Everyone else was doing it, so I just went along with the crowd." "If God didn't want me to eat that food, why did He put it on the earth?" Taking responsibility for our actions is the first step toward changing what needs to be changed so we can make and keep our commitments to God.

In "The Success Principles" by Jack Canfield, he devotes the entire first chapter in his book to taking 100 percent responsibility for everything in your life. As I read this chapter, it really made me realize how important it is to take 100 percent responsibility for my actions. He shares how we never want to look at where the real problem is–ourselves. Jack shares a story about working in 1969 for W. Clement Stone, the publisher of Success Magazine. W. Clement asked Jack if he took responsibility for his life. Jack replied, "I think so." Mr. Stone said, "This is a yes or no answer. You either do or you don't." He then asked questions I feel none of us would want to admit to: "Have you ever blamed anyone for any circumstance in your life? Have you ever complained about anything?" I feel certain we can all answer yes, just as Jack did. Mr. Stone said, "Okay, then, that means you don't take one hundred percent responsibility for your life." W. Clement continued to teach Jack how to take full responsibility for all results in his life, whether they were successes or failures. He shared how we have created our current conditions; and if we created them, we can un-create them! To read more about taking 100 percent responsibility, you can order Jack's book from www.thesuccessprinciples. com or from another online source or bookstore.

Integrity means we are willing to be honest with ourselves and with God about what we have or have not done. It also means we are reliable. If we say we are going to do something then we follow through and do it.

> *Whoever walks in integrity walks securely, but he who makes his ways crooked will be found out.* (Proverbs 10:9)

There are times in life when situations may tempt us to compromise our stand and even make excuses for not honoring a commitment. Read the story of Job and see how much this man had to endure. He basically lost everything, but look at what God says about this man.

> *And the LORD said to Satan, "Have you considered my servant Job, that there is none like him on the earth, a blameless and upright man, who fears God and turns away from evil? He still holds fast his integrity, although you incited me against him to destroy him without reason."* (Job 2:3)

Long before W. Clement Stone asked Jack Canfield if he took 100 percent responsibility, Job was an example for us. God said he was blameless yet Job took 100 percent responsibility. He was an upright man and feared God. Even though there was no reason for Job to go through what he went through, he did not blame God. What a lesson for us. He lost what we believe to be everything; however, he didn't lose his faith in God. Because of his faithfulness and gratitude, God showered him with another family and physical blessings.

Wouldn't we each like to have God say we are blameless and upright? I played the blame game. I didn't take 100 percent responsibility. I chose to let what others say make me feel unworthy and undeserving. As I write this, my heart aches and the tears come as I think of the time I wasted. I am so thankful for the patience God has had with me and how forgiving He is for the times I was critical of Him and of myself.

Are you willing to do what it takes to walk in integrity even in the area of what you eat and drink and how you treat your masterpiece? Will you take 100 percent responsibility for your life and the decisions you make regarding your masterpiece?

What do you want for your masterpiece? When God fearfully and wonderfully made you and designed all of your delicate, intricate parts, He also gave you talents and the ability to use those talents. His goal is for you to use the talents He has given you to help others and to glorify Him. If you aren't willing to take care of the masterpiece He created, are you going to be able to use your talents for Him? It's time to ask yourself some very important questions and then make some very important decisions. How you choose will make a big difference in how you live the rest of your life!

Ask Yourself:

What do you want for your masterpiece?

If you aren't willing to take care of the masterpiece He created, are you going to be able to use your talents for Him?

Are you willing to do what is necessary to have a healthy masterpiece?

Are you ready to say "yes" to feeling great, having energy, releasing weight, and proving to yourself you do have the self-control it takes to say "no" to unhealthy choices and to say "yes" to eating and enjoying healthy food?

Will you make a "true decision" to commit and make a promise to yourself to achieve the results you want?

Action Suggestion:

This answer is about being accountable and living with integrity! It's about making a decision and a commitment and then keeping your promises! Taking responsibility for your actions is the first step toward changing what needs to be changed so you can make and keep your commitments to God. Integrity means you are willing to be honest with yourself and with God about what you have or have not done. It also means you are reliable. If you say you are going to do something, then you follow through and do it. As you talk with God today, be honest with Him about what your struggles are. Make a decision and tell God you want to be the person He has called you to be. Then follow through with the commitments you make to Him. He will honor every step forward you take with Him. Thank Him today for being there with you every step of the way!

Answer 3: Understand There Is No Plan B

"Goal setting is the master skill of all lifelong success, yet it is practiced by less than 3 percent of the population." (Tommy Newberry)

Throughout these lessons, we have talked about eating healthy and eating to live instead of living to eat. Too many times when someone has decided to lose weight, they go on a diet and have a goal of a certain number of pounds they want to lose or an amount they want to weigh. Often though, once a person has achieved their goal weight, they go back to their old way of eating causing the discouraging yo-yo dieting pattern in their lives. Lose, gain, lose, gain is a vicious destructive cycle.

Most of the time on these weight loss types of diets, you feel so deprived of foods you can't wait to eat something from the "do not eat" list. When you are focused on losing weight, it creates a negative mindset in your thinking. When you lose something it usually means you want to find it.

However, when you focus on taking care of yourself physically to be your best spiritually, the goal is to focus on what you can eat because it will make you healthy and make you your best for God. Would you agree that's a better mindset? Would you be willing to change your thinking on how you view food? How about being focused on taking care of the masterpiece God has given you and eating the way God intended you to so your body can release the unnecessary weight?

I want you to continue to see yourself as the beautiful masterpiece God created you to be. I want you to cherish your body and want it to be healthy, not only for you, but for your family and for God. You only have one body. There is no plan B when it comes to the masterpiece God has created you to be. When you make the commitment to eat healthy the rest of your life, you can release the weight and begin to see the beauty of how God has made you!

In I Thessalonians 5:23, Paul is giving us a blessing and admonition in the last part of the book when he says, "May your whole spirit, soul, and body be preserved blameless at the coming of our Lord, Jesus Christ." In order to accomplish this, you have to follow God's plan in everything you do, in every area of your life. Your spiritual self needs to be fed and nourished through the reading and mediation of His Word. Your soul or mind needs to be filled with His truth which again can only be attained through spending time in His Word and in prayer with Him. Your body must be cared for by following God's plan for its care and maintenance.

When you read the instruction manual for a new appliance, does it give you several different plans for maintenance or does it say do this and you will get the best performance out of your new appliance? Many times the instruction manual will include a list of what not to do and give you the consequences of not following the prescribed instructions. There is no Plan B. You need to follow their Plan A if you want your new appliance to do what it was designed to do. The same is true for the masterpiece God has created you to be. Follow His Plan A and you will function at full capacity and do what you were designed to do.

God gave us the Bible, His Word, to help us understand the consequences of making godly choices versus ungodly choices. It also shows us how God will make a way for an individual who realizes they have made a poor choice and desires to get things back on track. It does, however, take a firm commitment and a willingness to get back on God's Plan A to achieve success.

It is also important at this point to make sure you understand that God's Plan A is not just for a few weeks or a few months. This is your life, the only one you have, and it is very important you take care of you! There is no place for excuses in God's Plan A.

"Commit to making your home and office an *excuse-free zone*. If a situation arises that previously called for an excuse, substitute the words, "I am responsible," where the excuse used to go." (Tommy Newberry)

Here is a powerful promise from our heavenly Father that has always helped me stay committed to God's Plan A.

> *No, in all these things we are more than conquerors through him who loved us. For I am sure that neither death nor life, nor angels nor rulers, nor things present nor things to come, nor powers, nor height nor depth, nor anything else in all creation, will be able to separate us from the love of God in Christ Jesus our Lord.* (Romans 8:37-39)

Ask Yourself:

> *Am I focused on taking care of myself physically to be my best spiritually?*

> *Am I willing to change my thinking on how I view food?*

> *Am I ready to stop making excuses and discover God's Plan A for me?*

> *Am I willing to make the commitment to eat healthy the rest of my life?*

Action Suggestion:

I want to invite you each day to take the time to pray and ask God for wisdom and help on your journey. Ask Him to help you when there are going to be foods available you know aren't the best for you to eat.

I believe the following suggestions are important to your success:

Write down what you eat, why you eat, and when you eat.

Savor the first bite, enjoy it, take your time, and really taste your food.

Pray before you eat and ask God to help you stop when you feel full!

Use the Strategic Daily Plan at the end of this book to get you started.

Answer 4: Realize Daily Decisions Do Make a Difference

"Self-discipline is the ability to funnel our desires and passions in a productive direction, for a sustained period of time in order to achieve our goals. It is the connective tissue that links ambition with achievement." (Tommy Newberry)

Do you know every little decision you make each and every day counts? Select what you eat with care as if your life depends on it because it does! Those little daily decisions you make will make a difference in your life and will grow to a final result. Deciding to follow God's Plan A will cause you to release the weight, feel good, love your masterpiece more, be a Christian example to others, and be your best spiritually for God!

"It takes less time to do things right than to explain why you did it wrong." (Henry Wadsworth Longfellow)[9]

Be Aware of How You Are Living

"Awareness is the first step on the ladder of positive change. You can only manage what you can label and bring to conscious awareness." (Dr. Arlene R. Taylor, "Age-Proofing Your Brain – 21 Key Factors You Can Control," Success Resources International, Napa, CA 94558 ©2009 ETB)

Becoming more aware of the way you are living your life can enhance your health, well-being, and balance. When you decide to take charge of your own life, you prevent others and circumstances from manipulating

9   http://www.values.com/inspirational-quotes/value/46-Right-Choices

you like a puppet on a string. Balance is a very important part of a high-level healthy lifestyle!

> "Everything you eat, drink, think, say, and do is a health-relevant behavior. Make thoughtful choices to achieve desired outcomes. Keep learning!" (Dr. Arlene R. Taylor, "Age-Proofing Your Brain – 21 Key Factors You Can Control" Success Resources International, Napa, CA 94558 ©2009 ETB)

Your lifestyle is as individual as you are and the choices you make on a daily basis can have a monumental impact on it. Refusing to make a conscious choice is a type of choice and can impact your life as well. If you refuse to choose others will make that choice for you.

The Bible speaks of making wise choices and the benefits of doing so.

> *"I call heaven and earth to witness against you today, that I have set before you life and death, blessing and curse. Therefore choose life, that you and your offspring may live, [20] loving the* LORD *your God, obeying his voice and holding fast to him, for he is your life and length of days, that you may dwell in the land that the* LORD *swore to your fathers, to Abraham, to Isaac, and to Jacob, to give them."* (Deuteronomy 30:19-20)

Joshua inferred we are each going to have to choose whom we will serve in our lives, "And if it is evil in your eyes to serve the LORD, choose this day whom you will serve, whether the gods your fathers served in the region beyond the River, or the gods of the Amorites in whose land you dwell. But as for me and my house, we will serve the LORD" (Joshua 24:15).

Joshua 24:1 says he issued this challenge before all the tribes of Israel. His decision was going to influence a whole nation! We read about the results of this decision by Joshua and the people he challenged and influenced in Joshua 24:29 where it says he lived to be 110. Then in verse 31 it says the people of Israel served God all throughout Joshua's lifetime. What an impact this one man's decision had on the nation of Israel.

The decisions you and I make will influence those around us. Our decisions are important to us and our own health as well as to those within our sphere of influence.

David wrote in Psalm 119:30-32, "I have chosen the way of faithfulness; I set your rules before me. I cling to your testimonies, O Lord; let me not be put to shame! I will run in the way of your commandments when you enlarge my heart!"

> "Learning is not attained by chance—it must be sought for with ardor and attended with diligence." (First Lady Abigail Adams 1744-1818)[10]

Beware of the Opinions of Others

When seeking the opinions of others, notice how their decisions have impacted their lives. Do you want what they have? Do you really want to do what they have done or not done? Many times we are tempted to try fad diets or the latest "lose weight quick plan" because a friend has recommended it. There are many choices out there that can have detrimental effects on our overall health. Slow down and take the time to evaluate your decisions, but do not slip into procrastination.

Making right choices requires developing the ability to view things from God's perspective. Since He created your masterpiece, He alone can give you the knowledge you need to make right choices on a consistent basis. Test every decision against God's design. The more knowledge you have about the intricacies of your body, the more wisdom you will have making choices especially in the area of what you put into your masterpiece. Look at both the short-term and long-term consequences of your choices.

> "You have only always to do what is right. It will become easier by practice, and you enjoy in the midst of your trials the pleasure of an approving conscience." (Robert E. Lee, General 1807-1870)[11]

---

10   www.great-quotes.com/quotes/author/Abigail/Adams

11   http://www.values.com/inspirational-quotes/value/46-Right-Choices

I used to think a little bite of this or just a taste of that would not make any difference in the overall scheme of things. I was wrong. When I began to honestly track all those little bites I had taken all day long, I was amazed at how much I had eaten that I was not even aware of. Every choice has a consequence, good or bad. This is one of the reasons it is so important to write down and track not only what you eat, but when you eat and why you eat. To make wise choices on a daily basis you must understand what triggers your decisions.

Are you really hungry or are you stressed? Do you need something right now or are you just bored and looking for something to do? Has a memory suddenly surfaced that has made you sad or mad and you just need comfort food to get through the next few minutes? Often emotions trigger our decisions and we make impulse choices that later put us in a cycle of guilt over our failure to exercise self-control.

> "There comes a time in the spiritual journey when you start making choices from a very different place. And if a choice lines up so that it supports truth, health, happiness, wisdom and love, it's the right choice." (Angeles Arrien, Anthropologist)[12]

Before you grab that fast food or snack Ask Yourself:

Am I really hungry or am I stressed about something?

Do I need food right now or am I bored and looking for something to do?

Has a memory suddenly surfaced that has made me sad or mad and I just need comfort food to get through the next few minutes?

Am I letting my emotions trigger my decisions and making impulse choices?

Is that really the way I want to live?

---

12   http://www.values.com/inspirational-quotes/value/46-Right-Choices

Action Suggestion:

Making right choices requires developing the ability to view things from God's perspective. Since He created your masterpiece, He alone can give you the knowledge you need to make right choices on a consistent basis. Spending time with Him will help you begin to test every decision against God's design. Seek more knowledge about the intricacies of your body, and look at both the short-term and long-term consequences of your choices. By writing your research in your journal, you can track your choices and begin to make better choices on your path to wholeness and health.

Health Hint: Dr. Kenneth Guiffre, author of "The Care and Feeding of Your Brain, says, "Exercise helps the brain to boot up efficiently." (NJ, Career Press Inc., 1999). Dr. Candace Pert, author of "Molecules of Emotion" says, "Twenty minutes of mild aerobic exercise at the beginning of the day can turn on fat-burning neuropeptides, the effects of which can last for hours" (NY, Scriber, 1997).

Chapter 10

HOW CAN I LOVE MYSELF?

———— ∞ ————

And he said to him, "You shall love the Lord your God with all your heart and with all your soul and with all your mind. [38] This is the great and first commandment. [39] And a second is like it: You shall love your neighbor as yourself. (Matthew 22:37-39)

W ho am I? What is my identity? When you first meet someone, there are introductions–names are given, where you live, etc. When you are shopping and you are asked to give your ID, you show them your driver's license, passport or something with your picture identifying who you are. All these things are your identity. It tells people who you are! Your friends know you by your face and your voice. But is all of this who you really are?

The truth is who you really are starts in the heart. In Psalm 51:10 David prayed, "Create in me a clean heart, O God." Proverbs 23:7 says, "For as he thinks in his heart, so is he" (NKJV). Throughout these lessons the focus has been on loving the masterpiece God created for you. You have learned to love yourself and you have realized God created you for good works in Christ Jesus. When you begin to focus on taking care of your masterpiece instead of feeding it, you begin to think new thoughts, and you will focus on your heart instead of your stomach. You will begin to see yourself from the inside out.

Answer 1: See Your Ideal Weight from the Inside Out

For as he thinks in his heart, so is he. (Proverbs 23:7 NKJV)

What does it mean to see your ideal weight from the inside out? I shared earlier how I lost my weight while I was in high school, but I didn't let go of the "fat girl" for over forty years. Physically, I was an ideal weight. Mentally, I was still seeing the fat girl. In my head I could not see that I was the ideal weight. Until I changed the head talk, I would never be the ideal weight from the inside out. I had to release the fat girl, release the negative head talk, and release the limiting beliefs I had put on myself. I knew it was vital for me to replace the negative with the love of God. A key for me was to replace the negative about my masterpiece with the understanding of how precious I am in God's eyes.

Just as you are known by your face and voice, God knows you from the inside out. Psalm 139 says God knew you before you were born. That is physical, but He also knows your heart and what you think about yourself. In 2 Chronicles 1:11 when God asked Solomon what he wanted, Solomon asked for wisdom and God gave him more than what he asked for because of what was in his heart. God knew Solomon's heart, just as He knows your heart. Jesus taught on this subject as well.

> *Do you not see that whatever goes into the mouth passes into the stomach and is expelled?* [18] *But what comes out of the mouth proceeds from the heart, and this defiles a person.* [19] *For out of the heart come evil thoughts, murder, adultery, sexual immorality, theft, false witness, slander.* [20] *These are what defile a person. But to eat with unwashed hands does not defile anyone."* (Matthew 15:17-20)

In Matthew 15:17-20 we are told what defiles a person. We are told the things that come out of our mouths and the words we speak were first in our hearts and this is what defiles a person. Our words tell on us by showing others what is really in our hearts. God knows it before we even speak it, though.

You can tell what things are in you by what you are saying about yourself. Are your words joyful or crushing? Proverbs 17:22 says, "A joyful heart is good medicine, but a crushed spirit dries up the bones." Proverbs 27:19 says, "As in water a face reflects face, so the heart of man reflects the man." What are you reflecting about your weight from the inside out? When your heart is happy, your face will reflect it.

> *A glad (merry) heart makes a cheerful (merry) face.*
> (Proverbs 15:13)

The great thing about the flaws we see on our faces is they can be covered up with make up or concealed, but the things of the heart can't be concealed. Oh, we may fool people for a while, especially if we are only with them for a short time, but on a regular basis we can't hide the reflections of our heart. People will know.

The physical heart is the lifeline and when it isn't functioning properly we die. The same is true of our spiritual heart. It is our lifeline and if it isn't functioning properly, we must do whatever it takes to repair it. Proverbs 4:23 says; "Keep your heart with all diligence, for out of it spring the issues of life."

> *Little children, let us not love in word or talk but in deed and in truth. [19] By this we shall know that we are of the truth and reassure our heart before him; [20] for whenever our heart condemns us, God is greater than our heart, and he knows everything.*
> (1 John 3:18-20)

It has been said that Satan is the father of discouragement. If Satan can discourage a Christian and keep her discouraged, he has won! When you are discouraged, you feel lifeless, you feel there is no hope, and you think, *Why even try?* Many times our hearts are heavy with discouragement and we feel so alone. We need to realize that we aren't alone because there are many other Christians just like you and me that need each other. God has promised He has given us everything we need to achieve our ideal weight from the inside out.

In I Chronicles 28:20, David was giving his son Solomon the plans for the temple and he said, "Be strong and of good courage, and do it; do not fear nor be dismayed, for the Lord God my God will be with you. He will not leave you nor forsake you, until you have finished all the

How Can I Love Myself?

work for the service of the house of the LORD." What wonderful words of encouragement and we can know those words are true for us today. Romans 8:31 assures us, "if God is for us, who can be against us?" We can win against the devil! We can change the way we see ourselves from the inside out. We can replace the negativity in our hearts and begin to see ourselves the way God sees us.

Be thankful and happy now for the body God created for you. When you show gratitude for who you are now, you will begin to love yourself and appreciate your masterpiece. This is having the ideal weight from the inside out. This will also help your thoughts about wondering if God loves you if you are overweight. God always loves us though He may not always be happy with decisions we make. However, just as a parent always loves their children, God always loves His.

> *You have a masterpiece inside you, you know. One unlike any that has ever been created, or ever will be. If you go to your grave without painting your masterpiece, it will not get painted. No one else can paint it. Only you.* — Gordon MacKenzie[13]

Ask Yourself:

> *What things are in my heart?*

> *What am I thinking about myself?*

> *Am I seeing myself at my ideal weight?*

> *What words do I use to describe myself?*

> *Are my words joyful or crushing?*

> *What do people learn about me from the words I speak about myself?*

---

13   http://www.positivequotes.org/selftalk/

Action Suggestion:

Begin to really think about the words that come out of your mouth, especially those you use to describe yourself. Remember that what you say and do is a reflection of what is really in your heart. Start changing how you think about yourself and watch the words you speak. Record what you observe about yourself in your journal. Perhaps ask a trusted friend to help you begin to monitor the way you speak about yourself. Ask them to gently remind you when you begin to bad mouth yourself. Thank God today for trusted friends and His help in changing you from the inside out.

Answer 2: Admit God Loves You Even if You Are Overweight

> *Everyone then who hears these words of mine and does them will be like a wise man who built his house on the rock. ²⁵ And the rain fell, and the floods came, and the winds blew and beat on that house, but it did not fall, because it had been founded on the rock. ²⁶ And everyone who hears these words of mine and does not do them will be like a foolish man who built his house on the sand. ²⁷ And the rain fell, and the floods came, and the winds blew and beat against that house, and it fell, and great was the fall of it.* (Matthew 7:24-27)

Is your thinking on a firm foundation? When we read the parable of the wise and foolish men in Matthew 7:24-27, we learn the importance of a firm foundation. Jesus doesn't emphasize a different opportunity for each of them. They each had the same opportunity to build on a firm foundation. There was nothing said about one being a better builder than the other. They had the same trials with the winds and floods. Jesus was putting emphasis on the foundation. In verse 24, Jesus says the one who hears His words and does them is like the wise man who built on the rock. But then in verse 26 it tells us the one who hears His words and does not do them is like the foolish man who built on the sand. When the storms came the wise man's house stood because it was on a firm foundation. However, the foolish man's house fell and great was the fall because he had not built on a firm foundation.

How Can I Love Myself?

Would you agree God's Word has given you a firm foundation for taking care of your masterpiece? Just as the wise and foolish men had a choice to make, you also have a choice. You can choose to eat whatever you want and not take care of yourself and when the storms come (illnesses, disease, etc.) you will find you have built on the sand and it's harder to get well. However, by taking care of yourself, you will have built on a firmer foundation and have a better chance of withstanding the storms when they come.

We are all terminal. However, isn't it wiser to build on a firm foundation by taking care of your masterpiece so you will be your best for God? Isn't it wiser to show God you love and respect your masterpiece by taking good care of it? The wise man in Matthew 7:24 heard, listened, and obeyed. The foolish man heard, but disobeyed. Are you wise or foolish?

In Matthew 22:37-39 we read the foundation we are supposed to build our lives upon. This is the kind of heart God wants for us. But as we have learned, God never tells us to do something without making sure we know that it can be done through Christ. He has told us to build our foundation on loving Him and loving one another as we love ourselves. There is no greater example of loving others than Jesus. Take the time to read the account of the death of Jesus in Matthew 26-28, Mark 14-16, Luke 22-24, and John 18-20, and let what Jesus did really sink in. Every time we read how Peter denied Him, Judas betrayed Him or how the disciples left Him alone, we are touched by the love He had for us. There is no way we can comprehend it. We also come to realize there is no way we deserve it, but He still gives us that love. He gives us that hope.

So if God looks at the heart, knows all about us from the inside out, and sent His Son to die for us on the cross, does He love us even if we are overweight? I do not read anywhere in the Bible where it says God withdraws His love from us. As a matter of fact, Romans 8:35 asks that very question, "Who shall separate us from the love of Christ? Shall tribulation, or distress, or persecution, or famine, or nakedness, or danger, or sword?" The answer is given in Romans 8:37-39, "No, in all these things we are more than conquerors through him who loved us. For I am sure that neither death nor life, nor angels nor rulers, nor things present nor things to come, nor powers, nor height nor depth, **nor anything else in all creation, will be able to separate us from the love of God in Christ Jesus our Lord"** (emphasis added).

Read Psalm 103. The whole chapter is uplifting. When we realize the love God has for us, how can we not love ourselves? I believe this scripture helps us see God loves us no matter what. His love is unfailing and the supply never runs out!

The only one thing I can change is myself, but sometimes that makes all of the difference.—Anonymous[14]

Ask Yourself:

Am I building on a firm foundation by taking care of my masterpiece so I can be my best for God?

Isn't it wiser to show God how thankful I am for His love by respecting the masterpiece He gave me by taking good care of it?

Does God love me when I am overweight?

How do I know?

Action Suggestion:

As suggested in this chapter, read the account of the death of Jesus in Matthew 26-28, Mark 14-16, Luke 22-24, and John 18-20, and let what Jesus did really sink in. How would you describe the love God has for you? Begin to tell yourself that God loves you just the way you are but He loves you too much to leave you where you are. He is going to continually move you toward His perfect will for you. Be willing and open to do what He leads you to do through your time with Him and time spent reading His Word. Continue to keep your journal. Thank God today for His love and guidance no matter where you are in your walk with Him.

Answer 3: Monitor Your Self-Talk

When you look in the mirror what do you think or say in your head to yourself? Do you complain or do you see the amazing creation you

---

14   http://www.positivequotes.org/selftalk/

are? When we whine, murmur, complain, and only see the negative in ourselves, we are not shining for Christ! The world is watching us and watching closely! Find the positive instead of the negative in everything.

I had someone share with me that when she was going through a hard time in her life, where nothing was right and everything was negative, she read a book that told her to carry a notebook around. She would stop every time she had a negative thought or said something negative and write it down. Then she would read it at the end of the day. She said after about a week, she was really tired of writing it down and decided that instead of being negative she would find the positive.

What a great idea! If you are a negative person, I want to challenge you to write down when you say something negative. Even if it is something as simple as, "It's so hot" or "it's raining again" can be a negative. It is sometimes in the tone of the voice. Stop and think how you and those around you are receiving what you are saying.

Maybe it is time you change your thinking and self-talk from the kind the devil wants. As a parent, wouldn't you be surprised if your child started using negative self talk and you knew they had not heard it in your home? Wouldn't you wonder who they were hanging around with? What does God think about the kind of thinking and self-talk we are using? Do we sound like God or do we sound like the devil?

The devil wants you to put limiting beliefs on yourself. The less you think of yourself, the more control you have given to him. The more you give God the glory and love the masterpiece He created for you, the more God can do in your life.

In Psalm 34:4 we read, "I sought the LORD, and He answered me and delivered me from all my fears." All those limiting beliefs that you speak about yourself are fears. God wants to deliver you from those fears and your limiting beliefs.

I have found, as a part of a direct sales business, that for many people, the deepest fear is the fear of success. However, each time I read 2 Timothy 1:7, I realize God didn't give me or you a spirit of fear. He gave us a spirit of power and love and self-control! There's no need to be afraid! Instead, step into becoming the person God intended you to be. Use the talents He gave you. Believe in yourself. Pay attention to the words you say to yourself because you are listening to every word! The words you say to yourself control the way you feel and act.

Ask Yourself:

Is my kind of thinking what the devil wants?

Am I giving too much control over my life to negative thinking?

Is my self talk a result of what I have let other people tell me about my identity?

Am I ready to change to the kind of thinking God wants?

Action Suggestion:

Try the process my special friend told me about. Stop every time you have a negative thought or say something negative and write it down. Read them at the end of the day. Decide to replace the negative with the positive. Remember it can even be something as simple as, "It's so hot" or "it's raining again." Stop and think how you and those around you are receiving what you are saying. Ask God to point these negatives out to you as you go through your day. Remember, the only thing you can change today is yourself, but sometimes that makes all of the difference. Be careful what you are saying to yourself because you are listening, too.

Answer 4: Replace Negative with Positive Affirmations

When you acknowledge the less than perfect parts of yourself, something magical begins to happen. Along with the negative, you'll also begin to notice the positive, the wonderful aspects of yourself that you may not have given yourself credit for, or perhaps even been aware of. -Richard Carlson (from "Don't Sweat the Small Stuff")

We have between 50-60,000 thoughts per day.[15] When we begin to learn to manage these thoughts, we can gain control of our beliefs. One of the methods I use in my coaching is to help people recreate beliefs,

---

15   http://wiki.answers.com/Q/How_many_thoughts_do_
people_have_each_day?#slide=1

and to go from limiting beliefs to empowering beliefs.[16] I got to thinking about all the people who were cruel in their words to me and how they treated me, and how I created limiting beliefs about myself because of these thoughts!

Some of the limiting beliefs I created were that I wasn't good enough, I wasn't smart enough, I wasn't talented, I wasn't pretty, and I was different. What I have learned is I need to find when and where these limiting beliefs started. Some of them started when I started gaining weight at the age of six. It was then I was made to feel different when the name calling started. Other limiting beliefs happened when teachers made comments about some of my class work or artistic ability (or lack there of). The limiting beliefs continued even into high school with the name calling and being made fun of.

Once you find when and where the limiting beliefs started, you recreate them. You see, even though people called me names and made fun of me, it doesn't mean that's who I was. There were other people in my life who loved me and cared about me. There were other teachers who encouraged me. They didn't care what I looked like. I had friends who loved me for who I was, not what I looked like. However, I focused on the negative stuff creating limiting beliefs on myself. Since I created them, I could un-create or recreate them. I could and I did turn them into empowering beliefs.

Are you one of these people who have "limiting beliefs" about your body and eating and how you feel God looks at you? Think about that for a minute and then see if you agree it is ridiculous to allow these limiting beliefs to control your life.

> *Don't listen to those who say, "It's not done that way." Maybe it's not, but maybe you will. Don't listen to those who say, "You're taking too big a chance." Michelangelo would have painted the Sistine floor, and it would surely be rubbed out by today. Most importantly, don't listen when the little voice of fear inside of you rears its ugly head and says, "They're all smarter than you out there. They're more talented, they're taller, blonder, prettier, luckier and have connections..." I firmly believe that if you follow*

---

16   This is something I learned from my business coach. He has a whole series called "Erase the Waste."

a path that interests you, not to the exclusion of love, sensitivity, and cooperation with others, but with the strength of conviction that you can move others by your own efforts, and do not make success or failure the criteria by which you live, the chances are you'll be a person worthy of your own respect.—Neil Simon[17]

Did you know you weren't born with your limiting belief? You actually created that belief by allowing it to enter into your thoughts and then your self talk. Since you created that belief, you can also un-create it and replace it with an empowering belief! Pretty powerful stuff! For example, have you ever thought to yourself or told someone, "I will be happy when I lose 20, 30, 40 pounds"? Or have you told yourself, "My life will be perfect once I _____"? (You fill in the blank.)

"Change of diet will not help a person who will not change his thoughts. When a person makes his thoughts pure, he no longer desires impure food. Obesity has become a major health threat as it has reached epidemic proportions according to the US Center for Disease Control. Despite the epidemic, the vast majority of those on a weight-loss diet today will fail. Even sadder is that virtually 100% of the people who fail won't know the REAL reason for their failure. Many will blame the diet they chose, the circumstances in their life, their lack of will power, and on and on. But the REAL reason — the ONLY reason they won't succeed is because they didn't change their thoughts. Their thoughts about themselves and the food they eat." (From "Day by Day With James Allen" by Vic Johnson, copyright 2003, 8th printing 2011. Page 22, Eighth Day)

I agree with Vic. I have seen many "yo-yo" in their weight. I have even heard people who are in the process of losing weight make the comment that they will gain it back because they always have. It is so important to get rid of the limiting beliefs you have surrounding your thoughts about your weight. I also believe many people feel they don't deserve to be healthy and release the weight. Vic shares how he believes you will never achieve sustainable success that exceeds the image you have of yourself. He says, "You must see yourself as a healthy, physically-fit person so you can release the weight and keep it off. Not only does this apply to weight-control, it applies to changing any habit."

---

17   http://www.positivequotes.org/selftalk/

How Can I Love Myself?

From his Inspirational Journal, "Total Wellness Cleanse" Yuri Elkaim recommends, "Remove, from your mind, the weeds of negativity and impossibility and plant only seeds that will empower you forward. Just like an apple seed will not produce a peach tree, poor thoughts will not produce the health and vitality you wish to have. The images in your mind become your reality" (From Day 2 of "Total Wellness Cleanse"). Yuri also shares how you speak your reality: "The more you speak of greatness, happiness, abundance and love, the more of it comes into your life. Speak great words that add intensity and passion to your life."[18]

Speak what you want to feel. Speak what you want to believe. The words you use will change your physiology and who you are as well. Speaking negative words creates acid in your body and weakens it. Conversely, speaking positive words of love, abundance, and joy will transform your body into something totally different–a physiology that is filled with love, happiness and health.

When you begin to love yourself, your self talk will change. Negative self talk is very disempowering and causes you to feel "less than" and unworthy. Before I released "the fat girl" my negative self talk was constant! I came to realize this was dishonoring God. Every time I complained or criticized my masterpiece, I was being critical of God. After I had this "Ah-ha moment," I changed my thought process. I became grateful for my masterpiece. I began thanking God for every part from the inside out. I showed gratitude for my organs on the inside to my hands, arms, legs, eyes, etc. on the outside. I began thanking God for creating me. The transformation was amazing.

Once you show gratitude for your masterpiece, you will become more aware of what you allow to go into your body. By expressing exceptional gratitude instead of routine gratitude for your masterpiece, it will be intentional and proactive. By being careful about what you say to yourself, you can be empowered to take control of your eating and every other activity in your life. As God's children, we must be happy, joyful, and positive every day. When we get up in the morning, we make a choice as to whether our self talk will be positive or negative. We can choose to rejoice and look for God's blessings or we can just get through the day.

---

18   From Day 5 of "Total Wellness Cleanse. Copyright @ Elkaim Health Fitness Solutions

We can thrive instead of survive. We have a responsibility to put on a happy face because people are watching.

Ask Yourself:

Have I created limiting beliefs about my body, my eating, and how I feel God looks at me?

Am I ready to start un-creating those limiting beliefs and replacing them with an empowering belief system one belief at a time?

Am I keeping my eyes open to God's new blessings each morning?

Do I begin my day with a thankful praising heart?

Action Suggestion:

Read Psalm 118:24 and Lamentations 3:22-23 when you get up in the morning. The psalms are filled with scriptures on praise. Begin each day with a thankful, praising heart. Express exceptional gratitude for your masterpiece. Let's be joyful, happy, positive, and filled with praise! Others will notice. Record how your days are changed when you begin your day with a positive instead of a negative. There are many positive quotes and scriptures in this chapter. Review them all and select the ones that you like the most. Make sticky notes out of them and put them where you will see them every morning as you start your day. Or take a dry erase marker and write them on your bathroom mirror so you see them every day. Begin to enjoy your masterpiece and others will enjoy being around you!

Health Hint: Vitamin D is available through food sources and dietary supplementation. The best dietary supplement form of vitamin D is vitamin D3 (also known as cholecalciferol). Many experts are now recommending the average American adult should get 1,000-5,000 IU of vitamin D3 daily year-round in conjunction with some regular sun exposure. When little or no daily sun exposure is available, individuals may need as much as 5,000 IU of vitamin D3 daily. More detailed guidelines on supplemental intake of vitamin D is available from the experts at the

Vitamin D Council (*www.vitamindcouncil.org*).

Conclusion

TAKE ACTION TODAY!

———∽∾∽———

- *Master the Guilt*
- *Change Your Brain Pattern*
- *Put Off the Old and Put On Your New Self*
- *Respond to God's Promises*

This book has given you all the spiritual and practical information you need to have PEACE in your life and live your life as God's Masterpiece. I encourage you to take each of the above actions and add them to your daily walk with God. Keep this book close by. At least once a week, open up the Table of Contents and look through the answers. Go to the chapter you feel will be most helpful that day, apply those scriptures throughout the week you feel will help you the most, and periodically go back through the **Ten-Week Devotional Journal**. This book is a tool that keeps on giving. Speaking of giving, give this book and your time to another person who you believe would be thrilled to discover that he or she is God's Masterpiece. In fact, become a mentor or coach to that person as they walk through the answers in this book. I also encourage you to start your own small group or use it to teach a Ladies' Bible class.

Thank you for purchasing "The Master's Masterpiece." Thank you for wanting to take care of yourself physically so you will be your best spiritually, and for cherishing your masterpiece. My prayer is that God has been glorified in this study, you have drawn closer to Him, and you have learned to love the masterpiece God created for you.

I invite you to post your results on our Facebook page, *The Master's Masterpiece.*

As you live your life, I pray you will keep God and Christ first. Stay in action with eating healthy every day and exercising. Have an accountability or power partner. Journal your prayers every day and ask God for wisdom and guidance to help you on your journey to being healthy. This is an amazing journey and I am so thankful to be a part of it with you. Even though we may never meet face to face, I am praying for every person who reads this book and puts this plan into action. May God bless you abundantly and may your life be filled with joy and exceptional gratitude.

10-Week Devotional Journal

PERSONAL OR SMALL GROUP GUIDE

This ten-week devotional journal section can be used individually or as a small group study guide. In using this journal, read through or review the entire chapter at the start of Day One of each week. Then, each day will review for you portions of that material and give you ways to think about, process, and act upon that material.

If you are using this journal with a partner or in a small group, you may want to bring your personal journal to the meeting to refer to for sharing and discussion.

Week One

AM I REALLY GOD'S MASTERPIECE?

DAY 1

Read or Review Chapter 1 – *Am I Really God's Masterpiece?*

This section can be used individually or as a group. A group facilitator can ask the questions and encourage group members to share and discuss each of the questions and answers.

Answer 1: Understand You Are Unique

Answer these questions:

> As you read Ephesians 2:10, did you ask yourself, "How in the world can I be God's masterpiece when I am overweight and out of shape?"

> What was your initial response to this question?

> What does the word masterpiece mean to you?

> Does it mean perfection?

> Does it mean you can never mess up?

If you do mess up have you ruined your masterpiece?

How do you know?

Have you looked in the mirror, focused on your flaws, and thought they made you a lesser person?

Define the word unique:

Do you believe God created you unique?

What has God shown you is unique about you?

Take the time each and every morning as you start your day to thank God for the unique way He made you.

Start keeping a journal of your prayers. Make them a letter to God as you start your day. Then at the end of the day, tell Him how that changed the way you felt about yourself and how it change your attitude toward everything you did.

<u>DAY 2</u>

Answer 2: Realize In God's Eyes You Are Perfect

When God created you in His eyes you were perfect.

What imperfections have happened because you have not made the best choices for your body?

What choices have you made that have caused the perfection to disappear physically?

How does focusing on these imperfections affect your attitude toward yourself and others?

In Matthew 22:37-38 Jesus said, "You must love the LORD your God with all your heart, all your soul, and all your mind."

What does that mean to you?

How do you know this is important to God?

Read Matthew 22:39.

How are you going to obey the commandment Jesus gave you in Matthew 22:39 if you don't love yourself the way God wants you to?

Begin to change the way you pray. Instead of complaining about the way you look, thank God for His love for you. Strive to obey Jesus and love Him back with all your heart, soul, and mind. Show Him you love Him by beginning to love the you He made.

Write your prayer of thanksgiving in your journal. Then at the end of the day describe what you did in obedience to Jesus' commandments in Matthew 22:37-39. Share with God how this changed your attitude about yourself and your relationship with others.

DAY 3

Answer 3: Love the Body God Gave You

The love we have for others is supposed to be equivalent to the love we have for ourselves.

Start by answering the question, "How much do I love myself?"

The way you care for your body gives you and God a clear picture of how much you love yourself.

How have you been caring for your body?

What is the message you are sending by your behavior?

Reread the scriptures given in this section.

God is clearly telling us to love others as we _____ _____.

Give an example of how this concept has been true in your life (i.e. If you are angry with yourself about what you ate, is your anger manifested toward others?)

If we hate ourselves instead of loving ourselves, what is our relationship with others going to look like?

Can we follow the other instructions Jesus left for us as His disciples if we cannot relate to others the way God has commanded?

Why or why not?

Begin to change the way you pray about others. Instead of complaining about the way they treat you, try to look back at why you are responding to them the way you are. Ask God to show you where **you are not loving** yourself and see if that is the cause of your attitude toward your neighbor.

It has to begin by loving the body God gave you and treating it with respect. The way you care for your body gives you and God a clear picture of how much you love yourself.

Write out in your journal how you are going to begin to treat your body with respect. God has promised to give you wisdom if you ask Him. Read James 1:5-6 and do what this tells you to do starting today.

<u>DAY 4</u>

Answer 4: Admit You Are Made in the Image of God

You were made in the image of God! How exciting! No other creature on earth has this characteristic!

Has anyone ever said, "You look or act just like your mother or your father?"

What positive physical or character traits do you feel you inherited from your parents?

Has anyone ever said, "You look or act like you are a child of God?"

If you were created in the image of God does it mean you are His child?

Wouldn't it make sense that you would have inherited His character traits?

What are some of the traits you have inherited from you heavenly Father?

Why is it so important that you begin to see this body God created for you as a treasure, not trash; as a mansion, not a shack?

Are you treating your body as a mansion or a shack?

Explain your answer.

<u>DAY 5</u>

God created you with a very special purpose! In I Corinthians 6:19 it says, "Do you not know that your body is the temple of the Holy Spirit who is in you, whom you have from God, and you are not your own" (NKJV).

Since God has called your body a temple, would you be willing to stop and think before putting foods in it which can be harmful?

Read 1 Thessalonians 5:23. Your masterpiece is more than flesh and blood. You are a three-part being – body, soul and spirit.

Are you taking care of yourself physically to be your best spiritually?

Explain your answer.

DAY 6

Begin to change the way you look at your body. Instead of asking God to change what you consider flaws thank Him for creating you in His image. Ask Him to forgive you for not treating your body as a mansion. Ask Him to show you how to respect your body as the temple of the Holy Spirit. Write down your prayer:

Write out in your journal how you are going to begin to treat your body as the temple of the Holy Spirit. Read God's promise in 2 Peter 1:3-4. Record what God has revealed to you about how He has created you in His image. Write down what you are going to do today to begin to manifest this truth in your life.

Week Two

DOES GOD REALLY CARE WHAT I EAT?

<u>DAY 1</u>

Read or Review Chapter 2: *Does God Really Care What I Eat?*

Answer 1: Understand You Were Bought With a Price

> Have you ever purchased something having a high price?
> How do you treat that item?
> Do you just put anything in it?
> Did you put it in places where you knew it might get broken?
> Did you protect it from obvious danger? Why?

Read 1 Corinthians 6:20 in *The Message Bible*:

Didn't you realize that your body is a sacred place, the place of the Holy Spirit? Don't you see that you can't live however you please, squandering what God paid such a high price for? The physical part of you is not some piece of property belonging to the spiritual part of you. God owns the whole works. So let people see God in and through your body. (1 Corinthians 6:20 MSG)

182

The Message Bible clearly brings out several key points as we consider whether God really cares about what we eat and put into our bodies. Fill in the missing words as you read this list:

1. Your body is a _____ place. It is the place of the _____ _____.

2. You _____ live however you please, squandering what God paid such a _____ _____ for.

3. The _____ part of you is not some piece of property belonging to the _____ part of you.

4. _____ owns the whole works.

5. Others see _____ in and through your body.

Take a moment right now and close your eyes. Take a deep breath and relax. Visualize yourself in a beautiful meadow, the grass is green, and the flowers are in bloom. Over to your right are trees with vivid green leaves. Over to your left is a creek where the water is running over the rocks making a very soothing sound. The sky is the bluest blue you have ever seen and the sun is shining. It's just the right temperature – not hot, not cold. As you are walking through this area you see someone up ahead coming towards you. It's a man and he has such a kind face. It almost seems as though he shines. You are drawn to see who it is. As you get closer you realize it's Jesus and He wants to see you. He gives you a hug and you feel so safe. He tells you how much He loves you and how special and important you are to Him. He talks to you about your masterpiece and how special you are to His Father – to God. He shares how God knew you even before you were born and how He knitted you together in your mother's womb and created your delicate, inner parts.

The Master's Masterpiece

Even though He knows the answer to this question, He asks you, "How are you taking care of the treasure, the temple, God created for you?"

What is your answer?

You know He knows; you know you can't lie!

Will you be embarrassed by your answer?

Will you feel it's none of His business?

Will you be able to tell Him you are doing everything possible to take care of this amazing gift His Father created for you?

Now open your eyes. What are you feeling?

Take action and think about ways you can change the way you are living so when the time comes you can answer God's questions in the positive about how you took care of the body for which Jesus paid such a high price. Write your ideas down in your journal. Begin each day by asking God to remind you to take good care of the masterpiece He created for you.

DAY 2

Answer 2: Realize You Are No Longer Your Own

You were bought with a price [purchased with a preciousness and paid for, made His own]. So then, honor God and bring glory to Him in your body. (1 Corinthians 6:20 AMP)

Have you ever borrowed anything from someone?

How did you treat that item?

Why did you treat it the way you did?

What was your motivation?

Does God Really Care What I Eat?

Have you ever loaned something to someone?

How did you expect to get that item back from them?

Who owns your body, soul, and spirit?

How can you apply this mindset, that you are not your own, to your body?

Read the Parable of the Talents in Matthew 25:14-30.

Who gave the talents to the three people in this parable (see verse 14)?

How did the owner decide how much talent to give each of these people (see verse15)?

What did the owner of the talents expect his people to do with what he loaned them (verse 19)?

How did the owner respond to the people who produced an increase with what they had been given (see verses 21-23)?

How did the owner respond to the person who did nothing with his talent (see verses 24-28)?

Who does the owner represent in this parable?

How important is it that we use the talents God has given us to produce fruit in our own lives and in the lives of those around us?

Begin to change your attitude toward the physical body God has loaned you. Picture yourself standing before God at the end of your life as He is asking you what fruit you produced with the talents He gave you. How would you answer Him today? How would you like to answer Him?

Make a list in your journal of your God-given talents. Begin to write out a plan to produce fruit for God using these talents. Be specific. Start with

The Master's Masterpiece

small steps and begin to implement one step each week until you are seeing fruit in your life and in the lives of those around you.

Here are some essential self-care factors to consider as you set up your plan to take better care of the body God has loaned you and produce fruit from the talents He has given you:

Am I living the life God intends for me?

Do I have a clear, compelling vision for my future?

Am I investing time alone each day with God?

Does anyone in my life hold me accountable to my best self?

Do I consistently make health-producing food and drink choices?

Am I exercising in some way almost every day?

Am I getting sufficient sleep most nights?

Do I have at least three close personal relationships?

Do I have 'extra time' or a margin built into my lifestyle?

Am I focused on progress rather than perfection?

Use your answers to help you pinpoint the areas where you need the most work. Develop a plan to get you where you want and need to be (taken from Chapter 4, "The 4:8 Principle" by Tommy Newberry, pages 71-72, *Practice Extreme Self Care*).

DAY 3

Answer 3: Remember Whose You Are

> "Deciding the value you place on yourself is another choice you have to make. Many people allow this decision to be made for them by their dominant capabilities, media, and other people." (Tommy Newberry)

Think about who or what you have let determine the value you place on yourself.

Have you allowed the media or other people to determine the value you place on yourself? Explain your answer.

Have you determined your value based on your dominant capabilities? Explain your answer.

Why do you believe God gave you those capabilities?

Were they meant to limit what you could accomplish in your life?

Do you believe you are important in God's plans for His kingdom here on the earth? Why or why not?

Tommy Newberry gave us some good advice when he said, "Dwell on the person God wants you to become. Visualize your best self. To accomplish this, first escape from the limitations of the current moment and shine your spotlight on your full potential."[19]

Read Luke 11:13.

> *If you then, evil as you are, know how to give good gifts [gifts that are to their advantage] to your children, how much more*

---

19   Newberry, Tommy. "The 4:8 Principle" by Tommy Newberry, p. 71.

will your heavenly Father give the Holy Spirit to those who ask and continue to ask Him! (AMP)

Begin to discover what it means to be a child of God. As you read about the privileges you have as the child of the King, write them down in your journal and ask God to reveal His purpose for your life in His kingdom as His prince or princess. Here are a few verses to get you started.

Declare each one of these truths over yourself!
   Romans 8:16-17 says I am _____

   How does this change how I am going to treat myself today?

   1 John 5:1 says I am _____

   How am I going to reflect this truth in my life today?

   John 16:27 says I am _____

   Do I believe this is true about me or am I different from others?

   Galatians 3:26-27 says I put on Christ by _____

   How have you put on Christ?

   1 Peter 2:4-5 says I am _____

   What do I need to do today to help this spiritual construction happen in my body?

Thank God today for the opportunity to become all He created you to be.

DAY 4

Answer 4: Admit Your Disobedience Is Sin

Read Genesis 1:26-31.

Who did Adam and Eve belong to?

Why did God give Adam and Eve a choice to obey Him or not?

Read 1 John 5:3-4.

Explain in your own words what this means to you especially as it relates to the way you treat your body.

Read Genesis 1:29, 2:9, and 2:16-17.

What were God's instructions to Adam concerning what he was to eat?

Does God care about what we eat?

Read Genesis 2:17.

What did God tell Adam was the consequence of eating something God told him not to?

Read Genesis 3:1-7.

What did Satan use to tempt Eve to disobey God?

What was the first sin in the Bible?

What does Satan tempt you with today?

DAY 5

Reread Romans 6:16-23.

What are the benefits of obedience listed in these verses?

What did you discover are the consequences of disobedience?

So is eating something God says is not good for our bodies in direct disobedience to Him? Why or why not?

How is this going to change your attitude toward food from now on?

What does eating what we know God would not approve show about our love for Him?

How is learning this going to change the way you eat?

Picture yourself living in the Garden of Eden. Look around at all the wonderful food God has provided for you to eat. Make a list in your journal of what you believe you would have to eat if you lived there.

<u>DAY 6</u>

Record in your journal how what you have learned in this chapter changed your attitude toward the food you eat. Start by making a list of the foods you know God wants you to eat and why, but don't stop there. Make a list of the foods God does not want you to eat and why. The list of what is good for you should be a lot longer than what is not good for you. Refer to the Strategic Daily Plan provided for you at the end of this book. Ask the Living God to guide you as you strive to be obedient to Him in all that you do.

Week 3

WHY DID GOD MAKE ME THIS WAY?

DAY 1

Read or Review Chapter 3: *Why Did God Make Me This Way?*

Answer 1: Acknowledge You Are Fearfully and Wonderfully Made

Have you ever asked, "Why did God make me this way?"

Is it God's fault you are fat?

Why is it so important that you take 100 percent responsibility for being fat?

Read Psalm 139:13-16. Explain this verse in your own words.

What does Psalm 139:15 say about how God wove you together in your mother's womb?

What are some of the expressive words used in this Psalm to describe God's process of creating us?

Why Did God Make Me This Way?

To understand how to care for what He has given us, we must understand and then acknowledge just how fearfully and wonderfully we have been made.

What does it mean that you are fearfully and wonderfully made?

Designed by the Master, our bodies are made of intricate parts which when taken care of properly work together. Just as the parts in a watch must be precise to work properly, God created the parts in our body to be precise with the heart pumping a certain amount of blood, the heart beating a certain number of times in a minute, and the blood flowing throughout the body at just the right speed. Every part of the body must be precise to make it work properly. When you don't take care of your watch, it can quit. Many times all it takes is a new battery to get it running properly again. The same is true with the body. Sometimes all it needs is a combination of the proper foods, the right amount of exercise and rest, and it will begin working properly again.

Think about how marvelous, wonderful, intricate, and complex the details of the human body are as you read over the intricacies of the human body. Highlight things on the list in this chapter you find the most marvelous.

What happens when we don't take care of any part of this intricate body God has given us?

What might be causing some of the parts not to work correctly?

Read 2 Timothy 2:21. How are you going to do what this verse says to do?

Begin to discover just how fearfully and wonderfully you have been made by God. Focus on how you were intricately woven together by God Himself. Learn about the intricacies of your human body and how to keep it in good working order. Just as you would do with any valuable piece of machinery, read the owner's manual and learn how God wants you to take care of what He so fearfully and wonderfully made. **Write a prayer thanking God for creating you:**

The Master's Masterpiece

Record in your journal how you are going to treat your vessel, your body, in a way worthy of your Creator. Use the Strategic Daily Plan at the end of the book to help you. Thank God just as David did in Psalm 139:14 every day by praying, "I praise you, for I am fearfully and wonderfully made. Wonderful are your works; my soul knows it very well."

<u>DAY 2</u>

Answer 2: Acknowledge God Knows All About You

Read Jeremiah 1:5.

Did God know you before He formed you in your mother's womb and approved you as His chosen instrument?

What did God have in mind for you to accomplish here on this earth even before you were born?

How did God intricately design you so you could accomplish your specific purpose?

Psalm 139:1 says God is what? _____ _____
_____ _____ and _____.

Why is that so important for you to know?

Read Psalm 139:2-4. What else does God know about you?

Read Psalm 139:5. Why is this such a key verse?

How does realizing God knows "where you are" and "what you do" make you feel?

It's kind of like "on star" on your car—they always know where you are and where **you have been!**

Begin to discover what God has chosen you to do. Ask Him for wisdom and guidance as you study His Word allowing the Holy Spirit to work. Record your thoughts in your journal as a prayer and open your eyes each day and watch how He mysteriously works in your life.

Why Did God Make Me This Way?

Record in your journal your own "Conversations with God." Ask Him the tough questions, and then see if you can find the answers as you study His Word and spend time in prayer. Record all of your conversations with God in your journal. Thank God that He knows all about you and loves you anyway! Tell Him you want Him to be an active part in your life from today on!

<u>DAY 3</u>

Answer 3: Acknowledge You Cannot Hide from God

Read Psalm 139:7-12.

Why is it important for you to understand there is no place you can be hidden from God?

How does it make you feel? Are you reassured or concerned?

Have you ever wanted to hide your sins and guilt from everyone including God?

Read Genesis 3:8-9.

When God called out for Adam in Genesis 3:9, did He know where Adam was?

Did He know why they were hiding?

How is this going to help you with your future decisions in all areas of your life?

Read Psalm 139:17-18.

What kind of thoughts does God have about you?

Read Psalm 139:10.

Why is God so intent on knowing where you are and what you are doing?

Do you want Him to be there to guide and support you every step of the way?

Read Proverbs 3:5-6.

What do these verses tell you to do?

If you do, what is your reward?

What do you need to do today to receive this guidance and support from God?

Begin to discover the wonders of having God always present in your life. Tell God today that you want to lean on, trust in, and be confident in Him with all your heart and mind. Ask Him to guide and direct your path. As you begin each day, acknowledge and welcome His presence in your life. All throughout the day thank Him for being there for you and with you. You will be surprised at the wisdom you will suddenly have about situations you face during the day. You will find great joy in knowing God is right there with you every step of the way!

Record in your journal in your Conversation with God section what you have tried to hide from Him. He, of course, already knows, but He wants to help you deal with it. Ask and receive His forgiveness. Then ask Him what you need to do to set things right. Record how you are making important changes in your life.

DAY 4

Answer 4: Acknowledge God Has a Plan for Your Life

Read Psalm 139:23-24.

> What revelation does David share with us in this wonderful Psalm?
>
> What amazing thing did David ask God to do for him?
>
> What did God say about David in Acts 13:22?
>
> Were you surprised at this once you learned about some of the things David did in his life time?
>
> How do you explain this relationship between God and David?

Below are some thought-provoking questions important to answer so you can begin to acknowledge God not only fearfully and wonderfully formed you, but also that He knows you from the inside out. We cannot hide anything from Him and we have to be willing to allow Him to expose anything that does not belong in our lives. Then even when we miss the mark and do something we know does not please God, we can pick ourselves up and continue on down the path God has set before us.

- *Do you want God to point out your sin?*
- *Do you want God to search you from the inside out?*
- *Do you want to know what thoughts offend God?*
- *Do you want God to lead you on a path of everlasting life?*

What does James 4:17 tell us about doing or not doing the right thing?

Do you know what is right to do?

Are you doing it?

If you are, what are your benefits?

If you are not what does the Bible say you are doing?

DAY 5

Begin to discover how powerful making Psalm 139:23-24 your prayer can be in your life. As you invite God to search your heart and reveal what He finds, be willing to make the necessary changes in your life to correct what needs correcting. **Write in your journal about what changes are happening right now in your life.**

DAY 6

Record in your journal in your Conversation with God what you have learned from Psalm 139. Go ahead and ask Him the hard questions and record the answers as you discover them. Also begin to carefully consider everything you put into your body. Take the time to ask yourself if what you are eating and doing could be offensive to God. Be willing to forego the food or activity if it turns out to be something God would not approve of for the masterpiece you are to Him. Consistently pray and ask for the Holy Spirit's guidance as you move forward with God's purpose for your life.

Week Four

How Can I Keep From Failing at Every Diet I Try?

———— ∞ ————

<u>DAY 1</u>

Read or Review Chapter 4: *How Can I Keep From Failing at Every Diet I Try?*

Answer 1: Understand He Has Given You What You Need

Read 2 Peter 1:3-4.

> Have you ever tried one of those fad, quick-fix weight loss programs or pills?

> How did that work out for you?

Do you know every little decision you make each and every day will make a difference?

> **"The food you eat today is walking and talking tomorrow."**
> **– Jack LaLanne**

We know from previous lessons that God designed our bodies to function in a certain way. They were designed to need a certain kind of fuel.

What did Hippocrates mean when he said, *"Let food be your medicine and medicine be your food."*

Thomas Edison, inventor of the light bulb, said, "The doctor of the future will give no medicine, but will interest his patients in the care of the human frame, diet, and the cause and prevention of disease."

Have you ever regarded your body as a machine that needs fixing?

Do you remember how we studied the intricacies of the human body and what a complex, divinely designed group of adaptive systems God has given us?

Does this confirm God has designed us and given us everything we need to live a long and healthy life?

What is the right kind of fuel important to keep our bodies running at maximum performance levels?

The evidence has been staring each of us in the face for decades: eating healthy will help us do what?

What kind of diets have you tried in the past?

Did they list many of the foods you want and like to eat on the "no, no list"?

Have you experienced the "yo-yo" life where you lost the weight, but then gained it back, sometimes gaining back even more?

What was your goal as you began these weight loss programs?

Was it to reach a certain number on the scale or a certain size?

What happened when you reached your goal weight or that dress size?

Have you come to realize how you eat is really about taking care of yourself physically to be your best spiritually?

What does that mean to your everyday decisions?

Why is focusing on losing weight usually not effective?

What would be a better focus?

Have you decided to make the commitment to eat healthy the rest of your life instead of going on another diet?

If you don't choose to take care of yourself and eat the way God intended what could happen to the body He has given you?

What message are you sending to yourself, to your family, to others when you don't give it the fuel it was designed to run on?

What message are you sending God?

Are you telling Him His creation isn't important and you don't care?

Why is it so important that you learn to work with God's design?

"Reality is that we are sons and daughters of the living God. We have His spiritual genetics within us. We haven't

simply been taught a better way, we have the Spirit of the true way living within us."[20]

Begin to discover just how amazing God has designed your body to handle life's ups and downs. The more you learn about this amazing body God has given you, the better job you can do taking care of it. There are many wonderful websites and resources out there that can help you become better informed on how your body works and what is the best fuel.

Record in your journal in your conversation with God how you feel about being His child. Thank Him for giving you His Spirit to show you the true way of living. Take the time each day to pray and ask God for wisdom and help on your journey. Ask Him to help you when you know there are going to be foods available you know aren't the best for you to eat. Write down what you eat, why you eat, and when you eat. Ask God to help you stop when you feel full! Use the Strategic Daily Plan at the end of the book to help guide your new eating habits.

<u>DAY 2</u>

Answer 2: Know It's Not Beyond What You Can Bear

People often tell me they have a hard time with weight loss because the temptations around them are so great.

What are some of those temptations you face every day?

Have you ever talked with God about these temptations? Explain your answer.

Did you ask Him to take them away or did you ask Him to help you walk through them?

Read 1 Corinthians 10:13.

---

20   (*Beloved Children* by Chris Tiegreen "Wonder of the Cross" by Chris Tiegreen, February 10 Tyndale Publishing, 2009.

What did God promise you in 1 Corinthians 10:13?

Were there any exceptions to this promise?

Do you feel you have been subjected to a temptation that is not covered by God's promise? Explain your answer.

When God says always does He really mean always?

How has learning this changed the way you look at your everyday temptations?

Read the story of Daniel (1:8-16) in the Old Testament.

What was Daniel determined not to do?

Because of Daniel's determination, what did God do to provide a way out of the temptation for Daniel?

What was the outcome Daniel and his friends experienced because they chose to obey God's commands concerning what to eat and what not to eat?

What kind of testimony did this provide for Daniel in regard to his witness to the heathen King? (Read Daniel 6:25-27.)

Do you remember the acronym WAIET? Fill in what each letter stands for based on our lesson:

W – W_____
A–A _____
I–I _____
E–E_____
T – T_____

Have you tried asking yourself this question when tempted to eat something you aren't supposed to?

What happened?

Have you tried eating only when you are really hungry?

Have you determined to eat the foods God intended for you to eat?

Begin to discover how reading 1 Corinthians 10:13 out loud to yourself is a powerful way to start your day. As you get this important truth deep inside of you and really begin to believe it, you will find yourself experiencing more and more victories over temptation. The secret to overcoming temptation is to trust God to show you the way out. A good way to get into this habit is to print this verse and tape it on your mirror so you see it as you are getting ready to begin your day.

> *The temptations in your life are no different from what others experience. And God is faithful. He will not allow the temptation to be more than you can stand. When you are tempted, he will show you a way out so that you can endure.* (1 Corinthians 10:13 NLT)

Record in your journal using the "I Did" and "I Didn't" Journal sample below.

MY DAILY I "DID" & I "DIDN'T" JOURNAL

This Journal is designed to help you stay focused on your accomplishments for the day.

Examples of "I Did."
    *I did eat a healthy lunch (write down what you ate)
    *I did enjoy the healthy food I ate.
    *I did have a potluck at work today; however, I took small amounts of food.

Examples of "I Didn't."
    *I didn't eat the cookie offered to me at break time today.

*I didn't eat burger and fries today.
*I didn't eat the desserts at the potluck at work today.

The goal is to find three "I Did" and three "I Didn't" per day.

If you gave in to the temptation during the day, write down why you think it happened and what could you do to keep it from happening again.

What I "DID" & "DIDN'T" do Today
Today's Date:_____
"For I am God's masterpiece...." Eph. 2:10

This is what I" DID" today:
1_____
2_____
3_____

This is what I "DIDN'T" do today:
1_____
2_____
3_____

Challenges from my day:
_____

Actions I'm willing to take to stay on track:
_____

Blessings from my day:
_____

What might come tomorrow I want to be prepared for?
_____

<u>DAY 3</u>

Answer 3: Realize Gluttony Does Not Honor God

> *So, whether you eat or drink, or whatever you do, do all to the glory of God.* (1 Corinthians 10:31)

How Can I Keep From Failing at Every Diet I Try?

What are we clearly told to do in this verse?

What does that mean to you personally?

What did the Apostle Paul tell his young disciple in 2 Timothy 1:7?

What does that have to do with the subject of gluttony?

Gluttony or self-indulgence is the opposite of

_____

How would you define gluttony?

What does Ezekiel 16:49 say about gluttony?

What is the advice given in Proverbs 23:19-21?

What is the warning given in Proverbs 28:7?

Our bodies are the temple of the _____.

We are to be an _____ to others.

We are to honor and glorify God with our

_____.

It is up to each of us to make the decision to exercise _____ and _____
_____.

God has given us all we need to be able to escape the corruption in the world caused by evil desires, but we have a part in the development of that self-control.

Read 2 Peter 1:5-10 to find out God's plan.

Let's look at the progressive list we have been given in this passage of scripture and look up the additional scriptures to help you get started on your road to victory.

- Add your diligence to the divine promises (1 Timothy 4:14-15)
- Employ every effort in exercising your faith to develop virtue-excellence, resolution, Christian energy (Colossians 3:1-14)
- In exercising virtue develop your knowledge (2 Peter 3:18, Proverbs 1:7)
- In exercising knowledge develop your self-control (1 Peter 5:8)
- In exercising self-control develop your patience, endurance (Romans 12:12)
- In exercising steadfastness, develop your godliness (1 Timothy 4:12)
- In exercising godliness, develop your brotherly affection (Colossians 3:12)
- In exercising brotherly affection, develop your Christian love (1 John 4:7-12)

Is it God doing the exercising and developing?

Read again 2 Peter 1:3-4 that precedes this list.

Are you to be an active participant in this process?

Why do quick-fix diets not work?

Have you stopped the yo-yo weight loss cycle? If so, how?

What does self-discipline or self-control mean to you personally?

Have you been showing self-control with your eating? Explain your answer.

Are you associating with those who encourage you to give in to gluttony?

If you answered yes, list their names.

Are willing to stop associating with them until you are strong enough to be a witness to them instead of being influenced by them?

Are you ready and willing to go through God's process to win the victory?

Begin to discover how much better you physically feel, and how much better you feel about yourself as you overcome this issue of gluttony. Use the progressive list given to you in 2 Peter 1:5-10 as a checklist to track your progress as you move forward in a positive direction toward your true goal which is to honor God in everything you do, including what you eat and drink.

Record in your journal in your Conversation with God the changes you want to make in your lifestyle to make sure everything you are doing, including eating or drinking, honors God. Ask God for wisdom to help you come up with a list and then ask Him to honor His promise to show you a way out of every temptation that comes your way. If you are associating with those who encourage you to behave in a gluttonous way, perhaps it is time to separate yourself from them until you can be a positive witness to them, instead of letting them influence your behavior. Pray daily for God's wisdom and favor and you will find you can overcome **every** temptation. Continue to use the "I Did" and "I Didn't" format in your journal.

<u>DAY 4</u>

Answer 4: Enhance Your Health with Moderation

> *Let your **moderation be known** unto all men.* (Philippians 4:5 KJV)

Have you heard the word moderation as you've tried to release weight and live a healthier lifestyle?

What does it mean to you to eat and exercise in moderation?

The Master's Masterpiece

What other words might also describe this concept of moderation?

No matter what word we use, it is something we have to learn to do.

Self-control means we learn to _____.

Who is doing the controlling?

Why is this important to God?

Has He asked you to do anything that He has not equipped you to be able to do? Explain your answer.

Are God's instructions for your own good? Explain your answer.

Read 1 Corinthians 9:25.

What is the prize we are competing for?

Is it worth being temperate in all things to attain it?

What is the warning in Proverbs 25:16?

What did Jesus criticize the Pharisees for in Matthew 23:25?

I finally realized God had big plans for me and when I didn't take care of the body He gave me, I couldn't be my best for Him. I want to be my best for Him!

Have you come to this same revelation?

DAY 5

What did you discover about yourself when you answered these questions?

Who draws the line between excessive and moderation in my life?

Who is my "moderation guide?"

Where do I discover the answers to my questions even about the food I eat?

Did you try and implement the suggestions given at the end of this chapter?

What were the results?

DAY 6

Record in your journal in your Conversation with God your efforts at moderation in your eating. Continue to think about what you have learned about gluttony and moderation. Think about honoring God in all that you do. If you need to take a break and leave the room during a meal or an activity focused around food in order to "coach" yourself during a particularly trying temptation, take a trip to the restroom and talk to yourself in the mirror about treating your masterpiece the way God wants you to. Continue to journal the revelations God gives you and daily ask the Holy Spirit to be your guide. Continue to use the "I Did" and "I Didn't" format in your journal.

Week Five

WHY DO I TURN TO FOOD FOR COMFORT?

DAY 1

Read or Review Chapter 5: Why Do I Turn to Food for Comfort?

Answer 1: Discover the Mindset behind Your Choices

In order to break the control food has over you, you will want to discover the mindset behind the choices you make when you eat. It's about *why, when, and what* you eat.

Define the following types of food choices listed below and indicate which ones you feel are part of the mindset behind your eating choices.

Confrontational Food–Is it your parent's fault you eat the way you do?

Cover-up Food–Did it really dull the pain or did it cause more in the long run?

Convenient Food–Did you eat healthier at lunch?

Celebration Food–You earned it, right?

Why Do I Turn to Food for Comfort?

Comfort Food–Have you ever had one of those days when people were rude and even mean to you so you went home and ate a quart of ice cream to make yourself feel better? How did you feel the next morning? Was it really worth it?

Conquer Food–I was determined to prove I could eat what I wanted. Ever try it? How did it go for you?

Begin to change your mindset by being honest with yourself about the reasons behind those mindsets. It has been said that doing the same thing over and over and expecting different results is the definition of insanity. If you don't change your mindset, nothing is going to change. Face these destructive mindsets head on and seek to replace them with the right ones.

Record in your journal what you have discovered about your mindsets concerning why, when, and what you eat. Ask God in your conversations with Him how to begin to replace these mindsets with godly ones. He has promised to direct your path and your mind toward what is right and healthy for you. Be honest and allow Him to be part of those decisions. Continue to use the "I Did" and "I Didn't" format in your journal. Pray and ask God for wisdom to give you the right mindset in your life.

<u>DAY 2</u>

Answer 2: Face Your Circumstances

Have you ever felt you could never achieve what you wanted in life?

Have you ever felt you were not worthy enough to have what you want so you try to compensate by eating whatever you want?

I faced the fact that I had issues and they were keeping me from losing weight and keeping it off. Are you ready to do that, too?

I discovered it's about taking care of myself physically to be my best spiritually. Is that your goal, too?

I discovered it's about loving and cherishing this amazing creation God gave me and wanting to honor Him with the way I ate and drank. Are you ready to take that step?

It will become easier and easier to say no to the foods that will harm your body and to focus on foods to fuel your body and keep you healthy.

Take a look at the chart again to see the risks with eating unhealthy. Are you willing to face the truth about the circumstances, make the right changes and implement them into your life?

Have you experienced fatigue, headaches, indigestion issues, heart problems, diabetes or any other health challenge?

Do you see that it is directly related to the fuel you put in your body?

What changes are necessary for you to start making?

Where have you been careless in your eating habits?

Do you agree everything you put in your mouth will have a beneficial or detrimental consequence based on the food choices you make?

The more you learn about the type of fuel your body needs the better choices you will make about the food you eat. Take the time to learn about the foods that benefit and strengthen your heart, muscles, and brain. Your body will reward you by staying healthy and strong. Eating sensibly, drinking lots of water, and regular exercise will reap wonderful benefits. You will enjoy life more when you are not constantly trying to repair the damage done to your masterpiece by the food choices you make on a daily basis. Consistently choosing wisely based on diligently seeking to know and understand how your body works will strengthen your body from the inside out.

It is vitally important to your health to begin to make better food choices. The Bible says people perish for lack of knowledge (Hosea 4:6). Science has proven this true when it comes to the way we treat our bodies.

What have you discovered about how the intricacies of your body work and the kind of fuel that will make it run more smoothly and efficiently?

Begin to face your circumstances head on by asking God to **take you through them instead of taking you out of them.** Realize that just like exercise, where you put pressure on your muscles to strengthen them, the pressure you face in walking through your circumstance will make you stronger in the long run.

Record in your journal what you are learning about the importance of the fuel you put in your body. Keep a list on your refrigerator of the best foods to eat to accomplish the goals you **want.** Foods such as avocados increase your energy level and raw nuts help you burn fat. God has offered you wisdom from above if you ask Him for it. Why not start every day by seeking wisdom for the fuel important to meet the challenges God knows you will face? Continue to use the "I Did" and "I Didn't" format in your journal and Strategy Daily Plan to start making right choices for the fuel your body needs. Keep a record of your successes in your journal and be willing to share them with others to help them on their journey as well.

<u>DAY 3</u>

Answer 3: Find the Stuff Beneath the Stuff

What I know to be true about someone who wants to release weight is how important it is to first get to the stuff beneath the stuff–the "meat" of the real issue for your weight issue. By getting to the core of the problem, you can also have a better mindset to release the weight and keep it off for life.

Confrontational Food–Even if your parents planted the seed in you as a child that dessert is a reward, what have you discovered happens when you continue to hold onto this idea?

> Would you agree God wouldn't want you eating things that are not good for your body even if you look at them as a reward for eating other things that are good for you?

Is our God a god of compromise?

Would you agree He wants you to take care of the beautiful creation, your masterpiece, in the best possible way so you can be your best not only for you, but for others and for Him?

The body you are living in is the only body you have.

Would you agree God would want you to focus on Him instead of always turning to food as your reward?

Read 1 Corinthians 13:11. What does this say God expects us to do?

Cover-up Food–Have you ever known someone who lost weight, was looking great and yet put the weight back on? What is the problem with the cycle of using cover up food to deal with inner pain?

Read Psalm 147:3.

What is God's promise to those of us that have suffered a broken heart?

What has caused your broken heart?

Do you believe God is there to help you through this and heal your broken heart?

Convenient Food–Read 1 Corinthians 6:19.

Are convenience foods the proper way to fuel your temple?

Is this really the way you want to treat it?

What kind of potential "inconveniences" have you learned may be a result of the convenience foods you have been using as fuel?

Why Do I Turn to Food for Comfort?

Read Proverbs 14:12.

What have you discovered from this verse?

How has that caused a change in your use of convenience foods?

Celebration Food–Were you led to believe sweets were the answer or "reward" when you accomplished something?

What happens with this mindset?

Have you ever said something like, "I deserve this piece of pie because I worked hard today"? Or, "I deserve chips and dip because I walked three miles today"?

What other reasons or excuses have you used to reward yourself with food?

Read Proverbs 14:15.
Which person would you rather be?

Read Jeremiah 17:10.
Isn't it time you focused on the real reward, the one God has for you, when you follow His plan and fulfill His purpose?
Who do you really want rewarding you when you accomplish great things?

Comfort Food–Just as some people choose to drown their sorrows in alcohol, have you chosen to drown your sorrows in food?

What have you learned is the problem with comfort food?

Has your comfort food actually made you uncomfortable? Explain your answer.

Read 2 Corinthians 1:3-4;

Who do you really want for your Comforter?
(see 2 Corinthians 1:3-4)

Conquer Food–Even though I got to a number on the scale and in a dress size I liked, I still struggled with keeping the weight off. More importantly, I struggled with my head talk. I had to deal with the fat girl issue within me, before I could conquer the control food had over me.

Read Proverbs 23:7b.

Are you dealing with this issue? Explain your answer.

Who would it be wise to listen to when making decisions about the best foods to eat?

Who has your best interest at heart?

How did you answer these questions?

Am I focusing on food or God for my reward?

Am I allowing childish ways to prevent me from becoming a productive adult?

Am I settling for short-term convenience instead of long-term health?

Am I constantly finding excuses to reward myself with food?

Am I stuck in a vicious cycle of weight loss and gain because I resort to comfort food instead of the comfort God offers me?

Have I allowed food to control me?

Begin to change your eating habits based on the way you answered the questions above. Remember every decision has a consequence which can be positive or negative. Begin by making small changes every day and see the difference even one decision a day can make in your life.

Record in your journal the ways you believe you could be a slave to food. Use your conversations with God to reveal the stuff beneath the stuff that you personally are dealing with. Ask Him to be your comforter and give you the reward of a healthy body and a sound, well-balanced mind. Also record the ways even the small changes in your eating habits have made in your level of energy and focus. Continue to use the "I Did" and "I Didn't" format in your journal to help you pinpoint which of the

Why Do I Turn to Food for Comfort?

"C's" you are dealing with in your eating. Implement and use the Strategic Daily Plan and keep a record of your progress.

<u>DAY 4</u>

Answer 4: Learn to Break Food's Control

Confrontational Food–Do you really believe God wants such chaos in our minds during a time of fueling our bodies?

When you pray and thank God for the food He has provided, thank Him for how unique and intricately He has made you (Psalm 139:14). Thank Him for providing food that will help the growth of your body.

Remember you are teaching your children and setting an example by the way you eat. As you exemplify how important taking care of your body is, others will learn by your example.

Don't bribe yourself or your children with unhealthy food.

Eat healthy food because you know it is the right fuel for the temple God has provided for you.

Give examples of what you have done to show God and others how important it is to take good care of the masterpiece He has given you. Be specific!

Cover-up Food–What if instead of drowning your sorrows in food, you turn to God?

Read Psalm 121:2. What does it tell you about where to seek help?

Have you found that when you cover up your pain with food, it's like digging a hole and going deeper and deeper? Explain your answer.

Read the words of Jesus in John 14:26-27. What did Jesus say He will give you?

Read John 16:33. What did Jesus say that can help you attain His peace?

When you turn to God instead of food you will find His peace, a peace food or any other source cannot give you. Then you can pull yourself out of the hole, love yourself again and never have to eat "cover up" food to hide your pain. Wow! Isn't that an amazing, peaceful way to live?

Convenient Food–If there's a lot going on and you feel you have to eat convenience food, what if you choose a restaurant with healthier choices?

What is it you really want to teach your children and others?

What are some of the potential major inconveniences you now know you may be forced to deal with as consequences of your choices?

Are you ready to focus on long-term released weight instead of short-term gratification?

Celebration Food–If you feel you have to reward yourself, what if you reward yourself with healthy food choices or relax with a book and a hot bubble bath?

Have you tried looking at yourself in the mirror and congratulating yourself with a "high five"? Have you ever wrapped your arms around you and given yourself a hug? It is an amazing feeling. I want you to take a moment and do this: stand up, wrap your arms around you as tight as you can, close your eyes, and lay your head over to one side so you are relaxed. Just enjoy hugging and loving on yourself just as you would hug your loved ones. Take a moment and thank God for creating you. This is a way to celebrate and reward yourself. Hugs are so important and this is one way you can feel special and appreciate your masterpiece.

How about sitting down and writing about what you did and be grateful for the victories you attained today?

What other ways have you discovered to celebrate the good times in your life?

Comfort Food–What if instead of drowning your sorrows and disappointments in comfort food, you choose instead to nurture and use the self-control you have through the Holy Spirit?

Read Galatians 5:22-23.

Read Exodus 15:26. What if you allow God to comfort and heal you?

Read Ephesians 2:14. What if you allow Him to be your peace?

How will this change the control Comfort food has had over you?

Conquer Food–Instead of being careless in your eating, begin to really care about what you allow to enter your masterpiece.

How has this chapter helped you learn to care about what you eat and drink?

Instead of feeling you have to be a "conqueror" with your food, have you chosen instead to conquer the deeper issues going on in your life?

Have you come to realize how special you are to God?

Do you see that in His eyes you are His Masterpiece? He loves you, and wants to help you with every circumstance that surfaces in your life.

You can choose to take control of your eating instead of letting food control you. Learn how to face what is going on in your life instead of turning to food for the answer. Get rid of the stuff beneath the stuff and release the weight forever.

Have you see TV commercials and media marketing telling us that living life to the fullest means eating and drinking whatever we want? Give some examples.

What does the Bible say in John 8:32?

Do you want to be set free from food controlling you?

How are you going to start? When will you start?

DAY 5

Begin today by making the right choices based on the truths God is revealing to you. Take the time to find out what foods benefit and strengthen your body. Find ways to prepare healthy foods. **Write down some of the right choices you are now making and thank God for the power to make right choices!**

DAY 6

Record in your journal your conversation time with God. Ask His help in staying true to your eating plan and record His answers. Continue to use the "I Did" and "I Didn't" format in your journal and write out your eating plan. Post it on your refrigerator and thank God at every meal for the healthy food He has made available to you. Think of ways you can share what you are learning with others. Helping others will help you to stay true to what you know God wants you to do—eat to live not live to eat!

Week Six

WHY ME?

———— ◈ ————

<u>DAY 1</u>

Read or Review Chapter 6: *Why Me?*

Answer 1: Learn to Focus on Your Inner Self

What did you personally relate to as you read my story?
How have you been treated by others?
Have you been holding on to the fat person inside?
What do you see when you look in the mirror?
How has your focus on your outer self affected your life?
How has it affected those around you like your children, family, and friends?
What kind of head talk are you using?

One of the things that really helped me begin the upward move toward improving my self-confidence and self-esteem was discovering how much I am worth to God. Remember we talked earlier about the value God has placed on us? Well, studying how much God says I am worth increased my own self-worth. Read the scriptures below and write out what they mean to you personally.

Proverbs 31:30 –
Matthew 10:29-31 –
1 Peter 3:3-4 –

Instead of asking, "Why me?" can you ask God, "How can I use what I've learned from my experiences to help others?"

What is the new thought process God is moving you toward?
How is this going to change your lifestyle?
How can God use what you've been through to help others?

Begin to change your mindset by asking God the right kind of questions in your conversations with Him. Begin to think of people in your life that could benefit from what you have learned.

Record in your journal all that you are learning about your amazing masterpiece and God's purpose for your life. Start making a list of people you can help through your testimony and look for ways to share your amazing discoveries with them. The more you pour out what God is giving you, the more He will give you. Ask Him to guide you every day to someone you can help from what you have been through and learned. Continue to use the "I Did" and "I Didn't" format in your journal. Today, add the name of someone you have shared with about what you have learned. How does it make you feel knowing you are making the difference in someone's life?

<u>DAY 2</u>

Answer 2: Discover Your Weight Grief

Did you know weight issues usually point to another deeper issue?

Doesn't it make sense that if you fix the deeper issue, you can fix the weight issue?

Since weight grief is one of these areas let's see if you can pinpoint specific areas where you need help.

What grief are you dealing with because of your weight?

Is it low self-worth?

Depression?

No Self-confidence?

Is your health suffering?

Are you experiencing high blood pressure, diabetes, heart issues or back issues?

Is it hard to walk because you are out of breath?

Is it hard to exercise?

What are you dealing with because you haven't been willing to make the right choices about taking care of your masterpiece?

These are very thought provoking questions. However, I encourage you to answer them openly and honestly. I invite you to be very honest with yourself and discover your own personal weight grief. To overcome the influence grief is having on your life, it's so very important to deal with it.

Here are some more very pointed questions that will help you pinpoint your specific area of weight grief.

Are you embarrassed when you buy clothes? Why?

Do you feel family members are embarrassed concerning you?

What has made you think that way?

Are you treated differently by others – do you feel they judge you? Give some examples:

Are you able to get on the floor and play with your children or grandchildren?

Are you missing out and not enjoying life because of your weight?

Have you gone through a crisis in your life and you chose to turn to food for comfort?

Explain your answer.

Read Psalm 6:7 and Psalm 31:9.

Describe David's grief:

Who is David turning to in his time of grief?

Have you ever had such deep grief?

Who or what did you turn to?

Who is the One to turn to?

Internal Emotional Response to Loss or a Problem:

As you read my testimony about carrying my fat girl around with me, did you discover you have allowed that fat girl to lurk behind you as well?

Do you think this might be why many have gained weight back over and over?

What are you going to do about this?

The Different Stages of Grief

Read through various stages of emotion when dealing with grief and determine where you are. Highlight the one that you think best describes your personal position.

Depression can many times cause you to eat more and more and start you on a vicious cycle.

Denial is when you try to convince yourself you are not that overweight. You are in denial and are choosing to pretend it's not a problem!

Anger manifests when you ask those why questions like, "How come I'm fat? Why can my friend eat anything she wants and never gain weight?"

Bargaining can be with yourself or with God.

Acceptance is deciding to accept you have a weight issue and you choose to make wise choices when eating. You have accepted the fact God wants you to nurture what He has given you.

Have you been using the acronym I suggested you use when you are being tempted to eat for the wrong reasons?

W – Why
A – Am
I – I
E – Eating
T – This

Share the ways using this acronym has helped you.

Begin to deal with the stage of grief you are in by first admitting where you are. Be honest with yourself and God. Share this with someone you trust and know will give you sound advice and help in dealing with this issue of grief.

Record in your journal the steps you have been taking toward dealing with your grief in this area of eating. Do you believe God wants you to learn self-control in this area so you will also have self-control in other areas? Do you believe He wants you to eat the healthy foods He has put on this earth for you? Record your conversation with God as you ask Him to walk you through the grieving process. Continue to use the "I Did" and "I Didn't" format in your journal and include a section on how you are dealing with your weight grief on a daily basis.

DAY 3

Answer 3: Let God Heal Your Broken Heart

Read each scripture contained in this chapter about grief. Write out what they mean to you and share how God has been helping you as you walked through the various emotional stages related to your weight grief.

Hebrews 12:1-2 says to me:
How has it helped you be more aware of what you are doing to your body?
How has it helped you make changes so you can be your best for God?

2 Timothy 2:3-5 and 7 says you are a _____ and an _____.
What insight has this given you to motivate you to persevere in your healthy eating and living plan?
How did the truth in verse 7 impact your life?

Galatians 5:22-24 lists the fruit of the Spirit.
One of the segments of the fruit of the Spirit is self-control which means _____

2 Timothy 1:7 says God has given you what?
Are you using this power?
Why or why not?
Explain your answer:

Why Me?

Galatians 5:24 says you need to be willing to do what?
Does this apply to the food you eat?
Explain your answer:
Are you willing to give up the passion for unhealthy food and create a passion for what God intended you to eat?

Ephesians 5:10 challenges you to _____
When you do what this scripture says what are you really doing?

Lamentations 3:22-23 gives you one of God's most amazing promises!
Write this promise out in your own words.
Are you enjoying these promises?
Why or why not?
Explain your answer:

Psalm 34:18 says

Psalm 147:3 says

Isaiah 61:3 reminds you

How have these verses helped you make the decision to take better care of the masterpiece God has given you?

Begin to change focus using all of the scriptures given you in this chapter. Declare one every day as you start your day and then take the time at night to record in your journal the impact that truth from God had in your life. Especially focus on how each one affected your eating decisions. Be willing to share this with others God sends across your path.

Check out any area where you are not experiencing peace in your life and search for the root cause of the chaos in your life. Then deal with it using all the resources God has given you. Thank Him for those He has provided in your life to help you walk through your grief.

DAY 4

Answer 4: Be Anxious for Nothing

In Matthew 6:25-34 Jesus talked about the fruitlessness of worry. He also talks about an unhealthy focus on food, drink, and the clothes we wear. He is not telling us to disregard them; He is saying there is a right way and a wrong way to focus in life.

Read this passage and describe the right way to focus our lives.

Jesus is inferring here that by worrying over food and drink and clothing shows the world what?

Focusing on food and drink in an unhealthy way _____ God. The right way is discovering _____ way of doing things and by doing so what do we achieve?

Read Philippians 4:6-7.
Be anxious for _____!
Does God really mean it?
Explain your answer.

Read Jeremiah 32:17 and Luke 1:37.
What did you learn about God in these two verses?

Read Philippians 4:8-9.
Why is this passage so important when it comes to dealing with worry?
What are you supposed to do with what you have learned in this chapter?
When you do, what will you reap in your life?
What practical help did you glean from reading this passage from the Message Bible?

Read Isaiah 53:3.
What does this verse assure you of?

Share how you answered the Ask Yourself questions:
What am I anxious about?

Am I making my request known to God or am I trying to handle everything on my own?
Do I really believe nothing is impossible for God?
If I do, am I showing Him I believe by my prayers and actions?
Do I seek His way of doing things?
Am I willing to put into practice what I have learned?

DAY 5

Begin to change your life and allow yourself to reach out and get the help you need instead of being weighed down in your grief. I have given you my contact information and information about what I do as a grief coach at the end of this book. Contact me if you are ready for more one on one help. Also, let your worries become prayers knowing with God nothing is impossible. Redirect your thinking by filling your mind with *the best, not the worst; the beautiful, not the ugly; things to praise, not things to curse.*

DAY 6

Record in your journal how you have been redirecting your thinking. Have you been experiencing God's most excellent peace? Be open to sharing what God has done in your life as He sends people across your path.

Week Seven

AM I DISRESPECTING GOD WHEN I EAT UNHEALTHY?

DAY 1

Read or Review Chapter 7: *Am I Disrespecting God When I Eat Unhealthy?*

Answer 1: Cherish Your Masterpiece

> *For no one ever hated his own flesh, but nourishes and cherishes it, just as Christ does the church.* (Ephesians 5:29)

When you love something you cherish it. When you learn to love your body, you will cherish and nourish it.

What does cherish mean to you?

What are some things you cherish in your life?

Write them down in your journal.

> *He makes the whole body fit together perfectly. As each part does its own special work, it helps the other parts grow, so that the whole body is healthy and growing and full of love.* (Ephesians 4:16 NLT)

Am I Disrespecting God When I Eat Unhealthy?

Part of cherishing your masterpiece is understanding your whole person.

What are the three parts of your whole person?

1.

2.

3.

How do you feed and nourish each one?

To really understand your whole person you need to:

Identify the _____ that impacts your sense of well being.

Uncover the sources of _____ that you may not have yet dealt with.

Deal with the _____ you have felt from others.

Choose sensible ways to _____ that will best meet your lifestyle.

Determine to _____ _____ by learning what is beneficial to the body you have been given.

Discover optimal health by caring for your _____, _____, and _____.

You support your soul by filling your mind with _____.

You feed and nurture your spirit by _____ _____.

You support your physical body through good _____ and _____.

The soul must be fed with _____ _____.

The spirit must be fed on _____ _____.

The · body must be nurtured and fed through the _____.

The World Health Organization has said, "Ignorance and complacency are the two most serious threats to our health."[21]

Define ignorance and complacency as it applies to cherishing your body:

---

21   http://www.iom.edu/-/media/Files/Activity%20Files/ Environment/EnvironmentalHealthRT/Smith.pdf

Have you ever faced a health crisis yourself or with someone you love? How did it affect how your treated your body?

Cherishing your masterpiece means you will do anything to protect it. In order to avoid a crisis in the physical realm, you will want to become a conscious competent.

What does it mean to be a conscious competent?

Generally how long does it take to develop a good habit?

Read James 1:22-25. What advice does this passage give when it comes to reaping good fruit in your health and developing good habits in everything you do in life?

*Do not merely listen to the word, and so deceive yourselves. Do what it says. Anyone who listens to the word but does not do what it says is like someone who looks at his face in a mirror and, after looking at himself, goes away and immediately forgets what he looks like. But whoever looks intently into the perfect law that gives freedom, and continues in it—**not forgetting what they have heard, but doing it**—they will be blessed in what they do.* (NIV emphasis added)

How do those around us know if we truly cherish the body God has given us?

Our _____ will clearly display just how much we value the gift God has given us.

Not only will we look and act differently, it is going to be obvious

_____

Read Titus 1:16.

What do those in this verse tell others with their words?

What do they tell others with their actions?

Is the condition of your body limiting your achievements?

Explain your answer.

Have you spent more time insuring your car and your house than you have cherishing your body as the masterpiece God designed it to be?

Explain your answer.

What does the way you treat your body tell others about how much you cherish it?

Begin to change your lifestyle starting today. Don't allow ignorance and complacency to let a health crisis happen in your life. Diligently study the Word of God to feed your spirit, think on the things listed in Philippians 4:8 to strengthen your soul, and study the intricacies of your body so you know the right fuel to give it.

Be a doer and use the knowledge God has made available to you to cherish the body He has given you. He has given you everything you need to stay healthy and prosperous. He has promised to give you wisdom from above if you feel you do not have the answers to your questions. Be a seeker and a doer and you will prosper. Record in your journal the things you are seeking to learn about the amazing body God has given you. Record the answers you receive to your questions and be prepared to share them with others. Enjoy the benefits of a healthy mind, body, and spirit. Continue to use the "I Did" and "I Didn't" format in your journal so you can better track the things you want to change or implement so you can cherish what God has blessed you with.

<u>DAY 2</u>

Answer 2: Respect God, Your Creator

> *Do your best to present yourself to God as one approved, a worker who has no need to be ashamed, rightly handling the word of truth.* (2 Timothy 2:15)

What does respect mean to you?
  I want you to think of someone you really respect.
  Why do you respect them?
  When you respect someone, how do you treat them when you are with them?
  How do you talk about them even when they are not right there with you?
  If they ask you to do something are you more than willing to comply?
  Isn't that one of the ways you show them your respect?
  If they give you a gift or are willing to give their time to you, how do you treat the gift and time?
  Do you pay close attention to what someone you respect says to you?

Do you value their opinion and their instructions?

Do you trust their advice?

How much do you know about the One who created you?

What does *Jehovah Elohim* mean?

What does *Jehovah El Elyon* mean?

What does *Jehovah Jireh* mean?

What does *Jehovah Rapha* mean?

What does *Jehovah Shalom* mean?

Why are these names of God important to you?

Why is our Creator worthy of our respect?

Reread Psalm 139:14 and Jeremiah 1:5. Are these reasons to respect your Creator?

Explain your answer.

Read these passages and begin to use them as ways to praise your Creator: Psalms 33:1, 34:1, 48:1, 100:4, 105:2, 150:2 and 6.

Read Hebrews 12:9 and Proverbs 13:13. What do these verses say about respecting God?

What do 1 Corinthians 10:31 and Colossians 3:17 remind us to do?

Why is it important to your health that you schedule time alone with God studying and reading His Word?

As you have spent time with Him and in studying His Word, what have you found out about what God likes and dislikes?

What pleases and displeases God especially concerning the way you treat your body?

What have you personally discovered about God's great love for you?

"All Scripture is inspired by God," the Apostle Paul is telling you today, "and is useful to teach us what is true and to make us realize what is wrong in our lives. It corrects us when we are wrong and teaches us to do what is right" (2 Timothy 3:16 NLT).

"For the word of God is living and active," Paul reminds you, "sharper than any two-edged sword, piercing to the division of soul and of spirit, of joints and of marrow, and discerning the thoughts and intentions of the heart" (Hebrews 4:12).

Can you like David say, "I have hidden your word in my heart that I might not sin against you" (Psalm 119:11 NLT).

Do you see it is disrespectful to God when you allow food to control you?

Why or why not?

Have you come to the conclusion that to be whole you must deal with your whole person; body, soul, and spirit?

Begin to change by scheduling time alone with God. Spend time studying and reading His Word. Take time to nurture your relationship with Him. God created you because He desires a relationship with you. Get to know what God likes and dislikes, and what pleases and displeases Him. Read the letters He has written to you and talk them over with Him during you conversations with Him.

Record in your journal what you learn about God during your time alone with Him. Start each day praising and thanking Him for creating you as His special masterpiece. Use the Psalms written by David to begin your prayer time each day. Continue to use the "I Did" and "I Didn't" format and target ways you respect God by respecting your body. Be ready to share what you have learned with those God brings across your path each day. Remember the way you treat your body shows others how much you respect the One who created you!

<u>DAY 3</u>

Answer 3: Develop a Healthy Self-Respect

God took so much love and care in creating your body, would you say He cherishes and respects it?

Do you respect your body as much as God does?

When you think of the things you cherish is your body one of them?

Does it seem strange to talk about cherishing your own body?

Does it seem strange to talk about respecting your own body?

When you hold a new born baby in your arms do you think about how you want to take care of him or her and how you want to keep them safe?

How did you select the food you wanted for your newborn?

How did you care for that child's body?

Did you teach your child the right and wrong way to treat him or herself?

Did you tell them you loved them and cherished them?

Did you want that child to grow and respect him or herself?

What about us now as grown adults? Have we gotten away from wanting to put the right foods into our bodies to make sure we grow and mature correctly?

Do we think because we've grown up we've arrived and it doesn't matter what is put into this body?

Read Psalm 139:13.

What does this verse say about the way God created you?

How are you treating those delicate, inner parts?

Are you treating them like a treasure or trash?

Do you really truly believe it's important to take care of your body?

Do you feel you can feed it whatever you desire and whatever happens, happens? Which attitude shows the kind of respect God would expect us to show the masterpiece He has created for us?

What is God's definition of self-respect?

Does it mean we are being selfish when we respect ourselves?

What does being selfish mean?

What is the difference in selfishness and self-respect?

What does self-worth mean?

What does having self-esteem mean?

How would you rate your self-worth and your self-esteem?

What kind of things happened in your life that damaged your self-worth and self-esteem?

Can we truly be self-controlled when it comes to eating properly if we do not have any self-respect?

Read 1 Thessalonians 4:12 and 1 Timothy 3:11. What do these verses say about how we are to present ourselves to others?

Does it sound like we should have a healthy self-respect?

Why is that important for others to see in us?

Having a healthy self-esteem and self-respect causes you to look at things from a different perspective. Remember when we were all encouraged to look at a situation through the eyes of Jesus and before we reacted to it ask ourselves, *What Would Jesus Do?*

What does it mean to look at things from God's perspective?

How would it change our levels of self-esteem and self-worth if we tried to look at ourselves from God's perspective?

What does God see when He looks at you?

It dawned on me one day that God knew all about me. He knew about my strengths and weaknesses. He saw my flaws and how imperfect I was, but He still gave me an opportunity to become His child through Jesus His Son. As a matter of fact, the adoption papers had already been signed. All I had to do was agree to the terms in Acts 2:38 and I would be called a child of the Most High God. The cool thing about adoption is many times the people who adopt you know all about you. They know your background and who your natural parents were, and yet they chose to adopt you. When we obey God's commandments, He still wants to adopt us even though He knows all about us and our weaknesses and sins. God chose to adopt you, too. When we obey God's commandments, He still wants to adopt us even though He knows all about us including our weaknesses and sins.

Read Ephesians 1:5. What does this say about God's plan to adopt you?

Read Romans 8:15-17.

What does this say about the purpose of God's adoption?

Doesn't it seem right to respect yourself and treat the body He has given you with respect?

In what ways have you discovered you have not been respecting your body through the food you eat, the things you drink, and perhaps the things you do not do?

What things are important for you to change in your life?

My prayer is that you will respect your body as much as God does and you will want to take better care of it. My mission is to inspire you to cherish and respect the body God gave you as your Masterpiece and to guide your thoughts about yourself so you will want to take care of yourself physically to be your best spiritually.

Begin to change your perspective of how you view yourself. Stop letting the words and actions of others damage your self-esteem. Remember God chose to adopt you. Begin to see yourself as God sees you. Begin to change the way you treat your body and show God you are grateful for the masterpiece He has made you!

Record in your journal the scriptures in this chapter writing them out in your own words. Use them to thank God for how He has chosen to adopt you and esteem you. Allow Him to minister to you in this area of self-respect and self-esteem. Continue to look for ways you can reach out and help others with what God has revealed to you in this lesson. Realize you are on a mission for the King of kings as His ambassador, as His child. Ask Him to use you in at least one person's life each and every day. Continue to use the "I Did" and "I Didn't" format to reveal areas where you are not respecting your body the way God does.

<u>DAY 4</u>

Answer 4: Develop a Healthy Respect for Food

Note: If you are leading a small group, prepare the smoothie given at the end of this chapter and have it available for your attendees to try.

"If you really want something you will find a way; if you don't you will find an excuse." Jim Rohn

Have you seen the dog food commercial talked about in this lesson?
How many food commercials have you seen that brag about being gluten free, sugar free, etc.?
What do most of the food commercials advertise?
How do you feel while watching that commercial?
Does it make you hungry?
Are you tempted to get up and go to the kitchen for a snack no matter what time of day it is?
Did you know there are good times and bad times to eat?
Would you describe yourself as a "nibbler or a grazer"?
What did you learn about the importance of the timing of the food you eat?

A root that has healthy nourishment produces good fruit. This is a basic law of nature.
When you think about how God made your delicate inner parts, does this inspire you to treat your body, your masterpiece differently?

Does it make you think about what you are doing to your heart, your lungs, your kidneys, your liver, and all your other parts by the food you put in your body?

How about the way food affects your brain function?

Is mental clarity a good reason to eat healthier?

Giving your body the right fuel can help you sharpen your focus and help you think more clearly. You can increase your creativity and your stress tolerance.

What is the best reason for having a healthy respect for the food you eat?

What are some ways we can begin to start respecting the food we eat?

Health Trivia: Beets and beet greens are both powerful cleansers and builders of the blood. Apples have calcium, magnesium, phosphorus, vitamin C, beta-carotene, and pectin.

Look for more health facts and share them with others, especially those in your support group.

Remember we are to eat to live, not live to eat, because food is the fuel our body needs to run all those delicate inner parts smoothly.

Science actually confirms that most cells in our body were constructed to last _____ years (SierraSciences.com).

Wisdom will multiply your days and add years to your life. If you become wise, you will be the one to benefit. If you scorn wisdom, you will be the one to suffer. (Proverbs 9:11-12 NLT)

Doing what we are *supposed to do* versus what we *want to do* will always bring us success, especially in the area of caring for the masterpiece God has given us. **When we follow the "owner's manual" with the right mindset, it will help us regain and maintain our health.** Logically speaking, the One who created us is the One to seek knowledge from if we want to live a long and healthy life.

What does this mean to us?

Why is it foolish to think we can abuse our bodies with poor nutrition, lack of exercise, and destructive thoughts and still live a productive and healthy life?

How would we personally answer these questions if God were to ask us them when we went to Him for healing?

Did you carefully follow the basic instructions?

Did you try to by-pass any of the steps listed in the manual?

Did you try to make it do something it was not designed to do?

Do you realize if you do not follow the instructions in the owner's manual your warranty may be made invalid?

The man considered wisest of them all once said, "Live wisely and wisdom will permeate your life; mock life and life will mock you" (Proverbs 9:12 MSG). Without a basic understanding of the instructions given by our Creator, life is just one health crisis after another. We are all creatures of habit, for better or worse. Bad habits create a poor quality of life. Good habits create an outstanding quality of life. If we do what we are designed to do, then success is the logical outcome. This concept spans every aspect of blessing, joy, and wellbeing in our lives. Basically, we are all slaves to our habits.

What kind of habits have you become a slave to?

Are they good habits or bad habits?

Explain your answers.

Why not be a slave to the good habits that can unconsciously and effortlessly lead us to obtaining good health and long life?

It has been said if we don't plan for success then we plan to fail. When our plan for success lines up with how we were engineered and designed, we will discover health and success! Greater blessings will be poured upon us than can be contained!

What does planning for success mean to you in this area of how you treat your body?

Do you remember reading about becoming a label reader in this chapter? What have you discovered as you have begun reading labels?

1 Thessalonians 5:21 says, "But examine everything carefully; hold fast to that which is good" (NASB). The Amplified Bible adds, "But test *and* prove all things [until you can recognize] what is good; [to that] hold fast."

Scientific Truth: "Eating carbohydrates for breakfast will promote fat storage, making weight loss more difficult despite exercise. Avoiding fructose and other grain carbohydrates is a critical element of a successful weight-loss strategy." (*Fat Burning Fitness*, ©2014 Elevation Health

Publications, North Richland Hills, TX 76182). Instead see my recipe for a great homemade healthy breakfast smoothie at the end of this chapter.

When we are abusive to our bodies whether it's eating, drinking or thinking negative thoughts are we cherishing and respecting His masterpiece, as much as He does?

Are we tempting God or daring Him when we continue to eat knowing the foods are harming us? Studies show the foods we eat can cause diabetes, heart disease, strokes, etc. Yet we are so controlled by the food we ignore the signs. Do we think, "This won't happen to me"? We continue to eat unhealthy foods, ignoring what can happen with an attitude of "I'll eat what I want" and play Russian roulette with our health! Jesus said, "On the other hand, it is written also, You shall not tempt, test thoroughly, *or* try exceedingly the Lord your God" (Matthew 4:7 AMP). Is this really the way we want to live?

Have you been tempting, testing, and trying God with the food you eat?

Explain your answer:

Get proper hydration: You can treat your water with lemon/lime and liquid sea salt which has iodine and supports your thyroid (one of your glands that is responsible for your metabolic rate). Slow, consistent saturation all day long is the most effective way to hydrate your body. Use water, not sports drinks, to properly hydrate your body. (*Fat Burning Fitness*, ©2014 Elevation Health Publications, North Richland Hills, TX 76182)

DAY 5

Begin to change your eating lifestyle by implementing the suggestions in this lesson. Use the information concerning the food you eat, when you eat, and continue to glean more information about what's in the food you eat by becoming an avid label reader. There are many resources on line to help you with what foods are best to eat and what to look for when reading labels. To make it even easier, I suggest eating fresh fruits and vegetables and lean meats. The more you learn the better choices you will make so you will enjoy a long and healthy life. **Keep a daily log of what you are eating to keep yourself accountable.**

DAY 6

Record in your journal your plan for success. Research more and more how your body is designed to function and the types of fuels it needs to give you a long and healthy life. Post the list of dos and don'ts on your refrigerator and have it handy when you go shopping for your groceries. Thank God for creating you and paying attention to every little detail of your inner parts. Thank Him for providing the type of fuel your body needs to run smoothly and efficiently for a long time! Remember, your health affects every part of your life. Do what you can today so you can enjoy a healthier tomorrow! Continue to use the "I Did" and "I Didn't" format especially in this area of respecting the foods you allow in your body. Look for recipes like the one below and share them with others. Perhaps offer to bring in something for your support group that you have found is good for your masterpiece. Start a recipe exchange with others you know are trying to change the way they are eating.

Week Eight

How Can I Stay in Control?

———⊰⊱———

DAY 1

Read or Review Chapter 8: *How Can I Stay in Control?*

God gave us a spirit not of fear but of power and love and self-control. (2 Timothy 1:7)

One thing I have learned as I've walked with God these many years is that if He tells us to do something then we are able to do it. If it says we have self-control and can live a life reflecting that power, then there is **a** way we can accomplish it.

Read Galatians 5:16-18 to start understanding how to overcome this lack of self-control and begin to live the life God designed us to live.

But I say, walk by the Spirit, and you will not gratify the desires of the flesh. ¹⁷ For the desires of the flesh are against the Spirit, and the desires of the Spirit are against the flesh, for these are opposed to each other, to keep you from doing the things you want to do. (Galatians 5:16-17)

What are we told in this passage to do so we don't keep giving into the cravings and desires of the flesh?

How are we to walk and live controlled by God's Holy Spirit and not our own fleshly desires?

Answer 1: Display the Fruit of the Spirit

Read Galatians 5:22-25.
Read I Corinthians 6:19.

Explain what these verses mean to you as far as gaining control over the cravings of the flesh.

What are the end results when we focus on allowing the fruit of the Spirit to shine forth and commit our daily life to God?

We are given this fruit primarily to find out if our fellowship with the Spirit is deep enough. Here is a brief description of what each segment of the fruit of the Spirit represents.

Read the scriptures suggested for each facet of the fruit of the Spirit and indicate whether you see that characteristic manifested in your life by circling yes or no.

Love – God's unconditional love (1 John 3:16) – [Yes or No]

Joy – Deeper than happiness, gladness (John 15:11)–[Yes or No]

Peace – **Security**. Safety, and tranquility (John 14:27)–[Yes or No]

Patience – Endurance, steadfastness, forbearance, and an even temper (James 1:4) - [Yes or No]

Kindness – Compassion and thoughtfulness (Romans 11:22)– [Yes or No]

Goodness – Uprightness of heart and life, benevolence (Romans 15:14) – [Yes or No]

Faithfulness – Covenant keeping (Psalm 119:90 and Proverbs 11:3) – [Yes or No]

Gentleness – Strength under godly control, meekness, humility (Philippians 4:5) – [Yes or No]

Self-control – Mastery of desires and passions, self-restraint (Proverbs 25:28) – [Yes or No]

We don't want our insufficiencies to lead us to search for more fruit, but instead to be in search of _____.

Read Galatians 5:19-21.

What does this list give us?

Why do we need this list?

What does all of this have to do with caring for the masterpiece God has given us?

Are you being kind to others and to your masterpiece?

Are you showing love to others and to your masterpiece?

Is there peace in your life?

Are you doing things the way God has instructed you to do them including your use of food?

Patience means you follow the procedure and not try to get a quick fix.

Have you been resorting to fads and quick weight loss diets?

If yes, how have these plans worked out for you?

Are you displaying God's faithfulness by faithfully caring for your body?

What are you showing the world about the character of God through the way you are treating your masterpiece?

Read Romans 7:15-21.

How does this encourage you in your struggle against your fleshly desires especially in the area of food?

Record in your journal what you have discovered through studying the fruit of the Spirit and God's character within you. This must be turned into practical application. As you see changes in your behavior based on what you learned in this lesson, keep a record of them in your journal. Be prepared to share what you have learned with others as God sends those in need across your path.

How Can I Stay in Control?

DAY 2

Answer 2: Commit Your Daily Life to God

Read Ephesians 2:10.

What has God continually impressed upon us about how and why He created us?

Read Ephesians 2:1-3.

How does God deal with the excuses people have for not walking in the Spirit and living the godly life He has prepared for us?

Can you see how well our Heavenly Father knows us?

The next set of verses starts out with "But God."

Ephesians 2:4-6 says, "But God_____

Genesis 8:1 says, "But God _____

Genesis 19:29 says, "But God _____

Genesis 50:20 says Joseph told his jealous brothers, "You intended to harm me but God _____ (see also Acts 7:9).

The Apostle Paul in Acts 26:22 tells us, "But God _____ Romans 5:7-8 says, "Rarely will anyone die even for a righteous man, but God _____

Read Ephesians 2:7-9.

Why did God save you by His grace when you believed?

How much of that grace is available to you?

Grace is receiving G_____ R_____ A___ C_____ E_____. It cost you _____ to receive it, but it cost Him _____ to give it. It is a gift more powerful than all of man's _____, _____, and _____ and it's yours as a gift from God.

Read 2 Corinthians 9:8.

What is the formula given here for a powerful, victorious life?

Do you see why He is giving you this grace?

What does Ephesians 2:10 say you were created to do?

Why?

What do you think those good works are?

So what does God require of us? Our answer is in Micah 6:8.

What is the description Jesus gave us in Matthew 5:14-16 that will help us understand what God desires of our lives here on this earth?

Here's your action plan:

Start out each day asking God what His plans are for your day.

Make your prayers aimed at finding out what His priorities are and set yours accordingly.

Totally commit your day to Him. Read Proverbs 16:3.

Avoid time and energy wasters and resist the traps and temptations through His plan for your day.

Instead of being the thermometer that is influenced by everything that is happening around you, become the thermostat and set the standard according to God's way of doing things.

The more we commit to Him the more His light shines through us and onto those we are called to influence in the world around us.

Read Psalm 37:5-6. What do you need to do daily?

Read 2 Timothy 3:16-17. What will reading the scriptures do for you?

Read Colossians 3:23. How can you please God today?

Begin this process today. Use Galatians 2:20 as your prayer today, "It is no longer I who live, but Christ lives in me." Commit everything you say and do to Him and watch Him do the miraculous in and through you.

DAY 3

Answer 3: Get Self Out of the Way

Read Colossians 3:1-15.

How does Colossians 3:5-9 describe putting off the old self?

What does Romans 6:6-7 say about our old self?

How does Galatians 2:20 apply to this concept?

Colossians 3:10 and 12 tell us to do what?

What is that supposed to include?

Is God doing it?

Does He strip us of the old self and then clothe us with the new one? Who has to do this?

Read Colossians 3:15-17.

What do we have to choose to do every single day?

What does verse 17 tell us to do?

What does 2 Peter 1:3-4 remind us?

How does 2 Peter 3:8-9 tell us to do this?

Then 2 Peter 1:10-15 says it is going to take _____ _____ and

_____

Our calling and election or our job as God's child is to present His _____, His _____ _____ to the world around us.

When we put off the old self and put on the new, we begin to _____ and _____ like our Heavenly Father. One of the ways to do this is to seek to reflect His great love for one another.

Do the visual suggested in the Action Suggestion part of your lesson.

Sometimes a visual of a spiritual concept helps us get a better feel for what these scriptures mean to us in the natural. Stand in front of the mirror and go through the motions of taking off that old self. Maybe take sticky notes and write the names of those desires you battle with and stick them on a coat you are wearing. Then take it off and strip off all of those fleshly desires and throw those sticky notes away. Maybe even burn them in a fireplace or charcoal grill. Then put the coat back on free of all of those fleshly desires. Record in your journal that this is the day you took that old self off. Ask God to show you how to show His love to those around you today.

The Master's Masterpiece

DAY 4

Answer 4: Realize It's All About Him

Read Matthew 22:37-40.
What did Jesus say is the first and greatest commandment?

What did He say is the second commandment?

It's all about Him! We have the mind of Christ and we are to display the character of God no matter where we are or who we are with. That is the only way we can manifest Him in our lives.

Read Philippians 2:5-11.
What does this powerful verse mean to you personally?

"When we allow the love of God to move in us, we can no longer distinguish between ours and His." (Austin Farrer)

So what is this God kind of love that we are to display with our lives?
If we do not take care of our masterpiece, showing that we love ourselves, how can we show this God kind of love to others as Jesus has instructed us to do?
The Apostle Paul has given us one of his famous lists in Romans 12:9-21. This is a long passage, but worth reading and studying regularly. Just as He has promised us, when God gives us a command He provides the instructions and the way to accomplish it.

DAY 5

Here is your action plan. Take the time to study everything on this list and write your own definition of how you will accomplish this in your life on a daily basis.

Let you love be genuine means I want to_____
Abhorring evil means I want to _____
Loving with brotherly affection means _____
Outdo showing honor means I look for ways to _____

Be zealous/work hard/serve the Lord where and when? _____
Rejoice in hope and be patient in tribulation means _____
Being constant in prayer means _____
Helping God's people means I get to _____
Showing hospitality means I get to _____
Bless those who curse you where and when? _____
Rejoice with those who rejoice where and when? _____
Weep with those who weep means I want to _____
Live in harmony with whom? _____
Don't be haughty or too proud to be in the company of ordinary people means_____
Don't be wise in my own sight and don't think I know it all means ___

_____

Never pay back evil for evil/do things so others see you are honorable means_____
Do all you can to live at peace with everyone even _____
Don't take revenge/let God take care of that means _____
Feed/clothe/give drink to your enemy means what to you? _____
Overcome and conquer evil with good means I _____

> "You will follow your passions. Our love for the Spirit must run deeper than our love for the world." ("Wonders of the Cross" by Chris Tiegreen devotional, January 8)

What do you offer yourself to?

Is it to the entertainment world, to the philosophies of our generation, to the passions of the flesh or to the pursuit of intellectual interests?

When you checked your day planner what did you discover your passions really are?

If you want to truly defeat the passions of the flesh you need to offer yourself to God each and every day. He will never lead you astray. A deep love for God is the ultimate defense against the temptation of forbidden fruit.

Read Romans 12:1-2.

Are you willing to surrender your will and ways to God?

The problem is _____ God's provision – the problem is always our _____.

DAY 6

Read 1 Corinthians 1:26-29.

Write in your journal how this week's decisions have helped you move forward in changing your behaviors from wrong to right, from unhealthy to healthy.

> Robert McGee writes, "What a waste to attempt to change behavior without truly understanding the driving needs that cause such behavior! Yet millions of people spend a lifetime searching for love, acceptance, and success without understanding the need that compels them. We must understand that this hunger for self-worth is God-given and can only be satisfied by Him. Our value is not dependent on our ability to earn the fickle acceptance of people, but rather, its true source is the love and acceptance of God. He created us. He alone knows how to fulfill all of our needs."[22]

---

22   Robert S. McGee. *The Search for Significance: Seeing Your True Worth Through God's Eyes* (p. 11). Kindle Edition.

Week Nine

HOW CAN I KEEP
MY COMMITMENTS?

DAY 1

Read or Review Chapter 9: *How Can I Keep My Commitments?*

"The world can be divided into feelers and doers. Feelers take action and initiative only when they feel like doing so. In other words, they feel their way into acting. If they don't feel like doing something that will advance their goals, they won't do it. If a feeler feels like exercising, he will. If he doesn't feel like exercising, he won't. If a feeler feels like watching television, he will... He is a prisoner of the desire for instant gratification, and naturally will suffer the long-term consequences of this short-term perspective... Doers, on the other hand, act their way into feeling. After determining what needs to be done, doers take action. They just do it. If they don't feel like taking action, they consider that emotion to be a distraction and take action in spite of it. They refuse to let their desire for short-term comfort divert them from their long-term goal."
(Tommy Newberry)

Answer 1: Be Willing to Make a Decision

Procrastinate means _____
To make a decision means to _____

> "Procrastination, which is the delaying of higher priority tasks in favor of lower priority ones, is more responsible for frustration, stress, and under-achievement than any other single factor." (Tommy Newberry)

Read Jeremiah 2:11-19.

The prophet Jeremiah was called by God to warn His people about the consequences of their decisions. They had wavered back and forth for many years trying to decide whether or not they wanted to worship and serve God exclusively.

What were some of the consequences of their decisions?

What does Ephesians 5:29 say?
How is that relevant when it comes to how you treat yourself?
How can we gain control over mindless eating?
Can you splurge once in a while and have something not so good for you?
How often is once in a while to you?
What would be a better way in making your decisions about splurging "once in while"?
Would you be willing to eat healthy for ninety days?

If your answer is yes, I recommend eating lean protein, vegetables, and one or two pieces of fruit per day. Eat three meals a day and only healthy snacks in between. No eating three hours before going to bed.

Read the story of Daniel in the Book of Daniel 1:8-19.
What was the decision Daniel and his friends made about what they would and would not allow into their bodies?
What were the results of that decision?

Read Romans 14:13 and 22.

What do these verses tell us about making decisions?
What does 2 Corinthians 9:7 say about the choices we make?
God has given us the ability to make a decision and choose the way we will do things.

Read Joshua 24:14-15. What do these verses tell us about making decisions?

What does Ecclesiastes 10:2 say is the difference between a wise man and a fool?

What did David say in Psalm 119:30 about his decisions?

Would you agree it's time for you to make some decisions about your eating habits?

Am I willing to commit to a ninety-day healthy eating plan?

Have I determined to live by God's rules?

Will I be wise and choose the right road?

Will I cheerfully give my body as a living sacrifice to God?

Record your daily decisions in your journal. Keep track of the blessing you experience as a result of each of those decisions. Thank God daily for His guidance and presence in your life. Be willing to share your victories with others as God sends people across your path who need to know what you have learned.

DAY 2

Answer 2: Be Willing to Live with Integrity

The integrity of the upright guides them, but the crookedness of the treacherous destroys them. (Proverbs 11:3)

The Master's Masterpiece

Being accountable means you are willing to be _____

Taking responsibility for our actions is the first step toward changing what needs to be changed so we can make and keep our commitments to God.

Integrity means we are willing to be _____

It also means we are _____. If we say we are going to do something then we _____.

> *Whoever walks in integrity walks securely, but he who makes his ways crooked will be found out.* (Proverbs 10:9)

Read the story of Job and see how much this man had to endure. He basically lost everything, but look at what God says about this man in Job 2:3.

> Wouldn't we each like to have God say that about us?
> Are we willing to do what it takes to walk in integrity even in the area of what we eat and drink and how we treat our masterpiece?
> What do you want for your masterpiece?
> Remember the story of W. Clement Stone asking Jack Canfield about taking 100% responsibility? Are you taking 100% responsibility for everything in your life?

When God fearfully and wonderfully made you and designed all of your delicate, intricate parts, He also gave you talents and the ability to use those talents.

> If you aren't willing to take care of the masterpiece He created, are you going to be able to use your talents for Him?

What important decisions are you willing to make as a result of this lesson?

How you choose will make a big difference in how you live the rest of your life!

Are you willing to do what is necessary to have a healthy masterpiece?

Are you ready to say "yes" to feeling great, having energy, releasing weight, and proving to yourself you do have the self-control it takes to say "no" to unhealthy choices and to say "yes" to eating and enjoying healthy food?

Will you make a "true decision" to commit and make a promise to yourself to achieving the results you want?

As you talk with God today, be honest with Him about what you are struggling with. Make a decision and tell God you want to be the person He has called you to be. Ask Him to help you take 100% responsibility for your life. Then follow through with the commitments you make to Him.

What kind of commitments are you making to God today?

How are you going to follow through with them starting today?

He will honor every step forward you take with Him. Thank Him today for being there with you every step of the way!

DAY 3

Answer 3: Understand There Is No Plan B

"Goal setting is the master skill of all lifelong success, yet it is practiced by less than 3 percent of the population." (Tommy Newberry)

Throughout these lessons, we have talked about eating healthy and eating to _____ instead of living to _____.

Why is that mindset important?

Has it begun to make a difference in your eating habits?

Explain or give an example.

The Master's Masterpiece

Too many times when someone has decided to lose weight, they go on a diet and have a goal of a certain number of pounds they want to lose or an amount they want to weigh.

Have you ever done this?

What were the results you experienced?

Would you agree changing your focus to taking care of yourself physically to be your best spiritually is a better mindset?

Have you begun to implement this change in thinking in your life?

What results have you experienced?

Do you think focusing on what you can eat because it will make you healthy and make you your best for God is a better way to go about weight loss?

Explain your answer.

Have you changed your thinking on how you view food?

Have you begun to see yourself as the beautiful masterpiece God created you to be?

Are you starting to cherish your body and want it to be healthy, not only for you, but for your family and for God?

What is the blessing and admonition given in 1 Thessalonians 5:23?

Your spiritual self needs to be fed and nourished through _____. Your soul or mind needs to be filled with

_____.

Your body must be cared for by following _____.

When you read the instruction manual for a new appliance, does it give you several different plans for maintenance?

If you don't follow this plan what might happen to your new appliance?

The same is true for the masterpiece God has created you to be. Follow His Plan A and you will function at full capacity and do what you were designed to do.

What has God given us to use as His instruction manual?

How long do we have to follow God's Plan A?

This is your life, the only one you have, and it is very important you take care of you! There is no place for excuses in God's Plan A.

What excuses have you used in the past thinking they gave you a way to deviate from God's Plan A?

How do you feel about these excuses after doing this lesson?

> "Commit to making your home and office an *excuse-free zone*. If a situation arises that previously called for an excuse, substitute the words, "I am responsible," where the excuse used to go." (Tommy Newberry)

Read Romans 8:37-39.

How does this help you in your determination to follow God's Plan A for your life?

Begin to change today by taking the time to pray and ask God for wisdom and help on your journey. Ask Him to help you when there are going to be foods available you know aren't the best for you to eat. Remind yourself He is right there with you and sees everything you do. Remind yourself of the consequences of not following God's Plan A.

Use the following suggestions and begin to change your mindset about food:

Write down what you eat, why you eat, and when you eat.

Savor the first bite, enjoy it, take your time, and really taste your food.

Pray before you eat and ask God to help you stop when you feel full!

Use the 90-Day Plan to get you started at the end of this book.

<u>DAY 4</u>

Answer 4: Realize Daily Decisions Do Make a Difference

> "Self-discipline is the ability to funnel our desires and passions in a productive direction, for a sustained period of time in order to achieve our goals. It is the connective tissue that links ambition with achievement." (Tommy Newberry)

Do you believe every little decision you make each and every day counts?

The Master's Masterpiece

Why do you need to select what you eat with care?

Deciding to follow God's Plan A will cause you to:
- release the _____
- feel _____
- _____ your masterpiece more
- be a Christian example to _____
- be your best _____ for God

> "It takes less time to do things right than to explain why you did it wrong." (Henry Wadsworth Longfellow)[23]

> "Awareness is the first step on the ladder of positive change. You can only manage what you can label and bring to conscious awareness." (Dr. Arlene R. Taylor, "Age-Proofing Your Brain – 21 Key Factors You Can Control," Success Resources International, Napa, CA 94558 ©2009 ETB)

Why is it important we be aware of how we are living?
It will enhance your _____, _____, and _____.
It will also help you take charge of your own life and you prevent others and circumstances from _____

_____.

Why do you think balance is such an important part of a high-level healthy lifestyle?

> "Everything you eat, drink, think, say, and do is a health-relevant behavior. Make thoughtful choices to achieve desired outcomes. Keep learning!" (Dr. Arlene R. Taylor, "Age-Proofing Your Brain – 21 Key Factors You Can Control" Success Resources International, Napa, CA 94558 ©2009 ETB)

Your lifestyle is as individual as you are and the choices you make on a daily basis can have a monumental impact on it.

---

23 http://www.values.com/inspirational-quotes/value/46-Right-Choices

What kinds of impact have you seen in your life as a result of the food choices you have made?

What happens if you refuse to make your own choices?

The Bible speaks of making wise choices and the benefits of doing so.

Read Deuteronomy 30:19-20.

What are the benefits listed here for choosing to do things God's way?

Read Joshua 24:15.

What important choice did Joshua make?

Read Joshua 24:1.

How many people did he influence with this decision?

Read Joshua 24:29 and 31.

What were the benefits for Joshua and the people he led as a result of this decision?

Read Psalm 119:30-32.

What were the choices David said he made?

I have chosen the way of _____

I have set _____ rules before me.

I will live in a way that follows God's _____

What did David go on to become and how many people did he influence in his lifetime?

> "Learning is not attained by chance-it must be sought for with ardor and attended with diligence." (First Lady Abigail Adams 1744-1818)[24]

What should we notice when seeking the opinions of others? Why?

---

24   www.great-quotes.com/quotes/author/Abigail/Adams

Making right choices requires developing the ability to view things from God's perspective. Since He created your masterpiece, He alone can give you the knowledge you need to make right choices on a consistent basis.

How can we begin to test every decision against God's design?

Look at both the short-term and long-term consequences of your choices.

> "You have only always to do what is right. It will become easier by practice, and you enjoy in the midst of your trials the pleasure of an approving conscience." (Robert E. Lee, General 1807-1870)[25]

Why is it so important to write down and track not only what you eat, but when you eat and why you eat?

DAY 5

To make wise choices on a daily basis you must understand what triggers your decisions.

What are the questions you can ask yourself when you are tempted to eat the wrong things at the wrong times?

Write down the questions and how you will answer them.

> "There comes a time in the spiritual journey when you start making choices from a very different place. And if a choice lines up so that it supports truth, health, happiness, wisdom and love, it's the right choice." (Angeles Arrien Anthropologist)[26]

DAY 6

Begin today to make right choices by developing the ability to view things from God's perspective. Since He created your masterpiece, He

---

25   http://www.values.com/inspirational-quotes/value/46-Right-Choices

26   http://www.values.com/inspirational-quotes/value/46-Right-Choices

alone can give you the knowledge you need to make right choices on a consistent basis.

Spend time with Him and test every decision against God's design.

Seek more knowledge about the intricacies of your body.

Look at both the short-term and long-term consequences of your choices.

Write your research in your journal.

Track your choices.

Begin to make better choices on your path to wholeness and health.

Health Hint: Dr. Kenneth Guiffre, author of "The Care and Feeding of Your Brain, says exercise helps the brain to "boot up efficiently" (NJ, Career Press Inc., 1999). Dr. Candace Pert, author of "Molecules of Emotion" says, "Twenty minutes of mild aerobic exercise at the beginning of the day can turn on fat-burning neuropeptides, the effects of which can last for hours" (NY, Scriber, 1997).

Week Ten

HOW CAN I LOVE MYSELF?

———∞———

DAY 1

Read or Review Chapter 10: *How Can I Love Myself?*

Answer 1: See Your Ideal Weight from the Inside Out

Read Proverbs 23:7.
> How does what you think about affect what you say?
> What do people learn about you by how you talk about yourself?

Read Matthew 15:17-20.
> What did Jesus teach about what defiles us?
> What are your words telling others about what is really in your heart?

Read Proverbs 17:22.
> Are your words joyful or crushing?
> Does it make a difference what is in our hearts?
> Explain your answer.

Read Proverbs 27:19 and Proverbs 15:13.
> What are you reflecting about your weight from the inside out?
> When your heart is happy, what does your face reflect?
> When your heart is sad or depressed what does your face reveal?

Read Proverbs 4:23.

What advice does this verse give us?

Why is this so important especially as we strive to be all that God has called us to be?

Read 1 John 3:18-20, 1 Chronicles 28:20, and Romans 8:31.

What do these verses reassure us about?

Why is this important to you?

Begin to declare God's truth:

I can win against the devil.

I can change the way I see myself from the inside out.

I can replace the negativity that is in my heart and begin to see myself the way God sees me.

I am thankful and happy for the body God created for me.

I love and appreciate my masterpiece.

I know God loves me.

> "You have a masterpiece inside you, you know. One unlike any that has ever been created, or ever will be. If you go to your grave without painting your masterpiece, it will not get painted. No one else can paint it. Only you." —Gordon MacKenzie[27]

Ask a trusted friend to help you begin to monitor the way you speak about yourself. Ask them to gently remind you when you begin to bad mouth yourself. Thank God today for trusted friends and His help in changing you from the inside out.

<u>DAY 2</u>

Answer 2: Admit God Loves You Even if You Are Overweight

Read Matthew 7:24-27.

Why did Jesus teach this parable?

---

27   http://www.positivequotes.org/selftalk/

The Master's Masterpiece

What does it have to do with learning how to care for your masterpiece?
Would you agree God's Word has given you a firm foundation for taking care of your masterpiece?
What happens when the storms of illness and disease come if you choose to eat whatever you want and not take care of yourself?

What happens if you are taking care of yourself?
Read Matthew 22:37-39.
What is the foundation we are supposed to build our lives upon?

What does the account of the death of Jesus in Matthew 26-28, Mark 14-16, Luke 22-24, and John 18-20 tell us about God's love for us?
How does that make you feel about yourself?
So if God looks at the heart, knows all about us from the inside out, and sent His Son to die for us on the cross, does He love us even if we are overweight? Explain your answer.

Read the question asked in Romans 8:35.
What is the answer to this given in Romans 8:37-39?

Read Psalm 103. What does this scripture passage help us to see?

> "The only one thing I can change is myself, but sometimes that makes all of the difference."—Anonymous[28]

What can you begin to do today to change yourself from the inside out?

Make a list and set some goals. It will make all the difference in your life!

---

28   http://www.positivequotes.org/selftalk/

DAY 3

Answer 3: Monitor Your Self-Talk

When you look in the mirror what do you think or say in your head to yourself?

Do you complain or do you see the amazing creation you are?

When we whine, murmur, complain, and only see the negative in ourselves, are we shining for Christ?

The world is watching us and watching closely! Find the positive instead of the negative in everything.

Do you remember the story of my friend who wrote down every negative word she said? I invite you to do the same. Even if it is something as simple as, "It's so hot" or "it's raining again." It is sometimes in the tone of the voice. Stop and think how you and those around you are receiving what you are saying. You have a choice. How will you choose today?

As a parent, wouldn't you be surprised if your child started using negative self talk and you knew they had not heard it in your home? Wouldn't you wonder who they were hanging around with? What does God think about the kind of thinking and self-talk you are using?

Do you sound like God or do you sound like the devil?

What kind of things do you say that sound like the devil?

How could you turn that around and talk like your Heavenly Father?

Read Psalm 34:4. What does this say about our fears?

I have found, as a part of a direct sales business, that for many people, the deepest fear is the fear of success. However, each time I read 2 Timothy 1:7, I realize God didn't give me or you a spirit of fear. He gave us a spirit of power and love and self-control! There's no need to be afraid! Instead, step into becoming the person God intended you to be. Use the talents He gave you. Believe in yourself. Pay attention to the words you say to yourself because you are listening to every word! The words you say to yourself control the way you feel and act.

Begin today to stop every time you have a negative thought or say something negative and write it down. Decide to begin to replace the negative with the positive. Stop and think how you and those around you are receiving what you are saying. Ask God to begin to point these negatives out to you as you go through your day. Remember, the only thing you can change today is yourself, but sometimes that makes all of the difference. Be careful what you are saying to yourself because you are listening, too. Perhaps ask a trusted friend to be your accountability partner when it comes to changing your negatives to positives.

<u>DAY 4</u>

Answer 4: Replace Negative with Positive Affirmations

When you acknowledge the less than perfect parts of yourself, something magical begins to happen. Along with the negative, you'll also begin to notice the positive, the wonderful aspects of yourself that you may not have given yourself credit for, or perhaps even been aware of.—Richard Carlson (from "Don't Sweat the Small Stuff")

We have between 50-60,000 thoughts per a day.[29] When we begin to learn to manage these thoughts, we can gain control of our beliefs. One of the methods I use in my coaching is to help people recreate beliefs, and to go from limiting beliefs to empowering beliefs.[30]

What are some ways you can begin to do this?

> *Don't listen to those who say, "It's not done that way." Maybe it's not, but maybe you will. Don't listen to those who say, "You're taking too big a chance." Michelangelo would have painted the Sistine floor, and it would surely be rubbed out by today. Most importantly, don't listen when the little voice of fear inside of you rears its ugly head and says, "They're all smarter than you out there. They're more talented, they're taller, blonder, prettier, luckier and have connections..." I firmly believe that if you follow a path that interests you, not to the exclusion of love, sensitivity, and cooperation with others, but with the strength of conviction*

---

29   http://wiki.answers.com/Q/How_many_thoughts_do_people_have_each_day?#slide=1

30   This is something I learned from my business coach. He has a whole series called "Erase the Waste."

that you can move others by your own efforts, and do not make success or failure the criteria by which you live, the chances are you'll be a person worthy of your own respect.—Neil Simon[31]

Did you know you weren't born with your limiting belief? You actually created that belief by allowing it to enter into your thoughts and then your self talk. What are some of your limiting beliefs? Since you created that belief, you can also un-create it and replace it with an empowering belief!

How can you change your self talk to un-create some of your limiting beliefs?

"Change of diet will not help a person who will not change his thoughts. When a person makes his thoughts pure, he no longer desires impure food. Obesity has become a major health threat as it has reached epidemic proportions according to the US Center for Disease Control. Despite the epidemic, the vast majority of those on a weight-loss diet today will fail. Even sadder is that virtually 100% of the people who fail won't know the REAL reason for their failure. Many will blame the diet they chose, the circumstances in their life, their lack of will power, and on and on. But the REAL reason —- the ONLY reason they won't succeed is because they didn't change their thoughts. Their thoughts about themselves and the food they eat." (From "Day by Day With James Allen" by Vic Johnson, copyright 2003, 8th printing 2011. Page 22, Eighth Day)

I agree with Vic. I have seen many "yo-yo" in their weight. I have even heard people who are in the process of losing weight make the comment that they will gain it back because they always have. It is so important to get rid of the limiting beliefs you have surrounding your thoughts about your weight. I also believe many people feel they don't deserve to be healthy and release the weight. Vic shares how he believes you will never achieve sustainable success that exceeds the image you have of yourself. He says, "You must see yourself as a healthy, physically-fit person so

---

31   http://www.positivequotes.org/selftalk/

you can release the weight and keep it off. Not only does this apply to weight-control, it applies to changing any habit."

DAY 5

Begin to change today by speaking what you want to feel and speaking what you want to believe. The words you use will change your physiology and who you are as well. Speaking negative words creates acid in your body and weakens it. Conversely, speaking positive words of love, abundance, and joy will transform your body into something totally different—a physiology that is filled with love, happiness and health. Choose to take control of your thoughts and words starting today!

Start by being grateful for your masterpiece. Thank God for every part from the inside out. Show gratitude for your organs on the inside and your hands, arms, legs, eyes, etc. on the outside. Thank God for creating you. Once you show gratitude for your masterpiece, you will become more aware of what you allow to go into your body. By being careful about what you say to yourself, you empower yourself to take control of your eating and every other activity in your life.

As God's children, we **must** be happy, joyful, and positive everyday. When we get up in the morning, we make a choice as to whether our self talk will be positive or negative. We can choose to rejoice and look for God's blessings or we can just get through the day. We have a responsibility to put on a happy face because people are watching.

Read Psalm 118:24 and Lamentations 3:22-23.

What are some of the other positive scriptures you are using to begin your day with praise?

Health Hint: Vitamin D is available through food sources and dietary supplementation. The best dietary supplement form of vitamin D is vitamin D3 (also known as cholecalciferol). Many experts are now recommending the average American adult should get 1,000-5,000 IU of vitamin D3 daily year-round in conjunction with some regular sun exposure. When little or no daily sun exposure is available, individuals may need as much as 5,000 IU of vitamin D3 daily. More detailed guidelines on supplemental intake of vitamin D is available from the experts at the Vitamin D Council (***www.vitamindcouncil.org***).

The Master's Masterpiece

DAY 6

Do you have any health hints you would like to share with others? Write them down on 3 x 5 cards and have them ready to give to those God sends across your path that could benefit from what you have learned.

Pray and then list the people you want to share this book with. Give it to them as a gift. Now pray and thank God (and your group if you have been sharing in a group) for giving you the power to walk through this Journal with Him.

> Heavenly Father, I thank you for fearfully and wonderfully making me. Please give me wisdom to make right decisions concerning my masterpiece. Thank you. I love you. Amen.

[END OF JOURNAL]

Strategic Daily Action Plan

To receive your free pdf version of the Strategic Daily Plan and the "I Did & I Didn't" journal, email Diane at <u>coachdianeburton@gmail.com</u>.

Daily:
    1- Devotional from this book:

        What was my verse for today?

        What did God reveal to me today?

        Prayer Requests:

        What action am I willing to take today?

2 – Eat Breakfast:

        Drink -

        Fruit -

        Protein -

        Other -

3 – Exercise: What exercise did I do today and for how long?

How much water did I drink?

4 – Lunch:

Vegetable -

Protein -

Fruit -

Drink -

Other –

5 – Snacks:

Water -

6 – Dinner:

Vegetable -

Protein -

Fruit -

Drink -

Other –

7 – Snacks:

Total Water for today –

8–Fill in My Daily "I DID" & "I DIDN'T" Journal

Strategic Daily Action Plan

Sean Smith is my business coach and gave me the idea for the mirror exercise and the concept of the "I Did & I Didn't" self-examination. I adapted his ideas into the following daily journal.

My Daily "I Did" & "I Didn't" Journal

This Journal is designed to help you stay focused on your accomplishments for the day.

Examples of "I Did"

*I did eat a healthy lunch (write down what you ate)

*I did enjoy the healthy food I ate.

*I did have a potluck at work today; however, I took small amounts of food.

*I did keep my mouth shut instead of saying some words that are offensive.

*I did (you fill in the blank of what you did positive helping you with your challenge.)

Examples of "I Didn't"

*I didn't eat the cookie offered to me at break time today.

*I didn't eat burger and fries today.

*I didn't eat the desserts at the potluck at work today.

*I didn't glare at the person who cut me off in traffic today.

*I didn't yell at my spouse.

*I didn't yell at my children.

*I didn't (you fill in with what you yielded to today.)

The goal is to find three "I Did" and three "I Didn't" per day.

There will be extra lines at the bottom of each page for you to write other victories or obstacles you had. If you gave in to the temptation during the day, write down why you think it happened and what you could do to keep it from happening again.

To contact Diane, you can visit her website at
www.themastersmasterpiece.com or
e-mail her at coachdianeburton@gmail.com.

What I "Did" & "Didn't" Do Today

Today's Date:_____

"For I am God's masterpiece...." Eph. 2:10

This is what "I DID" today:

1_____
2_____
3_____

This is what "I DIDN'T" do today:

1_____
2_____
3_____

Challenges from my day:

_____

Actions I'm willing to take to stay on track:

_____

Blessings from my day:

_____

What might come tomorrow that I want to be prepared for?

_____

Weight Control Tips:

By Kathleen M. Zelman, MPH, RD, LD WebMD Expert Column

Weight control is all about making small changes that you can live with forever. As you incorporate these minor adjustments into your lifestyle, you'll begin to see how they can add up to big calorie savings and weight loss. Here are my top 10 habits to help you turn your dream of weight loss into a reality:

1. **Evaluate your eating habits.** Are you eating late at night, nibbling while cooking, finishing the kids' meals? Take a look around, and it will be easy to identify a few behaviors you can change that will add up to big calorie savings.

2. **If you fail to plan, plan to fail.** You need a strategy for your meals and snacks. Pack healthful snacks for the times of day that you know you are typically hungry and can easily stray from your eating plan.

3. **Always shop with a full belly.** It's a recipe for disaster to go into the grocery store when you are hungry. Shop from a prepared list so impulse buying is kept to a minimum. Eating right starts with stocking healthy food in your pantry and refrigerator.

4. **Eat regular meals.** Figure out the frequency of your meals that works best in your life and stick to it. Regular meals help prevent bingeing.

5. **Eat your food sitting down at a table, and from a plate.** Food eaten out of packages and while standing is forgettable. You can wind up eating lots more than if you sit down and consciously enjoy your meals.

The Master's Masterpiece

6. **Serve food onto individual plates, and leave the extras back at the stove.** Bowls of food on the table beg to be eaten, and it takes incredible will power not to dig in for seconds. Remember, it takes about 20 minutes for your mind to get the signal from your belly that you are full.

7. **Eat slowly, chew every bite, and savor the taste of the food.** Try resting your fork between bites and drinking plenty of water with your meals.

8. **Don't eat after dinner.** This is where lots of folks pack on the extra pounds. If you are hungry, try satisfying your urge by drinking herbal tea. Brushing your teeth after dinner helps reduce the temptation to eat again.

9. **If you snack during the day, treat the snack like a mini-meal.** The most nutritious snacks contain complex carbohydrates and a small amount of protein and fat.[32]

Exercise!

In a study which involved eighty adults aged twenty to forty-five that were diagnosed with mild to moderate depression, the researchers looked at exercise alone to treat the condition and found the depression symptoms were cut almost by half in those individuals who participated in thirty-minute aerobic exercise sessions, three to five times a week after twelve weeks. The results of this study are similar to that of other studies, which involved patients with mild or moderate depression being treated with antidepressants or cognitive therapy – **"proving patients need not rely on drugs to treat depression."** (*American Journal of Preventive Medicine* January 2005;28 (1):1-8 (Free Full-Text Article) *Medical News Today* January 24, 2005).

Good brain and body communication and good fitness are very important. People who walk and exercise thirty minutes a day, 3-5 times a week for ninety days, slash their stress ration by 50 percent. That's huge! There are no drugs that can do that!

Superfoods

---

32   http://www.webmd.com/diet/features/top-10-habits-that-can-help-you-lose-weight

Weight Control Tips:

Here is a shortlist of superfoods for a super you! They are packed with a high concentration of essential nutrients and antioxidants, while being low in calories.

Sweet Potatoes–One sweet potato provides you with over 300% of the recommended daily intake of Vitamin A, which takes care of your body in every which way; from supporting your immune system and vision to helping your lungs, heart, kidneys, and other organs work properly.

Kale – Kale contains high amounts of lutein and zeaxanthin that may help prevent macular degeneration and cataracts. Reap its benefits by adding it to salads, soups, and sandwiches.

Avocado – Yes, there is such a thing as a good fat! Avocados help you watch your weight, keep you satisfied, and help you absorb the fruit's nutrients that help reduce high cholesterol. Brush a halved avocado with olive oil and grill one minute. Serve with red onions, sliced grapefruit, and balsamic vinegar for a great and nutritious treat.

Blueberries – They may be small but they are packed with a combination of antioxidants and vitamin C. Add them to salads, blend them in smoothies, plop them in your cereal or oatmeal, or just grab a handful for nutrition when you are on the go.

Cashews and Walnuts – Cashews and walnuts are the perfect snacks for busy people. They are a rich source of magnesium which is essential for energy and protein production. Turkey, salmon, walnuts, hazelnuts, sunflower seeds, garlic, spinach, coconut oil, and avocados have a lot of B6 and a lot of good fats for the brain. Omega 3 in walnuts is great for the brain. Five or ten little walnuts every single day will go a long way to balancing your brain to be able to handle stress. Magnesium rich foods help with muscle relaxing.

Salmon – This is a classic superfood that is nutrient dense and calorie sparse. It is a great source of Omega-3.[33]

---

33   http://www.webmd.com/food-recipes/features/10-everyday-super-foods

Recommended Reading

To learn about Jordan Rubin's Daniel Diet or the daily, weekly and monthly cleanse, order his book, "The Maker's Diet Revolution" from your favorite bookstore or you go to www.mybeyondorganic.com

"It Starts With Food" by Dallas & Melissa Hartwig

"The Virgin Diet" by J.J. Virgin

About the Author

Before The Master's Peace *After The Master's Peace*

Diane Burton is a Certified Grief Coach and the 2013 Coach of the Year for the Grief Coach Academy. Diane has taught Ladies' Bible Classes and Cradle Roll (a class for babies from birth to two years) at every congregation where Ken has preached; and also speaks at Ladies' Retreats and Ladies' Day events. Diane has been a leader in a Direct Sales company for over twenty years.

She is married to Ken, a minister for over forty years. They have two married children and two of the cutest, most adorable grandsons.

To contact Diane, you can visit her website at www.themasters masterpiece.com or e-mail her at coachdianeburton@gmail.com.

Why is Diane the right coach for you?

One reason Diane is the right coach for you is because she is a certified From Heartbreak to Happiness® grief coach. Her mission is to inspire and encourage women to cherish their body as God's masterpiece. Another reason Diane is the right coach for you is because she has been through the pain of being the fat girl and being made fun of. She understands what it's like to not feel like she belonged and the heartache of name calling. You know the saying, "sticks and stones will break my bones, but words will never hurt me." That is a lie! The words hurt, they hurt badly and they stay with you forever!

Diane now helps women focus on how special they are and helps them figure out ways to eat healthy and enjoy healthy foods as the weight comes off. One of my clients shared how from one idea I gave her she lost ten pounds! Another client shared how she has now stopped overeating. Do you know what this could mean to you? It could mean not only releasing the physical weight, but also emotional weight. You could fall in love with yourself again. You can learn to cherish and respect the body God gave you and have peace of mind!

When you coach with Diane, your experience will be caring and confidential. Diane will listen to your story. It will be all about you and how we can bring you to a place of peace, joy, happiness, and fulfillment. If you want to learn to love and cherish yourself more, contact her at her website:

www.themastersmasterpiece.com
or coachdianeburton@gmail.com.

CPSIA information can be obtained at www.ICGtesting.com
Printed in the USA
LVOW13s0759020714

392555LV00003B/4/P